ICSC's Dictionary of Shopping Center Terms

INTERNATIONAL COUNCIL OF SHOPPING CENTERS

NEW YORK

Published by
International Council of Shopping Centers
Publications Department
1221 Avenue of the Americas
New York, NY 10020-1099

Text design: Joseph Rutt
Cover design: Design Plus

ICSC Catalog Number: 212
International Standard Book Number: 1-58268-023-X
Printed in the United States of America

About the International Council of Shopping Centers

The International Council of Shopping Centers (ICSC) is the trade association of the shopping center industry. Serving the shopping center industry since 1957, ICSC is a not-for-profit organization with more than 39,000 members in 77 countries worldwide.

ICSC members include shopping center

- owners
- developers
- managers
- marketing specialists
- leasing agents
- retailers
- researchers
- attorneys
- architects
- contractors
- consultants
- investors
- lenders and brokers
- academics
- public officials

ICSC sponsors approximately 200 meetings a year and provides a wide array of services and products for shopping center professionals, including publications and research data.

For more information about ICSC, please contact:

International Council of Shopping Centers
1221 Avenue of the Americas
New York, NY 10020-1099
Telephone: (646) 728-3800
Fax: (212) 589-5555
ICSC.org

Contents

About This Book

ICSC's Dictionary of Shopping Center Terms brings together in one book hundreds of definitions of shopping center terms compiled from ICSC and other publications that cover the following major industry disciplines:

- Management
- Marketing
- Development
- Leasing
- Retailing

Financial, operations, insurance, e-commerce, research, and other terms are also included.

This book has been compiled for use by anyone who needs a definition of a shopping center term. The guide will assist newcomers in learning the jargon of the industry. Seasoned professionals can refer to this guide to find definitions of new industry terms, to get further explanation or clarification of a term they are not clear on, or to understand the language used by a shopping center colleague in a shopping center discipline other than their own.

This new volume features a helpful translation guide that translates the terms in four languages: French, German, Portuguese, and Spanish.

The dictionary that follows lists key terms and definitions. The terms are defined within the context of the shopping center subject area in which they originally appeared, and to further assist the reader, the specific subject area is identified within brackets following the term.

In some instances a word or phrase has been added to clarify a term that needed explanation after being taken out of the context of its original subject area, or to give greater depth to a definition.

Terms have numerical footnotes accompanying them to indicate the source from which they are reprinted. Readers can thus understand the context in which a term was originally used and can access the definition's original source for further information if desired.

Sources of
Shopping Center Terms

The terms and definitions contained herein have been updated and edited for clarity and style from content matter depicted in books, news articles, educational sessions, and meetings of professionals in the shopping center and other related industries, including but not limited to the following sources:

ICSC Sources

1. *ICSC Research Quarterly,* "Shopping Center Definitions."

2. *Marketing Your Shopping Center,* S. Albert Wenner.

3. *Fundamentals of Shopping Center Management.*

4. *ICSC Keys to Shopping Center Marketing Series.*

5. *Fundamentals of Shopping Center Marketing.*

6. *Market Research for Shopping Centers,* edited by Ruben A. Roca.

7. *ICSC Keys to Shopping Center Management Series.*

8. *Preparing a Budget for a Small Shopping Center,* Alan A. Alexander, CSM.

9. *Shopping Center Lease Administration,* Alan A. Alexander, CSM.

10. *The SCORE: ICSC's Handbook on Shopping Center Operations, Revenues & Expenses,* 1993.

11. *Construction Management Techniques,* Ray G. Simms.

12. *Carpenter's Shopping Center Management,* edited by Robert J. Flynn, CSM.

13. *Advanced Shopping Center Management: Roofs.*

14. *Advanced Shopping Center Management: Parking Lots.*

15. *Finance for Shopping Center Nonfinancial Professionals.*

16. *The ICSC Temporary Tenant Handbook.*

17. *Shopping Center Redevelopment and Renovation.*

18. *Shopping Center Management.*

19. *The Art and Science of Outlet and Off-Price Retailing & Development.*

20. Glossary of Financial Terms, *Value Retail News.*

21. *Keys to Shopping Center Management Series: Maintenance.*

22. *Keys to Shopping Center Management Series: The Security Process.*

23. *Critical Issues Facing Small Shopping Centers.*

24. "Maximizing Revenue from the Lease Administration Process," presented by Barbara J. Knode, February 3, 2000, at ICSC's University of Shopping Centers, Atlanta, Georgia.

Additional Sources

25. Dictionary of Real Estate Terms, Homes 101.net, © 1999–2000. http://www.homes101.net/r/dic/a.htm.

26. *The Carlson Report for Shopping Center Management,* February 1998.

27. Webopedia, © 2000, 2001 by internet.com Corp. http://e-com.webopedia.com; http://webopedia.internet.com.

28. Glossary of E-Commerce Terms, Oregon Innovation Center. http://www.oregoninnovation.org/pressroom /glossary a-c.html.

29. Securitzation Glossary of Terms, Special Report, Institutional Real Estate, Inc.

30. Glossary, National Association of Real Estate Investment Trusts® (NAREIT). http://www.nareit.com/changing facesite/glossary.htm.

ICSC's Dictionary of Shopping Center Terms

A

ABC Report [RESEARCH] Audit Bureau of Circulations Report. An audited report of newspaper circulation researched and published by this independent firm.[4]

absorption (rate) [LEASING] The percentage of a particular type of real estate that can be sold or leased in a particular location during a certain period of time.[25]

abstract [LEASING/LEGAL] A summary. A shortened version outlining the main points of a document.[3]

accelerated depreciation [ACCOUNTING/FINANCE] The method(s) of depreciation for income tax purposes that increases the write-off at a rate higher than under the straight-line method of depreciation.[25]

access time [MARKETING] The half hour in prime time television (7:30 P.M. to 8:00 P.M. Eastern Standard Time Monday–Saturday) that the networks have been required to turn back to the local stations. Network-originated programming in prime time is only three hours per night Monday through Saturday, four hours on Sunday.[5]

account executive [MARKETING] One who supervises client use of print and electronic media as advertising agency representative.[2]

accounts payable [ACCOUNTING] Cash amounts owed on open accounts, whereby the buyer pays cash sometime after the date of sale.[15]

accounts receivable [ACCOUNTING] All income that has been billed and is still owed at any point in time.[4]

accrual [ACCOUNTING] The entry made to record a bill not yet received or an income item not yet collected.[15]

accrual basis of accounting [ACCOUNTING] The method of accounting whereby revenues and expenses are identified with specific periods of time, such as a month or year, and are recorded as incurred, along with acquired assets, without regard to the date of receipt or payment of cash; distinguished from cash basis.[3]

An accounting method that tracks expenditures against the budget for a given time frame, indicating amounts already received and paid as well as anticipated receipts and planned expenditures.[4]

accrued liabilities [ACCOUNTING] Amounts recognized for wages, salaries, interest, and similar items not yet payable.[15]

accumulated depreciation [ACCOUNTING] The portion of the original cost of fixed assets that has already been charged to operations in an expense.[15]

activity report [OPERATIONS/SECURITY] A written record of openings, closing, and alarms for a protected area over a set period of time. The report is usually compiled by the security staff.[22]

ad grid [MARKETING] A system of presenting rates that assigns various values to each time period. Broadcast time can be offered and sold in terms of grids.[2]

adaptive re-use [DEVELOPMENT] Adapting a building for retail use. Examples: old factories, school buildings, warehouses, sometimes turned into outlet retail projects.[19]

add-on rent charges [ACCOUNTING] Additional charges to the rent, which may include service charges for maintenance of common areas, merchants' association fees, contribution to the marketing fund, HVAC (heating, ventilation, and air-conditioning), and electric charges, trash, insurance, or taxes.[4]

ADI [RESEARCH] *See* area of dominant influence.

adjacency [MARKETING] On a television or radio station, the period of time immediately following or preceding a regularly scheduled program. Also used almost interchangeably with "spot," thus "the Dallas adjacency at 9:00 P.M."[5]

A program or time period that immediately precedes or follows a scheduled program on radio or television.[2]

administration fee [ACCOUNTING] The cost of actually administering the common area of a shopping center; a standard addition to the overall cost of common-area maintenance (CAM), typically set at 15 percent of tenant CAM contribution but may vary due to negotiation between landlord and tenant.[15]

administrative marketing costs [ACCOUNTING/MARKETING] The cost of payroll, benefits, rent, and bookkeeping and other administrative costs attributed to marketing.[10]

advance [MARKETING] A story, feature, or copy of a speech distributed to the media before the event takes place.[4]

advance rental [ACCOUNTING] Money paid up front and applied to tenant's first month's rental.[24]

advertising [MARKETING] The nonpersonal communication of a sales message to actual or potential purchasers by a person or organization selling a product or service, delivered through a paid medium for the purpose of influencing the buying behavior of those purchasers.[3]

advertising campaign [MARKETING] Advertising and related efforts used on behalf of a shopping center in the attainment of predetermined goals.[2]

advertising fund [ACCOUNTING/MARKETING] A fund set up by the shopping center developer for producing special ad campaigns or catalogs for the shopping center.[4]

advertising plan [MARKETING] A description of the message, themes, and creative elements of an advertising campaign. It includes a budget for creative and production services.[4]

agate lines [MARKETING] A newspaper advertising unit of measurement. An agate line is one column wide by one-fourteenth inch deep.[2]

aggregate [OPERATIONS] Gravel, crushed stone, slag, or marble embedded in a flood coat of hot bitumen as the top surface for built-up roofs.[13]

aided recall [RESEARCH] A research technique that uses prompting questions or materials to aid a respondent's memory of the original exposure situation.[2]

air check [MARKETING] A tape of an actual television or radio broadcast that serves as file copy and which the sponsor may use to evaluate the content.[2]

alarm system [OPERATIONS/SECURITY] The network of alarms or monitoring devices designed to detect and alert guards to abnormalities within a center or retail space.[22]

alligatoring [OPERATIONS] *Also known as alligator cracks.* Shrinkage cracking of the bituminous surface of a built-up roof, producing a pattern resembling an alligator's hide. It results from solar radiation and exposure to the elements.[3]

alteration costs [RETAIL] Costs incurred in altering and finishing merchandise to meet the needs of customers at the time of sale.[4]

amortization [ACCOUNTING/FINANCE] The repayment of a portion of the principle before the end of the term of the loan; the opposite of an interest-only loan; such expenses, related to intangible assets, are recorded on an operating statement after net operating income (NOI), or "below the (bottom) line."[15]

The act or process of extinguishing a debt, with equal payments over regular intervals over a specific period of time.[29]

anchor store　[RETAIL] A major store (usually a chain store) in a shopping center having substantial economic strength and occupying a large square footage.[3]

A major department store branch in a shopping center.[2]

The stores and other uses that occupy the largest spaces in a center and serve as the primary traffic generators. Freestanding anchors are excluded.[10]

ancillary charges　[ACCOUNTING] Charges to tenants beyond minimum and percentage rent, typically CAM, insurance, real estate taxes, HVAC, trash hauling, promotional.[17]

angle　[MARKETING] The emphasis or slant of a story.[4]

annual basic rental　[ACCOUNTING/LEASING] The annual rent per square foot, one twelfth due on the first day of each month.[24]

annual percentage rent　[ACCOUNTING/LEASING] A percentage of tenant's sales over a predetermined sales threshold.[24]

answer print　[MARKETING] A composite print of sound, music, and opticals leading to a master print from which duplicates are made for distribution.[2]

apportionment　[ACCOUNTING/FINANCE] A division or allocation of responsibility among two or more persons.[25]

appraisal　[ACCOUNTING/FINANCE] Various methods in which the value of a property is determined.[15]

appraisal rent　[ACCOUNTING/LEASING] An amount based on sales potential as affected by the appraisal of a property at a given point in time; sometimes used interchangeably with *market rent*.[15]

approach (outdoor)　[MARKETING] The distance measured along the line traveled from the point where an advertising poster becomes visible to a point where the copy ceases to be readable.[2]

arbitron　[MARKETING/RESEARCH] American Research Bureau (ARB). The company which produces local spot television and radio audience reports. All spot television and radio buys should be made using ARB audience figures.[5]

A device for recording when the television is on; a part of a research operation.[2]

area of dominant influence (ADI) [RESEARCH] A group of counties in which the majority of the households watch television stations broadcasting from a particular transmitter city. The U.S. is divided into 208 mutually exclusive ADIs. No county can be in more than one ADI.[5]

A geographic area designated by the Arbitron Ratings Company, which defines a television or radio market for the purpose of measuring viewing and listening audiences.[4]

artificial breakpoint *See* unnatural breakpoint.

as-built plans [ARCHITECTURE/CONSTRUCTION] The final blueprints used by an architect when constructing a shopping center or tenant space. As-builts contain the most up-to-date information about a center.[21]

asphalt [OPERATIONS] A highly viscous hydrocarbon derived from residue after distillation of petroleum; used as a waterproofing agent in certain built-up roofs and for other purposes.[13]

asphalt emulsion [OPERATIONS] A method of sealer used to coat an asphalt parking lot. The emulsion is usually a diluted mixture of water, mineral filler, ash, and rubber added to a coal tar or asphalt sealer.[21]

assault and battery [OPERATIONS/SECURITY] An attempt or threat, with force or violence, to do corporal harm to another. Under common law, assault and battery are two separate crimes. An assault under the common law definition occurs if there is no actual touching or injury of another or corporal harm, merely an attempt. If there is touching of the other person, or injury or corporal harm, then the act is battery rather than assault.[3]

asset [FINANCE] Any owned physical object (tangible) or right (intangible) having a monetary value.[5]

What the business owns. *See* current assets and fixed assets.[4]

asset turnover [ACCOUNTING/FINANCE] A ratio determined by dividing net sales by average total assets.[15]

assignee [LEASING/LEGAL] New tenant that assumes the rights and responsibilities of the original tenant under the existing lease. Landlord approval usually required.[18]

assignment [LEASING/LEGAL] The transfer to another party of all a tenant's interests in a lease for the remainder of the lease term. It is distinguished from a sublease, in which some portion of the terms of the lease remains with the primary tenant.[3]

attractive nuisance   [OPERATIONS] A potentially hazardous object, such as a swimming pool, or a condition, such as an open pit on a parcel of land, that is inviting and potentially dangerous to young children.[25]

audience   [MARKETING/RESEARCH] All those who see some part of the editorial content of a publication, or listen to or see some part of a broadcast program, or have the opportunity to read an outdoor, transit, or point-of-purchase advertising message. Synonymous with total audience.[5]

   People who make up the primary and secondary market areas.[2]

audit trail   [ACCOUNTING] An explicit set of documentation by accountants illustrating how each entry made its way into "the books."[15]

avails   [MARKETING] The abbreviation for "availabilities." Avails list all television or radio programs available for commercial insertions, ratings for the program or time period for the market or for a target audience, cost per insertion, cost per rating point, and more.[4]

   A list of spots with their audiences, which a television or radio station has available for purchase.[5]

average   [ACCOUNTING] *See* mean. A measure of central tendency used to indicate the size of the data taken as a whole as compared with that of particular items.[6]

average household income   [GENERAL] Estimated average income (salaried income) per household.[6]

average inventory   [RETAIL] An average of the stock on hand at representative dates throughout the year or season.[4]

average quarter-hour persons (AQH)   [MARKETING/RESEARCH] An estimate of the average number of people in a demographic group listening to the radio for at least five minutes during a fifteen-minute period.[4]

B

back of the house or **back room** [OPERATIONS/LEASING] Nonselling area of a store that includes stockrooms, rest rooms, etc.[19]

back-to-back [MARKETING] Describes the situation where two commercials or programs directly follow each other.[2]

bad debt allowance [ACCOUNTING] *Also known as credit loss.* The allowance for uncollectible tenant billing balances.[10]

balance sheet [ACCOUNTING] A statement of financial position of any economic unit disclosing as of a given moment in time its assets, at cost, depreciated cost, or other indicated value; its liabilities; and its ownership equities.[3]

The portion of a financial statement showing a company's financial position—its assets, liabilities, and equity—at a particular point in time, analogous to a scorecard. On a balance sheet, assets equal liabilities plus equity; equity equals assets minus liabilities.[15]

See cash flow statement.[4]

balloon risk [FINANCE] The risk that a borrower will not be able to make a balloon (lump sum) payment at maturity due to a lack of funding.[29]

bank reconciliation [ACCOUNTING] A comparison of the cash disbursements journal with the bank's account record.[4]

banner heading [MARKETING] A print media term for a heading positioned across the top of box ad page(s) listing the theme, length of event, and other pertinent details.[2]

banning [SECURITY] A policy by which center security is able to bar a lawbreaker from the shopping center for a finite amount of time.[7]

base rent [ACCOUNTING/LEASING] *See* minimum rent.

base sheet [OPERATIONS] A heavy sheet of felt, asbestos, or organic material, often used as first ply in built-up roofing. Often saturated and factory coated with asphalt. Also used for roof insulation underlayment.[13]

basis [ACCOUNTING/FINANCE] The point from which gains, losses, and depreciation deductions are computed.[25]

baton   [SECURITY] A long, slender but sturdy stick used by center security as a nonlethal weapon. Also known as a billy club or nightstick.[7]

benchmarking   [RESEARCH] The process of measuring a business's performance in a particular area against some standard, which can be that of the industry as a whole, that of a competitor, or one related to the same business's overall performance.[15]

Best Company ratings   [INSURANCE] The A.M. Best Company quantitatively and qualitatively evaluates the financial condition of insurance carriers. Its ratings reflect company management with an alphabetical rating ranging from A+ down to C. These letters are followed by a financial numerical rating, which reflects the size of the carrier's surplus (equity).[7]

big-box   [LEASING/RETAIL] A single-use store, typically between 10,000 to 100,000 square feet or more, such as a large bookstore, office-supply store, pet store, electronics store, or toy store.[17]

bill-backs   [ACCOUNTING] All expense items enumerated in the lease—such as common area, taxes, insurance, and maintenance—that are paid by the landlord and then billed to the tenant.[8]

billboard   [MARKETING] The common name for an outdoor sign.[2]

A radio or television credit naming the sponsor and a slogan, used at the start or close of a program.[2]

In outdoor advertising, a term formerly used generally to mean poster.[5]

In television advertising, the term refers to special commercial positions at the start and close of a telecast to announce the name of the sponsor.[5]

birdbath   [OPERATIONS] A term used to describe a low area in asphalt paving which tends to collect water.[3]

bitumen   [OPERATIONS] The generic term for a semisolid mixture of hydrocarbons derived from petroleum or coal; used to waterproof roofs. The two basic bitumens used in roofing are asphalt and coal tar pitch.[3]

A hydrocarbon-based substance that is used as the waterproofing element in built-up roofs. Bitumens are either coal-tar based or asphalt based and are the by-products of the oil-to-gasoline production process.[7]

blanket or **rolling wrap-up**   [INSURANCE] A type of wrap-

up, or owner-controlled insurance, covering a series of renovation projects, often considered when total construction
costs exceed $100 million.[17]

bleeding   [OPERATIONS] *Also known as fat spots.* Sticky black
spots that appear on the parking lot pavement surface in
warm weather. They can be very slippery when wet.[14]

blistering   [OPERATIONS] The formation of air- or gas-filled
swellings in a roof membrane.[3]

blue line   [MARKETING] A press proof sheet containing all
the elements of an ad, including where color will go.[4]

bodily injury   [SECURITY/INSURANCE] Part of general liability coverage that insures the policyholder against physical
injury, including bodily injury, sickness, disease, or death to
a third party.[7]

boiler and machinery insurance   [INSURANCE] Coverage
for damage caused by or to boilers and machinery, including business interruption caused by boiler explosion or
machinery breakdown.[7]

boilerplate   [LEGAL] Those clauses of a contract that are
generally felt to be typical, standard, prescribed, representative, established, or accepted.[3]

bookkeeping   [ACCOUNTING] The process of analyzing,
recording, and classifying transactions for the purpose of
establishing a basis for recording and reporting the financial affairs of the enterprise and the results of its operations.[3]

bottom line   [ACCOUNTING] A measurement of profit (or
loss) in a budget or operating statement, typically expressed
as net operating income (NOI), as earnings before interest,
taxes, depreciation, and amortization (EBITDA). Funds
from operations (FFO) fall below the NOI line reflective of
cash flow.[15]

box ads   [MARKETING] A print media term meaning advertisements, generally uniform in size, grouped together under
a banner heading and promoting a cooperative event.[2]

break   [MARKETING] The commercial position between two
television or radio programs. Spots "on the break" are to be
distinguished from "in program" commercials. In general,
"in program" commercials are thought to have higher recall
value than spots "on the break."[5]

break even point   [FINANCE] The amount of rent or the
occupancy level needed to pay operating expenses and dept
service. Also called default point.[25]

breakpoint   [ACCOUNTING/MARKETING] Sometimes referred to as natural or actual breakpoint. In percentage rent, the point at which rent due from a specific percentage of sales equals the minimum rent.[7]

Theoretically, the point at which a tenant breaks even on expenses and sales, and thereafter begins to make a profit (a percentage of which is sometimes required to be paid to the landlord); also called a *sales breakpoint* or *natural breakpoint.*[15] *See* unnatural breakpoint.

bridge/mezzanine   [FINANCE] Financing for a company expecting to go public usually within six months to a year. Often bridge financing is structured so that it can be repaid from proceeds of a public underwriting.[20]

British thermal unit (BTU)   [OPERATIONS] A BTU is the amount of heat required to raise one pound of water one degree Fahrenheit.[7]

Broker   [LEASING] A licensed insurance professional who represents and acts on behalf of clients rather than an insurance company.[7]

brokerage   [LEASING/FINANCE] 1. The business of being a broker. 2. The commission received by a broker for his services.[25]

BTU   [OPERATIONS] *See* British thermal unit.

buckling   [OPERATIONS] Warping or wrinkling of the roof membrane.[13]

budget   [ACCOUNTING] An itemized listing and/or allotment of all estimated revenues anticipated and a listing (and segregation) of all estimated costs and expenses that will be incurred in obtaining those revenues over a fixed period of time.[7]

Any financial plan serving as an estimate of and a control over future operations.[5]

A summary of probable income and expenses for a given period of time.[8]

budget billing   [ACCOUNTING] In this method, the manager distributes copies of the applicable portion of the annual expense budget to the tenant and thereafter bills one-twelfth of the total for eleven months, with a final year-end charge adjusted for the by-then-established deficit or surplus.[12]

budgeted rent   [ACCOUNTING/LEASING] An amount based on sales potential, and representing the target approved by ownership for its annual plan; sometimes used interchangeably with *market rent.*[15]

building code endorsement [OPERATIONS/INSURANCE/CONSTRUCTION] An addition to property policies that includes coverage for work that might have to be done to comply with building code requirements enacted after the building is constructed.[7]

built-up roof (BUR) [OPERATIONS] A roofing membrane made of alternating layers or plies of felt adhered and made waterproof by the application of asphalt or coal tar bitumens.[7]

bulk mail [MARKETING] A quantity of third-class mail that must be delivered to the post office in bundles presorted by city, state, and ZIP code.[2]

bulk rate contract [MARKETING] Reduced advertising rate based upon annual linage used.[2]

bullet loans [FINANCE] Loans on which only the interest is paid for the term of the loan, with the full principal due upon maturity.[12]

bulletin [MARKETING] A billboard composed of multiple wooden panels on which a commercial message is painted. Bulletin billboards typically measure 14' x 48' or 10'6" x 36', with some exceptions.[4]

BUR [OPERATIONS] *See* built-up roof.

burglary [SECURITY] Forcible entry into a building with intent to commit a crime.[7]

business interruption insurance [INSURANCE] Covers loss of net income, other than loss of rents, that would have been earned, including expenses incurred to reduce that loss.[7]

business plan [FINANCE/OPERATIONS] A detailed, carefully prepared road map for the operation of a business for the coming year or years; it sets a direction and destination (strategy) for the business and plots the course (tactics) to get there. Typically contains operations, marketing, leasing development, and financial plan.[15]

buyout [LEASING] Funds provided to enable operating management to acquire a tenant that is underperforming to replace it with a more productive tenant.[20]

byline [MARKETING] The name of an article's writer or reporter, appearing above or at the end of an article.[4]

C

CAM [ACCOUNTING/OPERATIONS] *See* common area maintenance.

CAM administration fee [ACCOUNTING] Receipts from tenants for administering CAM common area maintenance charges.[10]

camera ready [MARKETING] A print media term. A finished, reproducible typeset paste-up of an ad.[2]

cancellation clause or **"kickout clause"** [LEASING/LEGAL] A contract provision that gives the right to terminate obligations upon the occurrence of specified conditions or events.[25]

cap [ACCOUNTING/LEASING] A maximum amount that a tenant must pay for certain expenses, no matter how much they actually increase; usually a set amount or a percentage of increase.[15]

cap (capitalization) rate [FINANCE] The rate at which net operating income (NOI) is discounted in determining the market value of a shopping center. It is one method to estimate property value. The ratio of income to price, determined by such factors as the market and the quality of a property, and used along with net operating income (NOI) to determine value; when two of three values are known (annual net operating income, cap rate, property value estimate), the calculations are: 1. Value = NOI/Cap Rate; 2. NOI = Value x Cap Rate; 3. Cap Rate = NOI/Value.[15]

A rate of return used to derive the capital value of an income stream. The formula is Value + annual income = capitlization rate.[25] *See* net operating income.

capital budget [MARKETING] Includes income from sale of assets, broken down as to gain or loss against book value, payments on the principal of a mortgage or other debt, and the year's outlays for repairs or additions to be capitalized for depreciation over future years. All numbers used in the capital budget are as estimated going in and as actual in the yearend report.[12]

An outline of expenditures for physical improvements to the property.[7]

capital costs [ACCOUNTING] Money spent on building improvements.[7]

capital expenditures [ACCOUNTING/OPERATIONS] Payments for something expected to last for several years, and recorded on a balance sheet as assets; for a shopping center, these include tenant improvement allowances, work by the landlord to improve a space, and commissions paid to the broker or management company, and operating expenditures such as parking lot resurfacing.[15]

capital expense [ACCOUNTING/OPERATIONS] A structural repair such as the replacement of a storm sewer system.[7]

The annual amount required to pay interest on and provide for the ultimate return (depreciation or amortization) of the investment.[7]

capitalization [FINANCE] The process of converting into a present value (obtaining the present worth of) a series of anticipated future annual installments of income.[7]

capsheet [OPERATIONS] The top ply of certain built-up roofs exposed to elements. Usually coated to provide weather resistance.[13]

captive brand stores [LEASING/RETAIL] Outlets selling brands that are not traded anywhere except in their own stores.[19]

captive insurer [INSURANCE] An insurance company that is sponsored or owned by another entity whose primary purpose is to insure the exposures of its founders.[7]

capture rate analysis [RESEARCH] An analysis that assumes retail centers attract expenditure levels relative to their size and location. Thus, a center is more likely to attract a shopper if the center is larger, if it is located nearer the shopper's residence than other centers, or both.[6]

card holder or sign holder [MARKETING] A plex or metal holder used to display informational signs within the shopping center or store. Available in many sizes for both floor and counter signage.[19]

carded [MARKETING/RETAIL] Describing merchandise that is delivered to the retailer attached to a display card, like jewelry, small toys, etc.[19]

carrier [INSURANCE] An insurance company.[7]

cart [LEASING/RETAIL] A merchandising display unit for a temporary tenant. Carts, often known as pushcarts or retail merchandising units (RMUs), are mobile, usually metal and/or wooden, and sometimes supplemented with fixtures to provide the tenant with adequate display areas.[16]

case history   [GENERAL] A study of similar projects elsewhere with a view to understanding commercial successes—and avoiding commercial failures.[17]

cash basis   [ACCOUNTING] An accounting method that, unlike the accrual basis method, recognizes revenues and expenses as they are actually received or paid, not as they are earned or owed.[15]

cash disbursement journal   [ACCOUNTING] A monthly record of all payments.[4]

cash discount   [ACCOUNTING] Percentage off billed price; concession for paying bills within the time period indicated on the invoice. (For example, 2/10 means 2 percent is deductible from the bill if it is paid within ten days of the invoice date.)[3]

The discount for prompt payment of purchases earned on the goods sold during a specified period.[7]

cash flow   [ACCOUNTING] Sometimes referred to as funds from operations. *See* funds from operations. The amount of spendable income available after all payments have been made for operating expenses and mortgage principal and interest; it is a way of recognizing the timing of receipts and payments.[15]

cash flow analysis   [ACCOUNTING] A projection of anticipated income and expenses according to the actual or anticipated times of receipt and disbursement. It indicates a positive or negative cash flow and allows for any necessary adjustments throughout the year.[4]

cash flow statement   [ACCOUNTING] A financial picture for a determined period of time. It provides an overview of assets and liabilities, and any variance between them. Also called a balance sheet.[4]

cash method   [ACCOUNTING] This report indicates exactly what was received and what was paid to date and relates specifically to the projected cash flow prepared with the budget.[4]

cash-wrap   [LEASING/RETAIL] The front counter/checkout area of a store or retail merchandising unit (RMU) that houses the cash register and wrapping section.[19]

CBD   [GENERAL] *See* central business district.

census tracts   [RESEARCH] Small areas into which large cities and adjacent areas are divided by the Census Bureau. They are designed to be relatively uniform; the average tract has about 4,000 residents.[6]

center mayor   [GENERAL] *See* mall mayor.

center-owned   [GENERAL] The square footage that is owned by the center and is the leasable area designed for tenant occupancy, including any owned freestanding buildings, plus basements, mezzanines, or upper floors. This does not include the square footage of buildings that are owned by anchor stores.[10]

center rate   [MARKETING] The reduced advertising rate arranged between the center and a publication for use by tenants during cooperative centerwide advertised events.[2]

center spread   [MARKETING] An advertisement printed across the two facing center pages, including the gutter inside margin white space. Outdoors, two adjacent panels using coordinated copy.[2]

central business district (CBD)   [GENERAL] Historically, the main shopping or business area of a town or city.[6]

central city   [GENERAL] The major city around which Standard Metropolitan Statistical Areas (SMSAs) are defined.[6]

central/urban city center   [GENERAL] Located in a major city in one of the U.S. Census Bureau's metropolitan statistical areas, or in a large urban core city in Canada. A center can be located anywhere inside the boundaries of a central/urban city, not just in its downtown area.[10]

centralized administrative system   [ACCOUNTING] An administrative system in which all financial systems, including payroll, accounts receivable and payable, and purchases originate from a home office rather than from individual shopping centers. *See* decentralized system *and* hybrid decentralized system.[7]

certificate of insurance   [INSURANCE] A document that is evidence that an insurance policy has been issued.[7]

A document that verifies the type and amounts of insurance carried by a policyholder.[7]

certificate of occupancy   [CONSTRUCTION] A document issued by a local government to a developer permitting the structure to be occupied by members of the public. Issuance of the certificate generally indicates that the building is in compliance with public health and building codes.[25]

chain of command   [OPERATIONS] The ordering of a security force by rank or importance. The order of management rank from the highest level of authority, usually a chief operating officer (U.S.) or managing director (U.K.).[22]

chart of accounts   [ACCOUNTING] A systematically arranged list of accounts applicable to a specific concern, giving account names and numbers, if any.[5]

An organized list of a company's financial activity codes, the "financial DNA." [15]

Christmas decor/events   [MARKETING] The cost of seasonal decor and special events during the Christmas season. It includes labor, decorations, signs, point-of-purchase materials, and special entertainment attributable to the Christmas season.[10]

chuckhole   *See* pothole.

circular/shopper   [MARKETING] A preprinted special advertising section with a cover paper followed by ads relating to a specific center and event; hand delivered or inserted into an area publication.[2]

circulation   [OPERATIONS] To the Audit Bureau of Circulation, this means paid copies of a publication. In broadcast, it means the number of television set–owning families within range of a station signal. In outdoor advertising, it means the number of people passing an advertisement who have a reasonable chance of seeing it.[5]

The number of copies of a newspaper or circular sold and distributed.[2]

circulation plan   [LEASING/OPERATIONS] A diagram showing the expected route customers take throughout a store or project. In a store, it determines the location of fixtures, displays, and counters to ensure maximum exposure of merchandise to a maximum number of customers.[19]

city zone   [GENERAL] An area of distribution as defined by the newspaper, typically taking in the city plus surrounding residential areas.[4]

civil liability   [INSURANCE] The legal responsibility one citizen has to another. It is liability law which applies to an individual who is considered a victim even though no law has been broken. Civil liability is decided in a civil court of law.[7]

claim   [INSURANCE] A demand to recover payment under an insurance policy; the amount of the loss.[7]

Class A/B/C rates   [MARKETING] Rate structure determining rates for the most to the least desirable advertising time periods.[2]

close   [MARKETING] In print media to reach the final stage of preparing to publish, at which time no editorial matter or advertisements can be inserted. Also a noun: the close.[4]

closing entries [ACCOUNTING/OPERATIONS] Special entries in a journal, made to reverse all account balances in preparation for the next accounting period.[15]

cluster-shaped shopping center [GENERAL] An early form of regional center design. Stores are arranged in a rectangular area, with parking on as many as four sides of the center and with service provided through a tunnel or shielded service bays or a combination of both. Early cluster centers were built as open centers, although some have since been enclosed. The design results in a series of malls. A single-anchor cluster would probably have its anchor store extending from the periphery to the center of the cluster.[12]

clutter [MARKETING] An overabundance of visual and/or audio messages in a given medium.[4]

CMBS [FINANCE] Commercial Mortgage-Backed Securities. Securities collateralized by loans on commercial real estate. Yield on the mortgages is passed through to the investors, less a service charge by the issuing organization.[29]

coal tar [OPERATIONS] One of two types of bitumen used to construct built-up roofs.[7]

Bitumen derived from coking of coal. Used as waterproofing material for minimally sloped built-up roofs.[13]

COD (cash on delivery) [OPERATIONS/RETAIL] A transaction in which the customer or buyer agrees to pay when the goods are received.[3]

coinsurance clause [INSURANCE] A clause penalizing the insured if the amount insured for is less than a pre-agreed specified percentage of the value of the property insured.[7]

collateral [ACCOUNTING/FINANCE] Generally, the guaranteed backup source of a loan repayment if the investor does not repay the loan as specified in the loan documents; this security ranges from property to a personal guarantee.[15]

color key [MARKETING] A proof that indicates both where color is in an ad and the percentages of color that will be applied.[4]

column depth/width [MARKETING] A print advertising term. Example: one column wide by one inch deep.[2]

Depth: The dimension of a column measured from the top of the page to the bottom, in either agate lines or inches.[2]

The basic newspaper unit of measurement.[4]

combination rate [MARKETING] A single rate charged for insertion in two or more publications, usually owned by the same publisher.[2]

commencement date   [LEASING/LEGAL] The day on which a tenant's lease term begins; not to be confused with occupancy date.[7]

commercial general liability policy   [INSURANCE] A broad form of third-party insurance that covers the policyholder in the event of bodily injury, personal injury, and property damage claims.[7]

commercial length   [MARKETING] In broadcast, the duration of a commercial, expressed in seconds.[5]

common area   [ACCOUNTING/OPERATIONS] The walkways and areas onto which the stores in a center face and which conduct the flow of customer traffic.[2]

The portions of a shopping center that have been designated and improved for common use by or for the benefit of more than one occupant of the shopping center.[5]

common area HVAC energy   [MARKETING] Heating, ventilation, and air-conditioning (HVAC) energy expenses for the common area only.[11]

common area maintenance (CAM)   [OPERATIONS/ACCOUNTING] The amount of money charged to tenants for their shares of maintaining a center's common area.

The charge that a tenant pays for shared services and facilities such as electricity, security, and maintenance of parking lots.[7]

The area maintained in common by all tenants, such as parking lots and common passages. This area is often defined in the lease and may or may not include all physical areas or be paid for by all tenants.[7]

Items charged to common-area maintenance may include cleaning services, parking lot sweeping and maintenance, snow removal, security, and upkeep.[12]

community acceptance   [MARKETING] Recognition of a shopping center by its market area as an integral part of the community, as well as a purveyor of goods and services.[2]

community center   [MARKETING] A community center typically offers a wider range of apparel and other soft goods than the neighborhood center. Among the more common anchors are supermarkets, superdrugstores, and discount department stores. Community center tenants sometimes include off-price retailers selling such items as apparel, home improvement/furnishings, toys, electronics, or sporting goods. The center is usually configured as a strip, in a straight line, or as an "L" or a "U" shape. Of the eight center types, community centers encompass the widest range of formats. For example, certain centers that are anchored by a large discount department store refer to themselves as discount centers. Others with a high percentage of square footage allocated to off-price retailers can be termed off-price centers.[1]

A shopping complex constructed around a junior department store or variety store. Such a center usually lacks a full-line department store. The average size is 150,000 square feet of gross leasable area.[6]

In addition to convenience goods and personal services, community centers typically offer a selection of apparel and home furnishings. Anchors commonly consist of a junior department store and/or a large variety store in addition to one or more supermarkets. The size ranges from 100,000 to 300,000 square feet of GLA and the land area from 10 to 30 acres.[12]

community rooms [MARKETING] An area for public use ranging from bare halls equipped with folding chairs capable of seating perhaps 50 persons, to quite elaborate facilities accommodating several hundred and providing kitchens, tables, stages, special lighting, and sound equipment.[12]

compaction [OPERATIONS] The squeezing of a layer of asphalt by the addition of another asphalt layer or lift. Dense asphalt is usually required for parking lots and roadways.[7]

comparative lease analysis [FINANCE/LEASING] A method of quantifying the economic differences between a proposed lease and a baseline, such as the development pro forma, for the same space.[15]

comparison goods [RETAIL] Merchandise offered by department stores, apparel, furniture, and other stores in sufficient variety to permit a wide range of choice and comparison between the merchandise offered by one store and another. Comparison-shopping trips are made less often than shopping trips for convenience items.[6]

competing business [LEASING/GENERAL] A policy that limits tenant from opening competitive stores in the vicinity (within 50 miles) of the shopping center. Protects landlord from a reduced percentage rent; commonly referred to as *radius restriction*.[24]

competitive effectiveness [GENERAL] That portion of the total sales capacity of a competitive unit or group of stores that the unit or group obtains from *within* the subject trade area. In the predevelopment stage, that term refers to the estimated effect existing competitive facilities will have in the subject trade area after the proposed shopping center is constructed.[6]

competitive evaluation   [MARKETING] An inventory of the competition and other retail in the market to pinpoint a center's strengths and weaknesses and determine its competitive position in the market.[4]

competitive facilities   [GENERAL] Existing or known future retailing facilities either within or near the trade area that offer merchandise similar to that which will be offered in the proposed center. Note that "low-end" facilities should not be considered in the assessment of competition for higher-quality projects, and vice versa.[6]

compound interest   [ACCOUNTING] The interest on interest; interest earned during a given period is added to the principal and included in the next period's interest calculation.[7]

comprehensive   [MARKETING] A rough sketch of the idea for an ad.[4]

compressor   [OPERATIONS] The workhorse of an HVAC (heating, ventilation, and air-conditioning) unit. The compressor is the hardware that "pushes" hot or cold air out of the system and into the center space.[7]

concession   [LEASING] The privilege of maintaining a subsidiary business within certain premises.[3]

consequential loss coverage   [INSURANCE] The coverage for consequential loss should include all income derived from tenants. Loss of overage rent is readily computed on the basis of past performance. The loss should be computed on an actual monthly basis rather than treated as one-twelfth of the annual total. Coverage should also include loss of common area maintenance payments and any other tenant charges subject to abatement by lease terms.[12]

consideration   [LEGAL] Something tangible, usually money, that has been promised or done that binds a legal obligation and makes it enforceable.[7]

constant dollar projections   [ACCOUNTING] Dollar projections that account for only real growth and not for inflation.[3]

construction allowance   [FINANCE/LEASING] Money or financial incentives given to tenants for the cost of constructing their store space in a center.[7]

construction management [CONSTRUCTION] Construction management is a form of contracting. The construction manager acts as an agent for the developer or owner, taking no risk or financial responsibility for the outcome of the project, which is different from the responsibilities of a general contractor. The construction manager supervises, coordinates, and administers the work on behalf of the developer; however, all contracts are executed directly between the various trade contractors and the developer, with the construction manager signing as an agent of the owner. The construction manager might hire a general contractor or enter into multiple prime contracts with a variety of trade contractors. In either case, if there is a loss or overrun, the dispute is between the developer and the trade contractors, not between the developer and the construction manager.[11]

construction manager (CM) [CONSTRUCTION] An agent of the owner who supervises, coordinates, and administers construction work on a renovation or redevelopment but takes no risk or financial responsibility for its outcome, unless hired as a construction manager at risk.[17]

constructive eviction [LEGAL] The legal term describing a situation in which a lessor's breach of a lease contract causes the lessee (tenant) to cancel the contract and vacate.[25]

consumer benchmarks [RESEARCH] Comparative standards of shopping patterns and store-related performance.[4]

consumer market research [RESEARCH] Research based on questionnaire administration of two key types: a random sample survey, generally conducted by telephone within a designated geographic area (the primary trading area of the proposed facility); and an on-site survey of an existing competitive facility.[6]

Consumer Price Index (CPI) [ACCOUNTING/LEASING] An indicator of rising prices or inflation used to measure the impact of inflation upon consumers; published by the Bureau of Labor Statistics at the end of every month.[6]

Various statistical indexes gathered and published by the federal government as economic indicators.[7]

The most widely known of many such measures of price levels and inflation that are reported to the U.S. government. It measures and compares, from month to month, the total cost of a statistically determined "typical market basket" of goods and services consumed by U.S. households.[25]

Consumer Price Index adjustment (CPI) [ACCOUNTING/ LEASING] An adjustment to agreed-upon tenant charges such as marketing contributions based on changes in a consumer price index, generally released by government entities.[18]

consumer survey [RESEARCH] A study, either face-to-face (intercept survey) or by telephone, to determine shoppers' preferences and buying habits.[17]

contingency plans [SECURITY] Procedures to be implemented by security and center staff during an emergency.[7]

continuity [MARKETING] An advertising message that runs consistently; used for image-building.[2]

continuous occupancy clause [MARKETING/LEGAL] A requirement to fully operate a store during mall hours without interruption or closing.[7]

continuous scheduling [MARKETING] A consistent and ongoing presentation of the advertising message designed to reach a given audience repeatedly. For example, a commercial that airs every Thursday and Friday between 6 A.M. and 8 A.M. for 13 weeks.[4]

contra-asset account [ACCOUNTING] An account on a balance sheet that complements an asset account; additions to this type of account are recorded as credits, in the right-hand column.[15]

contract [OPERATIONS] An agreement by which two legally competent persons promise to obligate each other to do something.[3]

In media usage, a written agreement (usually one year's duration) to use a specified amount of space (print) or air time (radio and TV).[2]

contract security [OPERATIONS/SECURITY] An outside security force hired by the center manager on a contract basis.[7]

contractors [OPERATIONS/CONSTRUCTION] Prior to actual construction, the contractor advises the owner, architect, and engineers on alternative methods of construction, prepares the project's construction budget and master schedule, and provides information and guidance on government approvals, safety requirements, bonding, insurance, local labor agreements, wages, and work rules. During the construction phase, the contractor provides on-site organization and supervision for all elements of the work, provides cost statements and progress billings, and exercises overall financial and administrative control of the project.[11]

Laborers who are hired by center managers for certain tasks. They are called contractors because the work is done according to a written agreement or contract.[7]

convenience goods [RETAIL] Goods from drug, grocery, liquor, and hardware stores; services from beauty, barber, and bake shops; and services from laundry and dry cleaning establishments.[6]

convenience shopping center [GENERAL] Planned development in which the predominant retailing elements are devoted to providing day-to-day necessities.[6]

conversion [DEVELOPMENT] Taking a conventional retail mall or center and "converting" it to another type of shopping center such as value-oriented retailing by re-leasing to value-oriented tenants. Frequently done in conjunction with physical renovation of the property.[19]

cookie [E-COMMERCE] An e-commerce term for a message given to a Web browser by a Web server. The browser stores the message in a text file called cookie.txt. The message is then sent back to the server each time the browser requests a page from the server. The main purpose of cookies is to track Web page visits and identify users and in some cases prepare customized Web pages for them.[27]

cooperative pages [MARKETING] Single or facing pages divided into equal-size box ads, headed with a banner giving event details. All ads are in the same typeface; no logos are permitted.[2]

cooperative section [MARKETING] *See* circular/shopper or mailer.[2]

copy and layout [MARKETING] The visual and copy components of an ad to be typeset by a publication; usually requires a proof.[2]

copy and layout deadline [MARKETING] The lead time required to produce an ad and furnish a proof prior to publication.[2]

copy research [MARKETING] *Also known as copy testing.* Research to determine the effect of an advertisement or campaign, either before it is disseminated (pretesting) or afterward (posttesting).[6]

core samples [OPERATIONS/CONSTRUCTION] A testing process used to determine the condition of roofs or asphalt parking lots and roadways. A core is used to take a vertical sample of the roof or parking lot in question. An expert then surveys the layers to determine if the work was completed as agreed.[7]

cost   [RETAIL] The price at which goods are purchased in the wholesale market.[7]

cost approach   [FINANCE] A method in which the value of a property is derived by estimating the replacement cost of the improvements, deducting the estimated depreciation, and adding the value of the land, as estimated by use of the market-data approach.[7]

The value of a property obtained by estimating the replacement cost of the improvements, deducting the estimated depreciation, and adding the value of the land, as estimated by the use of the market-data approach. A high percentage of appraisals include the cost approach in the analysis, and, in some states, it is obligatory for the assessor to include it in his considerations.[12]

cost of capital   [FINANCE] The weighted average of the cost of equity. Generally expressed as the interest rate one must pay to borrow the necessary capital to make an investment. True cost of capital is considered the investors' expected rate of return on their investments. If the capital is already available through cash flow, the cost of the capital is the opportunity cost in terms of not being able to use that amount for alternative investments.[15]

cost per thousand (CPM)   [MARKETING] The cost of reaching a thousand people with an ad. The formula is: Total ad cost divided by number of thousands of people reached. For example, if the total cost for a newspaper ad is $500 and the ad is read by 100,000 people, the cost per thousand is five dollars.[4]

Used in comparing media costs. Can mean cost per one thousand readers, viewers, or listeners.[2]

The advertising cost of reaching 1,000 consumers.[4]

The cost of reaching 1,000 individuals in a demographic group. The lower the CPM (cost per thousand) the more efficient the spot. CPM is developed by dividing the cost of a spot by the thousands of homes reached. (*See* efficiency.)[5]

cost-plus contract   [OPERATIONS/CONSTRUCTION] A cost-plus contract has no fixed price. Rather, the owner pays the contractor whatever costs are incurred plus a fee for indirect overhead and profit. The fee is either a fixed dollar amount or a percentage of the total project cost.[11]

co-tenancy [LEASING] A term that refers to a clause inserted into a tenant's lease stipulating that a reduced rent or no rent be paid until an agreed-upon percentage of the center is occupied.[7]

course [OPERATIONS] Thickness and build-up of composition flashing, consisting of alternate layers of roof cement and felt.[13]

covenant [LEGAL] Words used in a contract whereby the person who is getting or giving something binds himself to the other for the performance (or nonperformance) of a particular act.[3]

cover page [MARKETING] The lead page of a cooperative special advertising section that promotes the theme, event day, center hours, and other pertinent information.[3]

coverage [MARKETING] The portion of an area, community, or group that may be reached by an advertising medium.[2]
The extent of the insurance provided by a policy.[7]

CPI Consumer Price Index adjustment [ACCOUNTING/ LEASING] An adjustment to the agreed-upon marketing contribution based on changes in the consumer price index.[4]

CPI Consumer Price Index rents [ACCOUNTING/LEASING] Rents that are pegged to rises in the consumer price index.[7]

CPM [MARKETING] *See* cost per thousand.

CPM/PCM [MARKETING] Cost per thousand per commercial minute.[2]

CPR [OPERATIONS/SECURITY] Cardiopulmonary resuscitation.[7]

credit [ACCOUNTING] A bookkeeping entry recording the reduction or elimination of an asset or expense, or the creation of or addition to a liability or item of net worth or revenue.[5]

credit loss [ACCOUNTING] *See* **bad debt allowance**.

credit tenants [LEASING] Generally, national chains with strong financial balance sheets, to which an appraiser might apply a different rate, based on lower risk, than to smaller, undercapitalized local operators.[15]

cricket [OPERATIONS] A roof slope or swell designed to run rainwater in a certain direction.[7]

Crime Prevention Through Environmental Design (CPTED) [DEVELOPMENT/SECURITY] A discipline involving designing a center or project with security in mind; specialists can help a project retain its desired look while minimizing the risk of crime and improving how people feel about the space.[17]

criminal liability [OPERATIONS/SECURITY] Liability occurring when a person is harmed by someone who is breaking the law. Redress for criminal liability is argued in a criminal court of law.[7]

critical mass [DEVELOPMENT] refers to the high number of retailers and square-footage needed in one center or in one market to create enough excitement to attract a high volume of shoppers.[20]

critical path method (CPM) schedule [CONSTRUCTION] The common scheduling method used for construction projects today, it includes the first and last activities, and all others in between, that combine to establish the overall duration of the project (the longest path in time from start to finish); any change in a critical path activity will delay or shorten the overall project duration or establish a new critical path.[17]

cross-collateralization [FINANCE] A grouping of mortgages or properties that serves to jointly secure one debt obligation. The concept that each of the partners in a property with more than one owner is personally responsible for full repayment of a loan, even though each partner may own only a small percentage of the property. It also applies to a group of properties covered by multiple loans, in which case any deficiency in income from—or even the loss on the sale of one property—in the group may be required to be made up by the income or sale of another property.[15]

cross-promotion [MARKETING] A promotion of two different retailers or advertisers whose products are unrelated and noncompetitive.[4]

cross-shopping [RESEARCH] Purchasing complementary items at different stores or in different departments of a single store.[4]

cume [MARKETING] Abbreviation for cumulative. The unduplicated audience a program or commercial gets if played two or more times in the same environment over a fixed period of time.[2]

The number of unduplicated people and/or homes reached by a given schedule over a given time period.[2]

The number of different persons or households reached by a number of advertising messages in one media vehicle or a combination of media vehicles over a period of time. Also called net audience or unduplicated audience.[5]

An estimate of the number of different people in a demographic group listening or viewing at least once during a specified time; comparable to a newspaper's circulation.[4]

cumulative attraction [MARKETING/LEASING] Refers to the sales advantage generated when two or more compatible retailers group together.[19]

curb stone [OPERATIONS] A brace system designed to keep HVAC (heating, ventilation, and air-conditioning) units from touching a roof.[7]

current asset [FINANCE] Unrestricted cash or other asset held for conversion within a relatively short period into cash or other similar asset, or useful goods or services. Usually the period is one year or less.[6]

Assets that can be converted into cash within 12 months.[7]

current dollar projections [FINANCE] Dollar projections that account for both real growth and inflation.[6]

current liability [ACCOUNTING] A short-term debt, regardless of its source, including any liability accrued and deferred, and unearned revenue that is to be paid out of current assets or is to be transferred to income within a relatively short period, usually one year or less.[5]

Those things owed and due within 12 months.[7]

current ratio [ACCOUNTING/FINANCE] The ratio of current assets to current liabilities; a current ratio of 2:1 (meaning two dollars of current assets for every dollar of current liabilities) is generally considered adequate.[15]

customer profile [RESEARCH] A composite estimate of the demographic characteristics of the people who buy certain products and the purchase patterns they will produce.[2]

cutline [MARKETING] A photo or illustration caption.[4]

D

daypart [MARKETING] In electronic media, a designated segment of the broadcast day—for example, "Prime."[4]

daytime business population data [RESEARCH] Demographic and economic information obtained for the worker population of a market area.[4]

DB [MARKETING] *See* **delayed broadcast**.[2]

debentures [FINANCE] Debts, such as bonds, notes, and loans, that are formal certificates of indebtedness indicating a company's promise to pay interest at a specified annual rate.[15]

debit [ACCOUNTING] A bookkeeping entry or posting recording the creation of or addition to an asset or expense, or the reduction or elimination of a liability.[5]

Entered in the left-hand column of each account, this is an addition to an asset account or an expense account, or reduction in a liability account.[15]

debt coverage ratio [FINANCE] The relationship between projected net operating income and expected debt service, expressed as NOI divided by debt service. A ratio of 1.0 (NOI equals debt service) means there is no margin of error, because any drop in NOI will leave insufficient cash to pay the debt service. The higher the ratio, the higher the margin of error, and the greater the chance that the loan will be repaid.[15]

debt service [ACCOUNTING/FINANCE] The payments consisting of amortization of and interest on a loan.[7]

decentralized administrative system [ACCOUNTING] An administrative system maintained at individual shopping centers (bookkeeping, accounting, purchasing). Each center is responsible for its work but may follow a standardized system. *See* **centralized system** and **hybrid decentralized system**.[7]

deck [OPERATIONS] The base on which roofing insulation is laid.[13]

declaration [INSURANCE] The "housekeeping" page on the front of a policy that identifies the policyholder, policy dates, and type and limits of coverage.[7]

deductible [ACCOUNTING] The portion of first dollar loss assumed by the insured.[7]

default [LEGAL] The failure to perform on an obligation previously committed to. For example, failure to pay rent on a specific date may place a tenant in default of obligations under his lease.[7]

Failure to comply with the terms of a lease.[7]

default rate [LEGAL] The rate of penalty charge tenant is charged when tenant is in default.[24]

delamination [OPERATIONS] A built-up roof membrane failure due to separation of felt plies, often resulting in wrinkling and cracking.[13]

delayed broadcast (DB) [MARKETING] The airing of a particular program or segment at other than its regularly scheduled broadcast time.[2]

demising studding [MARKETING] Steel supports located at the extremities of the leased space where a demising wall or drywall will be attached. Demising wall separates one tenant from the next.[17]

demographic characteristics [RESEARCH] Basic objective data about the shoppers of a center or residents of a market area. The statistics might include age, gender, income, education, and occupation.[4]

demographic market [RESEARCH] A demographic group or segment from which a shopping center draws its shoppers and sales.[4]

demographic multiplier [RESEARCH] An estimate of average household size and school-age children for various sizes and configurations of housing.[6]

demographic study [RESEARCH] A study of socioeconomic facts concerning individuals or households—such as car ownership, income, age, marital status, and education—studied by advertisers and merchandisers in order to make their sales and advertising programs more effective.[5]

demographics [RESEARCH] Vital statistics of the marketing area; that is, average income, age, number of children, cost of homes, education, and ethnic factors.[2]

Basic objective data about the shoppers in a geographic market area. Demographic statistics include age, sex, income, education, and occupation.[7]

The statistical characteristics of population groups, sorted out by such things as age and income, used to identify markets.[7]

department store type merchandise (DSTM) [RESEARCH] DSTM includes the kind of goods sold in shopping centers, such as apparel, shoes, jewelry, gifts, and other merchandise usually found in department stores and shopping centers. DSTM excludes personal services, entertainment, food service, drugs, groceries, and automotive, all of which may be found in shopping centers. DSTM sales potential is a component of a center's share of market calculation.[4]

DSTM includes merchandise normally found in variety, apparel, furniture, and appliance stores, and in other outlets such as jewelry, sporting goods, stationery, luggage, and camera stores, as well as department stores.[6]

General merchandise, apparel, furniture, and other merchandise (GAFO) as defined by the Department of Commerce, *Census of Retail Trade*.[6]

depreciation [FINANCE] The process of estimating and recording lost usefulness. Loosely, any wasting away of a physical asset and hence its cost, especially where not accompanied by a change in outward appearance, as in a slow-moving inventory of styled goods; functional loss of value.[5]

A loss from the upper limit of value caused by deterioration and/or obsolescence.[7]

The amount the value of a property deteriorates in a year, how much the total value is reduced by wear and tear.[7]

Expenses, or lost value over time, related to tangible assets; this is recorded on an operating statement after net operating income (NOI), or "below the (bottom) line."[15]

depth of selection [RETAIL] A merchandise line's variety of styles, colors, sizes, and prices.[19]

design criteria [ARCHITECTURE/CONSTRUCTION] A number of different elements set out in a center's design criteria manual, including guidelines for store design; mechanical, electrical, plumbing, and structural requirements; and the different responsibilities of tenant and landlord.[17]

designated market area (DMA) [RESEARCH] A geographic area designed by the A. C. Nielsen Company that defines a television market for the purpose of measuring viewing audiences.[4]

development area [DEVELOPMENT] Parcels of land owned by landlord, situated contiguous or adjacent to the shopping center. This is the land on which landlord pays taxes.[24]

difference-in-conditions insurance [INSURANCE] A separate insurance package written to cover catastrophic risk.[7]

differential advantage [MARKETING] A benefit—feature, location, or concept—that will distinguish your shopping center in the mind of the consumer. A differential advantage may be real or perceived.[4]

digital cash [ACCOUNTING/E-COMMERCE] An e-commerce term for a system that allows a person to pay for goods or services by transmitting a number from one computer to another. Similar to the serial numbers on dollar bills, the digital cash numbers are unique. Each one is issued by a bank and represents a specified sum of real money. One of the key features of digital cash is that, like real cash, it is anonymous and reusable. When a digital cash amount is sent from a buyer to a vendor, there is no way to obtain information about the buyer (as opposed to credit card systems). Another key difference is that a digital cash certificate can be reused.[27]

digital certificate [E-COMMERCE] An e-commerce term for an attachment to an electronic message used for security purposes. The most common use of a digital certificate is to verify that a user sending a message is who he or she claims to be, and to provide the receiver with the means to encode a reply.[27]

digital wallet [E-COMMERCE] An e-commerce term for encryption software that works like a physical wallet during electronic commerce transactions. A wallet can hold a user's payment information, a digital certificate to identify the user, and shipping information to speed transactions. The consumer benefits because his or her information is encrypted against piracy and because some wallets will automatically input shipping information at the merchant's site and will give the consumer the option of paying by digital cash or check. Merchants benefit by receiving protection against fraud.[27]

direct writing company [INSURANCE] An insurance company whose sales force represents only that one company.[7]

directors and officers liability insurance [INSURANCE] Protects a company's directors and officers in the event of a suit brought by stockholders or the public for negligence in the performance of their responsibilities.[7]

discount-anchored shopping center [GENERAL] A retail development in which a discount store is the major tenant in the development, with additional retail space usually consisting of smaller retail tenants.[7]

discount rate   [FINANCE] An interest rate commensurate with perceived risk; used to convert future payments or receipts to present value.[7]

discount retailing   [RETAIL] In softgoods, the sale of non-branded goods at prices less than that of branded goods in the same merchandise category.[19]

discounted cash flow   [FINANCE] The principle of discounted cash flow is that a dollar in hand is of greater value than one to be received at a future time, and the future value progressively diminishes as receipt is further deferred.[12]

display advertising   [MARKETING] Newspaper and magazine advertisements designed to attract attention by layout, variety of type, illustration, and relatively large space, and not grouped according to classifications, as in classified advertising.[5]

A print ad bound by a border or an implied border, as opposed to classified or line advertising.[4]

disposable income   [RESEARCH] That portion of an individual's income after all taxes and Social Security have been deducted; it is the portion which will be invested or spent.[6]

distribution   [MARKETING] Area covered by the circulation of a publication.[2]

DMA   [RESEARCH] *See* **designated market area**.

documentation   [OPERATIONS/SECURITY] The written or taped recording of the results of an investigation, survey, patrol, or any other activity.[7]

door busters   [MARKETING] Small groups of sharply reduced merchandise, with incomplete assortments.[2]

double decker   [MARKETING] Outdoor advertising erected one above the other.[2]

double-entry bookkeeping   [ACCOUNTING] The method usually followed for recording transactions. It involves formal bookkeeping records, consisting of journals, ledgers, or their equivalent, and supporting documents and files.[5]

double-dumbbell shaped   [DEVELOPMENT/GENERAL] Essentially a dumbbell-type center. One dumbbell runs longitudinally and a second dumbbell runs latitudinally, forming malls that cross in a central court. This design accommodates four anchor stores and provides parking on four sides of the center and in the intervening U-shaped areas. Service to stores is available through a tunnel or service bays.[12]

double truck [MARKETING] The two centerfold facing pages of ads, including gutter space.[2]

draw tenant [MARKETING/LEASING] A store that attracts a large volume of customers to the center.[4]

dress code [SECURITY] A regulation that defines the type of dress a security officer is to wear while on duty.[7]

drive time [MARKETING] Automobile commuting time, usually 7:00 to 9:00 A.M. and 4:30 to 6:30 P.M.[2]

A radio daypart comprising the hours of 6 A.M. to 10 A.M. and 3 P.M. to 7 P.M. (called morning drive and afternoon drive). These periods are generally characterized by the greatest audience levels of any daypart in terms of total listenership.[5]

dry sheet [OPERATIONS] An unsaturated felt or paper often used on wood decks to prevent asphalt or pitch from penetrating joints. An underlaymerit.[13]

DSTM [RETAIL/RESEARCH] *See* department store type merchandise.

due diligence [FINANCE] Activities carried out by a prospective purchaser or mortgagee of real property to confirm that the property is as represented by the seller and is not subject to environmental or other problems. Due diligence is a reasonable investigation by the parties involved to confirm that all statements within the document are true and that no material facts are omitted.[29]

dumbbell-shaped shopping center [DEVELOPMENT/GENERAL] A double strip of stores placed face-to-face along a mall, with anchor stores placed at both ends of the mall, and with parking on all sides. The dumbbell is designed so that the anchors draw traffic along the mall in an effort to achieve maximum interchange of shoppers.[12]

E

early fringe [MARKETING] The time period in television or radio usually preceding Prime Time.[2]

EBITDA [FINANCE] An acronym for *e*arnings before *i*nterest, *t*axes, *d*epreciation, and *a*mortization, this approximates the total cash from operations; used in the supplemental disclosures accompanying a financial statement, it is an attempt by analysts to measure a company's operations by eliminating certain charges (such as depreciation) and focusing on the results from operations without either interest revenue or expense.[15]

e-commerce [E-COMMERCE] The practice of selling goods or services over the Internet or World Wide Web; also refers to conducting business online (this can include customer service functions, sales, marketing, PR, advertising, and more).[28]

economic base [RESEARCH] The analysis of employment, population, income, retail sales, and other demographic factors that indicate the strengths and weaknesses of a market. Analysis of the economic base aids in determining the need for a regional center.[6]

EDI [E-COMMERCE] An e-commerce acronym for *e*lectronic *d*ata *i*nterchange. This system provides the communication of data from company-to-company and computer-to-computer in a standard data format. It permits the receiver to perform the function of a standard business transaction. E-commerce is often between business-to-business (B2B) and business-to-consumer (B2C).[28]

EDI Gateway [E-COMMERCE] An e-commerce term for the location of entry or exit of EDI data into or out of a company.[28]

EDLP [RETAIL] An acronym for *e*very *d*ay *l*ow *p*rice, a retail strategy that emphasizes low prices year-round, rather than relying on periodic sales.[19]

effective circulation (outdoor) [OPERATIONS] The number of people who have an opportunity to see a billboard: one half of the pedestrians, one quarter of the automobile riders, and one quarter of the surface public transportation riders is considered an effective viewing mix.[2]

effective date [LEASING/LEGAL] The latest date appearing on the signature page of the lease and the date upon which the lease contract goes into effect. *See* lease commencement date.[24]

effective reach [MARKETING/RESEARCH] The number of consumers, viewers, or listeners exposed to a message enough times (three or more) to be motivated to act on it.[4]

effective rent [LEASING/GENERAL] A combination of the minimum and percentage rent paid by a tenant.[7]

efficiency [MARKETING] The cost to reach 1,000 individuals in a demographic group. Generally referred to as CPM, or cost per thousand. To calculate, divide the cost per spot by the audience reached (expressed in thousands).[5]

elasticity factor of spending [RESEARCH] The increment in spending by a population with higher than average income, but not in direct proportion to income differential; varies from one income group to another and, to some extent, for different retail categories. Generally amounts to 60 percent of income differential for comparison retail. The higher the income, the smaller the elasticity factor (diversion of income to categories other than comparison retail).[6]

eligibility list [OPERATIONS/SECURITY] List of candidates for police employment compiled by local police departments. Candidates most likely to become police officers are at the top of the list. The lists are available, upon request, to the public.[22]

emergency book [OPERATIONS] A pamphlet given to new tenants that gives important telephone numbers and outlines procedures for various emergencies.[7]

enclosed common area [GENERAL] A term applied to enclosed malls and measured in square feet of floor area. It includes the mall, public rest rooms, receiving and distribution facilities for the common use of tenants, and other enclosed common areas.[10]

enclosed mall [GENERAL] An enclosed mall has a walkway or mall that is enclosed, heated and cooled, insulated, and lighted. The mall corridor is flanked on one or both sides by storefronts and entrances. The configuration of the center may vary, but on-site parking is usually provided around the perimeter of the center.[10]

end-of-month (EOM) dating   [RETAIL] Dating that requires the retailer to pay within a certain number of days from the end of the month during which the goods were shipped. When a bill is dated the 26th of the month or later, EOM dating begins from the end of the following month.[3]

endorsement   [INSURANCE] A written addition to a policy.[7]

engineering design forms   [ARCHITECTURE/CONSTRUCTION] Forms completed by the tenant's engineering consultant, in conjunction with working drawings, to allow the landlord to verify that the tenant's HVAC, electrical, and plumbing systems comply with the landlord's criteria.[17]

entertainment complex   [GENERAL] A shopping center that emphasizes theaters, restaurants, and related retail.[17]

EOM   [GENERAL] End of month.

EOP   [ACCOUNTING] End of period.

equity   [FINANCE] The net value of a property, obtained by subtracting from its total value all liens and other charges against it. The term is frequently applied to the value of the owner's (as opposed to the lender's) interest in the property in excess of all claims and liens.[7]

The owner's interest in a company after all obligations are met; analogous to the difference between the value of your home and the balance of your mortgage.[15]

equity offerings   [LEGAL/FINANCE] Raising funds by offering ownership in a corporation through the issuing of shares of a corporation's common or preferred stock.[20]

equity related loan   [FINANCE] A loan that is convertible into equity ownership or collateralized with equity positions.[20]

errors and omissions coverage (E&O)   [INSURANCE] Insurance that protects against liability arising out of errors and omissions in the performance of professional services.[17]

escalation clause   [ACCOUNTING] A provision in a lease that requires the tenant to pay more rent based on an increase in costs. Same as stop clause.[25]

estoppel letter   [LEGAL] The tenant or the landlord represents as to the current relationship of the tenant and landlord; that is, an estoppel letter will set forth whether there are any defaults or whether rent has been paid in advance. This document would have each party agree that the lease is in full force and effect and that no covenant has been breached.[7]

excepted property [DEVELOPMENT] The basic fire and extended coverage policy, with rare exceptions, does not cover boilers and certain other kinds of machinery on which the insurance is written separately with companies specializing in that field. Also excluded are trucks, sweepers, and similar mobile equipment, the coverage of which is customarily made part of the casualty insurance. Losses sustained from theft, burglary, and embezzlement are also included in casualty, and all of these things will be spelled out in the excepted property clause of the fire policy.[12]

excessive force [SECURITY] The use of too much force by a guard during the apprehension or search of a criminal suspect. Determined case by case in a court of law.[7]

exclusion [INSURANCE] A provision of an insurance policy identifying those things not covered by that policy.[7]

exclusives [LEASING/LEGAL] A term referring to a store's being given the exclusive right to sell a particular category of merchandise within a shopping center.[7]

An existing tenant may have negotiated the right to be the only one in the center to offer particular goods or services, and therefore space may not be leased to another tenant offering the same goods or services in competition with the first tenant.[7]

exclusivity clause [LEASING] A lease clause that limits the number of stores that can open in the shopping center competing with the lessee.[20]

exhibits [LEASING/LEGAL] Attachments, usually to the end of an original lease, specifying the location, legal description, and tenant's construction specifications.[7]

expansion [DEVELOPMENT] An increase in a shopping center's gross leasable area (GLA), usually done in conjunction with the addition of an anchor store.[17]

expansion contribution [FINANCE] Tenant's contribution to any expansion funds.[24]

expense recovery [ACCOUNTING] Total receipts from tenants to recover operating expenses for maintenance and repair, utilities, security, insurance, taxes, and other expenses.[10]

expenses [ACCOUNTING] Charges involved in running the business. *See* fixed expenses and variable expenses.[7]

expiration date [LEASING/LEGAL] The date on which a tenant's lease term is complete.[7]

export   [RESEARCH] Refers to the export of consumer dollars, usually from an area of limited retail activity to an area of greater retail activity.[6]

exposure   [OPERATIONS] That part of the felt on a built-up roof covered directly by the bitumen flood coat.[13]

extended coverage insurance   [INSURANCE] A fire and extended coverage insurance policy routinely includes, in addition to fire, numerous other perils such as windstorm, hail, explosion, riot, and smoke. The same policy customarily also includes the vitally important coverage against what is variously known as consequential loss, use and occupancy, or rental value—the income lost during a restoration period.[12]

F

face out [RETAIL] Displaying clothing front forward rather than side hung.[19]

fact sheet [MARKETING] Material used to present essential facts about a subject, most often in nonnarrative, outline form.[4]

factory outlet [RETAIL] A store offering merchandise direct from the manufacturer at prices lower than standard retail. These stores are often contained in centers that specialize in factory outlets.[7]

fair market value [FINANCE] The price an informed person is willing to pay on the open market.[7]

fall [OPERATIONS] A measurement used for the installation of a drainage system in a parking lot. Fall is the slope or grade from one point, usually to a drain.[7]

fashion/specialty center [GENERAL] A center composed mainly of upscale apparel shops, boutiques, and crafts shops carrying selected fashion or unique merchandise of high quality and price. These centers need not be anchored, although sometimes restaurants or entertainment can provide the draw of anchors. The physical design of the center is very sophisticated, emphasizing a rich decor and high-quality landscaping. These centers usually are found in trade areas having high income levels.[1]

Retail facilities merchandising high-quality merchandise, usually high-priced, primarily apparel and accessories but also including other comparison facilities such as jewelry, luggage, and leather goods; sometimes referred to as high-quality specialty shops.[6]

fat spots [OPERATIONS] *See* bleeding.

feasibility study [DEVELOPMENT/RESEARCH] A feasibility study asks the question "Will it work?" Any feasibility study must explore all avenues of approach in determining whether the economic climate is favorable for active and effective implementation of a proposed business or real estate development. The feasibility study is a forecast of things that will most probably occur when the project is "open for business."[5]

feature story   [MARKETING] In the media a story based on human interest or a particular interest rather than on news.[4]

fee manager   [GENERAL] A manager or management firm that contracts to manage a shopping center for a fee or other consideration. A fee manager's relationship with the center's landlord is that of an independent firm hired to render specific services for a specified term of contract.[7]

felony   [SECURITY] Generally, an offense for which the sentence provided in the statute is death or imprisonment for one year or more. A crime can also be made a felony by a statement in the statute that the crime defined is felonious.[3]

felt   [OPERATIONS] A fabric manufactured by interlocking fibers mechanically and with moisture and heat. Roofing felts are used to give membranes tensile strength and elasticity. They may be organic or inorganic compounds and are a vital component of built-up roof systems.[3]

A fabric manufactured in a plant that brings fiberglass and binders together. Usually the binders are asphalt.[7]

FFO   [FINANCE] *See* funds from operations.[15]

fidelity bond   [INSURANCE] Employee theft insurance covering monetary loss to the employer caused by a dishonest act of an employee.[7]

field survey   [GENERAL] Gathering comprehensive information, in part through actual visits to other centers and stores, on the existing and future retailing and entertainment situation within the project's trading area. This involves such things as examining the site in terms of ingress and egress, adjacent land uses, visibility, parking and road patterns; taking an inventory of existing competitive retail, entertainment, service, and food facilities in close proximity to the center and possibly elsewhere in the greater market area; estimating the future competitive retail market; studying market rental rates and performance data; and evaluating the strengths and weaknesses of competition.[17]

FIFO   [ACCOUNTING/RETAIL] *See* first in, first out.[15]

fills   [OPERATIONS] Materials added to the substrate roof deck to alter its contour; e.g., to achieve slope or to smooth out substrate.[13]

financial reports   [FINANCE] Monthly statements of how much an account had at the start and the end of the month; they provide both budgeted and actual information for the current month and year to date.[4]

financial statement [ACCOUNTING/FINANCE] A summarized report of accounting transactions, composed of the balance sheet, the operating (or income) statement, and the statement of cash flows.[15]

A written statement of the financial position of a person or company, showing total assets and liabilities as of a certain date. Many lenders require a financial statement as part of a loan application.[25]

finished mechanical [MARKETING] The completed pasteup of an ad in which visual and copy components are ready for reproduction by the print medium.[2]

fire insurance [INSURANCE] A standard fire policy, often written with an extended coverage endorsement and a vandalism and malicious mischief endorsement.[7]

first in, first out (FIFO) [ACCOUNTING/RETAIL] An accounting method that assumes inventory acquired earliest is sold or used up first. Thus, the "Monday" inventory item is deemed to have sold before the "Tuesday" item, regardless of which actual item is delivered to the customer. In times of rising prices, use of this method usually results in the largest gross profits.[15]

first stage [FINANCE] Financing provided to companies that have expended their initial capital and require funds, often to initiate commercial manufacturing and sales.[20]

fiscal year [ACCOUNTING] Any twelve-month period for a lease (or any other financial purpose), such as July to June; if it is from January 1 to December 31, it is called a *calendar year*.

fixed assets [ACCOUNTING/FINANCE] Things used in a business that are not for sale.[4] *See* tangible assets.[15]

fixed contributions [ACCOUNTING] Insertion into the original lease of a provision limiting the landlord's contribution in the total real estate burden to a fixed amount—usually expressed as so many cents per square foot of GL A (gross leasable area)—with all taxes over that figure to be spread among the tenants pro rata to their share of the total GL A. The sum to be paid by the landlord is usually pegged at approximately the total amount anticipated for the first year.[12]

fixed expenses [ACCOUNTING] Also called indirect expenses, these are operating expenses that are not affected by increases or decreases in sales volume.[7]

fixed minimum rent [ACCOUNTING/LEASING] Also known as *base rent*. The amount of basic rent paid by the tenant, usually stated as an amount per square foot charged on an annual basis. This figure does not include any other fees or assessments typically charged in a shopping center. [4]

fixed position spot [MARKETING] In television, a commercial which is broadcast at a specified time for the length of the agreement. Often such spots are high-rated and carry a premium price. They differ from announcements in rotating schedules, which only specify placement in broad time periods but do not stipulate exact times for each commercial. In radio, very few stations offer fixed position spots any longer. [5]

fixed rate [FINANCE/ACCOUNTING] An interest rate set at the time of a loan and unchanging over the life of the loan. [15]

flashing [OPERATIONS] Any protective and waterproofing material used to seal the junction of a roof and a vertical wall rising above the roof, or a projection through a roof, such as a chimney, vent pipe, or skylight. [3]

flat rate [MARKETING] In advertising a uniform charge for space in a medium without regard to the amount of space used or the frequency of insertions. [2]

flat rent [ACCOUNTING/LEASING] A specific rent on square footage paid by a tenant for a specified period of time. [7]

flight [MARKETING] Also known as *flighting*. A series of promotions or events within a single-themed larger promotion to achieve greater impact by utilizing repetition. This is accomplished by enveloping various forms of media. [5]

A scheduling technique in which commercials are scheduled to air for a period of one week or a number of consecutive weeks, then do not air at all for a period of time, after which the schedule is resumed. [4]

floating rate [FINANCE] An interest rate that fluctuates over the life of a loan, based on some relationship to a benchmark such as a bank's prime lending rate. [15]

flood coat [OPERATIONS] A mopping of bitumen on exposed felts of a built-up roof to protect them from weather pending completion of the job. [13]

fluorescent light [OPERATIONS] Type of lighting commonly found in a shopping center. Light is produced when current passes through the low-pressure mercury vapor inside a fluorescent bulb. [21]

FOB [RETAIL] *See* free on board.

focus group [RESEARCH] A group representing a cross-section of the center's customers, brought together to discuss their needs and preferences.[4]

A group of consumers who are assembled to candidly discuss their opinions on a particular subject.[4]

follow-on/later stage [FINANCE] A subsequent investment made by an investor who has made a previous investment in the company—generally a later stage investment in comparison to the initial investment.[20]

food court [GENERAL] In enclosed malls, an area devoted to permanent vendor stalls offering a range of prepared foods for on-premises consumption and served by a common seating area.[10]

food court expenses [ACCOUNTING] All expenses specifically attributable to a food court operation. These include: 1. housekeeping labor—the payroll and employee benefits associated with the janitorial function of the food court, and 2. supplies/other—all costs of supplies and other miscellaneous expenses relating specifically to the food court.[10]

footcandle [OPERATIONS] A measurement of light. The equivalent of illumination produced by a candle at the distance of one foot.[7]

force majeure [LEGAL] Any uncontrollable act ("Act of God") that delays tenant's or landlord's obligations under the lease (cannot be due to lack of funds). Usually it is labor strikes, weather, earthquakes, or natural disasters.[24]

foreseeability [SECURITY] In the shopping center context, it means that the landlord should be aware that a particular type of crime is likely to occur on shopping center property.[7]

format [MARKETING] The pattern of an advertisement or publication; typeface, size, shape.[2]

four-way rack [RETAIL] A four-armed presentation rack used to display clothing at multiple levels.[19]

free on board (FOB) [RETAIL] A shipping term signifying that the vendor or shipper retains title and pays all charges to an FOB point. For example, FOB New York would indicate that a supplier in New York would not pay freight costs for a purchaser in California.[3]

freestanding stores [GENERAL] Retail stores not located in a planned shopping center or in association with a major business district.[6]

Anchors or nonanchors that are managed as part of the center but are physically separate from the main structure.[10]

frequency   [MARKETING] In media exposure, the number of times an individual or household is exposed to a medium within a given period of time. Frequency of an advertisement is based upon its opportunity for exposure to an audience; in print, the number of times an individual or household is exposed to the same or successive advertisements for the same product in one or different publications; in broadcast, the sum of audiences per telecast in a given time period (four weeks, for instance) divided by the net cumulative audience for that period.[5]

Refers to consistency of advertising; frequent advertising usually results in a rate reduction.[2]

fringe time   [MARKETING] The hours directly before and after Prime Time in television or radio. May be further specified as early fringe or late fringe.[2]

frontage   [LEASING/GENERAL] The amount of space, in linear feet, of a tenant store that is exposed to the common area of a shopping center, increasing the store's exposure and visibility.[17]

full position   [MARKETING] A special preferred position of an advertisement in a newspaper. Usually refers to an ad placed adjacent to editorial copy.[2]

funds from operations (FFO)   [FINANCE] A measurement favored by real estate investment trusts (REITs) that approximates the cash-generating power of a company appearing in an operating statement below the net operating income (NOI). FFO is intended to highlight the amount of cash generated by a company's real estate portfolio relative to its total operating cash flow. It consists of net income, excluding gains (or losses) from debt restructuring and sales of property, plus depreciation and amortization after adjustments for unconsolidated partnerships and joint ventures.[15]

future value (FV)   [FINANCE] A way of determining the eventual value of an investment, based on the amount of the initial investment, the reinvestment rate, and the number of years under consideration; analogous to figuring out how much a bank account paying a particular interest rate will be worth after a set number of years.[15]

FV   [FINANCE] *See* future value.

G

GAAP [ACCOUNTING] (U.S.) An acronym for *g*enerally *a*ccepted *a*ccounting *p*rinciples; an authoritative set of rules, adopted by the accounting profession, that dictates the way a business reports its financial condition and performance.[15]

GAFO [RESEARCH] An acronym for *g*eneral merchandise, *a*pparel, home *f*urnishings, and *o*ther merchandise (such as books, toys, and food sold away from home), which are normally sold in regional shopping centers.[6]

general and administrative expenses [ACCOUNTING] All expenses related to the management of the shopping center, office staff, office supplies, office equipment rental expenses, management fees, leasing fees and commissions, and professional services. Line items include bad debt allowances, leasing fees and commissions, legal and audit expenses, management fees, office equipment expenses, on-site payroll, and benefits.[10]

general conditions [CONSTRUCTION/GENERAL] Indirect costs primarily covering the contractor's on-site staffing and management; for example, preconstruction services, field superintendent, contractor's project manager, field office, temporary utilities, and the like.[17]

general contractor (GC) [CONSTRUCTION] A person who manages the construction process, holds the prime subcontracts, and guarantees completion for an agreed-on cost. Like a construction manager at risk.[17]

general ledger [ACCOUNTING] The place—in a book, today, in a computer—where an accountant or bookkeeper records, collects, and stores all accounts; also called a *ledger*.[15]

generally accepted accounting principles [ACCOUNTING] *See* GAAP.

GLA [GENERAL] *See* gross leasable area.

glossies [MARKETING] Reproducible prints of ads supplied to publications.[12]

Photographs with a shiny—as opposed to matte—finish.[4]

gondola [RETAIL] A display fixture usually configured as an "H" with a 48-inch-wide by 54-inch-high center panel and

36-inch-wide by 54-inch-high end panels. A base anchors the unit and shelves, or hangbars are used on all sides for merchandise presentation.[19]

goodwill [FINANCE/MARKETING] The excess of the cost of an acquired company over the sum of the fair-market value of its identifiable assets less its liabilities.[15]

graduated lease [LEASING/ACCOUNTING] A lease that provides for graduated changes, at stated intervals, in the amount of rent.[25]

grand opening date [GENERAL] The date of the opening of the shopping center or the applicable expansion, as in grand reopening.[24]

granules [OPERATING] Mineral particles of a graded size embedded in the coating asphalt of shingles and roofing.[13]

graphics [MARKETING] Descriptive techniques, including sketches, photographs, and all other visual components of an ad.[2]

grease pans [OPERATIONS] Metal reservoirs placed near ventilation units to catch grease before it touches the roof membrane.[7]

grooving [OPERATIONS] Rounded ruts in paving caused by automobile wheels; they may be seen in the main direction of traffic.[3]

gross collectibles [ACCOUNTING] The combination of all money transactions handled by the center management on behalf of the tenant. Taxes, minimum rent, percentage rent, and CAM (common area maintenance) fall into this category. This figure is used to determine the management fee of the center.[7]

gross floor area [LEASING/GENERAL] The total floor space of all buildings in a project.[6]

gross income [FINANCE] Revenues before deducting any expenses.[5]

gross leasable area (GLA) [GENERAL] Normally the total area on which a shopping center tenant pays rent. The GLA includes all selling space as well as storage and other miscellaneous space.[6]

The square footage of a shopping center that can generate income by being leased to tenants. This figure does not include the area occupied by department stores or anchor tenants.[4]

The measurement used to define how much space a tenant has leased in a center. GLA is determined by measuring the distance between the middle walls of a space and the distance between front outside wall to back outside wall.[7]

The total floor area designed for tenant occupancy and exclusive use, including basements, mezzanines, and upper floors. It is measured from the center line of joint partitions and from outside wall faces. In short, GLA is that area on which tenants pay rent; it is the area that produces income.[12]

gross lease   [LEASING] A lease in which the landlord pays 100 percent of all taxes, insurance, and maintenance associated with the operation of a shopping center.[7]

gross margin   [RETAIL] The difference between the sales and the total cost of merchandise sold.[7]

gross potential revenue   [FINANCE/ACCOUNTING] A figure used by appraisers to determine potential revenue, based on 100 percent occupancy.[15]

gross profit   [RETAIL] Net sales less cost of goods sold but before considering selling and general expenses, incidental income, and income deductions.[3]

Markup multiplied by sales price.[7]

gross rating points (GRPs)   [MARKETING] The number of rating points a program including commercials has on each area station, multiplied by the number of times it runs within a specified period; example: per week.[2]

The sum of all rating points in the schedule, indicating the estimated reach and frequency of the media buying schedule.[4]

A rating point is one percent of the total television or radio audience universe. *Gross* rating points are percents (or ratings) expressed on a gross (or duplicated) basis. Since 100 percent of the homes never have their TV sets turned on at the same time, gross rating points in any quarter hour never add up to 100.[5]

gross sales   [ACCOUNTING/RETAIL] Total sales from all transactions.[7]

GRPs   [MARKETING] *See* gross rating points.

guaranteed maximum price (GMP)   [OPERATIONS/CONSTRUCTION] An amount fixed in a contract, setting a limit on the reimbursement to the contractor for the cost of the work plus a fee; this hybrid of lump sum and time-and-material contracts has most of the advantages of the other types, with few of the disadvantages.[17]

gutter space   [MARKETING] The inside margins of facing printed pages.[2]

H

half run   [MARKETING] In transportation advertising, a car card placed in every other car of the transit system used.[2]

hard costs   [DEVELOPMENT/CONSTRUCTION] The brick-and-mortar elements of a redevelopment project, such as the land, the building, and building improvements; excludes architectural fees, overhead, etc.[15]

hard goods   [RETAIL] That class of merchandise, sometimes referred to as hardlines, composed primarily of durable items, such as hardware, machines, heavy appliances, electrical and plumbing fixtures, and farming machinery and supplies.[6]

head   [MARKETING] The headline or title of an article or story.[4]

head-on position   [MARKETING] An outdoor poster that directly faces the direction of traffic on a highway.[2]

heat pump   [OPERATIONS] A type of HVAC (heating, ventilation, and air-conditioning) unit, named for its internal mechanism, which runs on electricity.[7]

heating, ventilation, and air-conditioning (HVAC) units   [OPERATIONS] Fairly large machines that handle all the heating, cooling, and ventilation uses associated with a center.[7]

hiatus   [MARKETING] A break in the advertiser's broadcast schedule; a period between flights.[2]

high end   [RETAIL] Refers to tenants offering better quality and/or exclusive merchandise at higher prices.[7]

high income per capita   [RESEARCH] The total income of high-income families and individuals, divided by the total high-income population.[5]

hired car automobile liability insurance   [INSURANCE] Insurance that provides contingent coverage for short-term rental vehicles.[7]

historical sales performance (of tenants)   [ACCOUNTING/LEASING] One of the most important analytical tools in determining strong and weak merchandising areas in a center, and therefore which tenants should be retained, which ones should be relocated, and which ones should be replaced.[17]

---

hold-harmless agreement [INSURANCE] An indemnity agreement in which one party's legal liability for damages is assumed by the other party to the contract. It protects one against losses from someone else's failure to fulfill an obligation.[7]

holdup alarm [SECURITY] An alarm that indicates a holdup is in progress. This type of alarm is usually silent.[7]

house organ [MARKETING] A publication used for communication between management and its employees.[4]

household [RESEARCH] Includes all the persons who occupy a group of rooms or a single room that constitutes a housing unit.[6]

The total number of persons, both related and unrelated, residing in a household unit.[6]

housekeeping expenses [ACCOUNTING/OPERATIONS] The cost of janitorial services for the interior common area of the center, whether performed by mall personnel or an outside service. For mall personnel, it includes payroll, employee benefits, and materials and supplies. For outside service contracts, it includes time charges for labor and any charges for equipment use and maintenance supplies.[10]

housing unit [RESEARCH] A house, an apartment, a group of rooms, or a single room occupied or intended for occupancy as separate living quarters.[6]

hurdle rate [FINANCE] An investor's minimum acceptable rate of return[15]

HUT level [MARKETING] The percentage of Homes Using Television during a given time. This number is the sum of the ratings of all stations in a market for the time period.[5]

HVAC [OPERATIONS] *See* heating, ventilation, and air-conditioning.

hybrid decentralized administrative system [GENERAL] An administrative system that has the characteristics of both decentralized and centralized administrative systems. It takes advantage of computers that tie together such elements as bookkeeping and accounting, but a center manager may do purchasing and approvals, although the center's books are kept at a central location. *See* centralized administrative system and decentralized administrative system.[7]

I

image-building [MARKETING] A consistent program of advertising and publicity designed to favorably portray a shopping center to the market area in terms of community involvement and the availability of goods and services.[2]

import [RESEARCH] Consumer dollars from beyond the designated trading area of a retail facility—usually from an area of limited retail activity.[6]

inboard [DEVELOPMENT] That portion of a trade area lying in the direction of the central city. The effectiveness of a shopping center in attracting patronage from the residents of the inboard side is less than it is for those residents on the opposite, or outboard, direction, since patronage normally flows toward the direction of the central city from the outlying areas.[6]

incandescent lighting [OPERATIONS] A lamp in which light is produced by electrically heating a filament. Used sparingly because of its cost inefficiencies.[21]

inch [MARKETING] A unit of advertising measurement; a space one inch deep and one column wide. A column inch.[2]

incident reports [OPERATIONS/SECURITY] Written documentation, based on investigation, describing events that took place during an incident.[22]

income, net [ACCOUNTING] Difference between the shopping center's total effective income and total operating expenses.[6]

income, per capita [RESEARCH] Total personal income of residents divided by the resident population.[6]

income, real [RESEARCH] The amount of income one can spend on goods and services one may enjoy.[6]

income, total [RESEARCH] Money "cash" income, including wages, salaries, self-employment, Social Security, and retirement pension.[6]

income, total personal [RESEARCH] Money income plus noncash types of income, including food stamps and imputed income.[6]

income approach [FINANCE] An appraisal technique in which the anticipated net income is processed to indicate the capital amount of the investment that produces it. The capital amount, called the capitalized value, is, in effect, the sum of the anticipated annual rents less the loss of interest until the time of collection.[7]

A technique that takes the historical net income as a basis on which to calculate the capital value of the investment producing that net income. According to this method, the value of income-producing property, such as a shopping center, tends to be set by the amount of future income that can reasonably be expected, and the present value of the property is the present value of future income.[12]

income statement [ACCOUNTING] *See* operating statement.

indemnification [INSURANCE] Protection against a lawsuit or unanticipated expenses.[7]

indemnity agreement [INSURANCE] *See* hold-harmless agreement.

index [INSURANCE] A percent in relation to a norm of 100. For instance, a 123 index means that a number is 23 percent higher than the norm. An 83 index means that a number is 17 percent below the norm.[5]

industry averages [INSURANCE] Average national sales figures for a given retail category (broken down by year, month, or season).[7]

inflow market [INSURANCE] The geographic market located outside the primary and secondary markets from which a center obtains shoppers or sales. Also called tertiary market. *See* primary market and secondary market.[4]

in-house agency [MARKETING] An advertising agency installed by owner-developers with a group of shopping centers to create a desired image through the use of the various media; also to provide guidance to the various centers on their budget and promotion programs.[2]

initial assessment [ACCOUNTING/LEASING] A one-time assessment, equal to one year's dues, charged to new tenants in addition to the standard merchants' association annual dues.[4]

initial markup [RETAIL] The first markup placed on an item offered for sale.[7]

initial/seed [FINANCE/GENERAL] A relatively small amount of capital provided to an investor or entrepreneur, usually to prove a concept. It may involve product development, but rarely involves initial marketing.[20]

insert   [MARKETING] A preprinted section, delivered by insertion in a publication.[2]

insertion order   [MARKETING] Written instructions to a publication authorizing insertion of an advertisement and providing specifications.[2]

insolvency   [FINANCE/LEGAL] The inability or failure to pay debts as they become due. The condition of an individual or organization in which liabilities exceed the fair and realizable value of the assets available for their settlement.[3]

inspection   [OPERATIONS] A detailed examination of the various physical assets of a shopping center.[7]

institutional advertising   [MARKETING] Used to build the reputation of a center or a merchant as the most desirable complex or store in the area offering goods and services to the consumer.[2]

insulation layer   [OPERATIONS] A layer of roofing which lies between the deck and the roof itself.[13]

insurance   [INSURANCE] A contract between a risk-taker (the insurer) and another party (the insured) in which, for a fee (the premium), the insurer agrees to pay the insured for losses to something specific (the risk) due to named causes (hazards or perils). The insurer may also assume the obligation to pay a third party (the claimant) on behalf of the insured.[7]

insurance expense   [INSURANCE/ACCOUNTING] This major category includes all premiums and costs incurred for insurance covering structures, public liability, rental value, equipment, and bonding of employees. It includes the cost of an insurance consultant. Line items include: Liability insurance: the net premium cost of public liability insurance; Property insurance: the net premium cost of property insurance; Special coverage: the net premium cost of special coverage, such as earthquake or flood insurance; and Other: the net premium costs of other types of insurance, such as auto, boiler and machinery, bonding of employees, and insurance consultants, if any.[10]

insurance revenue   [INSURANCE/ACCOUNTING] Receipts from tenants to recover the cost of insurance for the center.[10]

insuring agreement   [INSURANCE] The section of an insurance policy that states what the policy covers.[7]

intangible assets   [FINANCE/ACCOUNTING] A class of long-lived assets that are not physical in nature; they are the

rights to expected future benefits deriving from their acquisition and continued possession. Examples include tenant
improvement allowances, goodwill, franchises, patents,
trademarks, and copyrights.[15]

integrated commercial   [MARKETING] A single broadcast
announcement in which the advertiser presents two products using the same announcer and locale. *See* piggyback.[2]

intercept survey   [RESEARCH] A study conducted by stopping shoppers, usually exiting a center, to gather information about their shopping patterns. Such studies are usually
more in-depth than telephone surveys, and conducting
them on-site permits a sufficient sample size. Its limitations
include not obtaining the opinions of nonshoppers or
potential future shoppers at the center.[17]

interest   [FINANCE] Money paid for the use of capital. It is
usually expressed as a rate or percentage of the capital,
called the interest rate.[7]

interest-only loan   [FINANCE] A type of loan, preferred by
some real estate borrowers, in which there is no amortization—no principal is paid back prior to the maturity of the
loan.[15]

interest rate   [FINANCE] The additional return, usually
expressed as a percentage of the unpaid balance, required
by the lender to make a given loan, due on a regular basis.[15]

internal controls   [OPERATIONS/ACCOUNTING] The safe-
guards a company puts in place to help detect accounting
errors and prevent employee dishonesty on financial statements.[15]

internal rate of return (IRR)   [FINANCE] A discount rate at
which the present value (PV) of projected cash flow exactly
equals the initial investment. This discounted cash flow
technique is used to determine the single rate of return that
equates capital outlays and cash flows to a present value of
zero.

Internet   [E-COMMERCE] A global network connecting mil-
lions of computers.[27]

inventory   [RETAIL] The goods on hand at a specified
accounting date. The term may refer either to the physical
goods or to their value.[4]

Physical inventory is determined by actual inspection of
the merchandise on hand in the store, stockrooms, and
warehouses.[3]

inventory average [RETAIL] An average of the stock on hand at representative dates throughout the year or season.[7]

inventory turnover [RETAIL] A ratio measuring the adequacy and efficiency of the inventory balance, calculated by dividing the cost of goods sold by the amount of the average inventory.[15]

investigation [SECURITY] The process by which center security officers determine the cause of a crime or accident. This is usually accomplished by interviewing eyewitnesses and documenting their statements.[7]

investment bank [FINANCE] An investment banking firm acts as underwriter or agent, serving as intermediary between an issue of securities and the investing public. Investment bankers handle the distribution of blocks of previously issued securities, either through secondary offerings or through negotiations, maintain markets for securities already distributed, and act as finders in private placements of securities.[20]

IPO [FINANCE] Initial public offering. A company's first offering of stock to the public. Sometimes referred to as a privately held company *going public*.[20]

IRR [FINANCE] *See* internal rate of return.

irregularity reports [OPERATIONS/SECURITY] Written documentation of irregular and unusual conditions noted by security officers.[22]

irregulars [RETAIL] Slightly flawed merchandise with appearance and function usually unaffected. Generally, these flaws are pulled threads, imperfect stitches, scratches, and nicks.[19]

J

jointly and severally [FINANCE/LEGAL] *See* cross-collateralization.

journal [ACCOUNTING] The book of original entry in which are recorded transactions not provided for in specialized journals.[5]

journal entry [ACCOUNTING] A process of recording detailed information about accounts in a journal.[15]

junior department store [RETAIL] A store that, in both size and selection of merchandise, can be classified as being between a full-line department store and a variety store.[6]

junior unit [MARKETING] In print media, a page size which permits an advertiser to use the same plates for small- and large-page publications.[2]

K

kettle [OPERATIONS] A vessel used to heat bitumen for roof application.[7]

key money [FINANCE/LEASING] Money from the tenant to the landlord for the right to operate a business in the center.[7]

keystone price [RETAIL] The price when a product that costs a retailer $1 is sold for $2. This doubling of the cost of goods to arrive at a sales price is called *keystoning* and is considered a 50 percent markup on cost.[19]

kick-out clause [LEASING/LEGAL] An option that allows a landlord or tenant to terminate the lease before the end of the term. In the tenant's case, generally tied to the presence of another retailer. *See* cancellation clause.[7]

king-size poster [MARKETING] An outside transit display placed on the side of a vehicle. Size: 30" x 144"

kiosks [LEASING/GENERAL] Booths located in the common areas of the center or mall and generally housing small-time merchandise or services; for example: hosiery, photo developing.[2]

L

L-shaped center [DEVELOPMENT/GENERAL] A strip center with a line of stores placed at a right angle to it, forming an L, with parking in front of the stores and service lanes behind them. Anchors are usually placed at the ends, but it is possible to place an anchor in the crook formed by the two lines of stores. The L shape is adaptable to corner locations and is used widely for both neighborhood- and community-type centers.[12]

land charges [ACCOUNTING] Some leases call for adding to the common area maintenance charge the increases over the base year of the taxes attributable to all of the land within the center, regardless of use.[12]

land use regulations [GENERAL/LEGAL] Zoning, ordinances, maps, and subdivision regulations that guide or control land development.[6]

landlord [GENERAL] The owner of real property (or of a leasehold interest in real property) who leases the property to a tenant for value consideration.[3]

landlord's building [GENERAL] All structures built or to be built by the landlord, excluding contiguous or adjacent parcels not owned by the landlord of the specific shopping center.[24]

landlord's floor area [ACCOUNTING/OPERATIONS] The total square footage of leasable floor area in the shopping center. This total is used in determining each tenant's proportionate share of common area costs associated with the shopping center (real estate taxes, trash services, landlord's operating costs, and insurance).[24]

landscaping expenses [ACCOUNTING/OPERATIONS] The cost of landscaping contracts, services or groundskeepers, and normal replacement of trees, shrubs, and flowers on the exterior and in the interior common area of the mall. It covers the cost of mall personnel, if any, performing these services.[10]

last in, first out (LIFO) [ACCOUNTING] An accounting method that assumes inventory acquired most recently is sold or used up first. This treats the most recent costs as the costs of goods sold, unlike FIFO, which associates the most recent costs with inventories. Many accountants believe that LIFO provides a more realistic income picture, because net income measured using LIFO combines current sales prices and current acquisition costs.[15]

layout   [MARKETING] The sketch and design of an ad.[2]

lead   [MARKETING] In print media the first paragraph of a release or story. It summarizes the most important elements of the story.[4]

leader   [RETAIL] A selected item deliberately sold at a price lower than the one at which the largest total profit on the item could be realized in order to attract customers.[4]

lease   [LEASING/GENERAL] A contract transferring the right to the possession and enjoyment of property for a definite period of time.[3]

The signed agreement between landlord and tenant that establishes responsibility, sets standards, and states what is recoverable from tenants for the maintenance process.[7]

lease abstract   [ACCOUNTING/LEASING/LEGAL] A short version of a lease, containing the most important facts about it in order to facilitate later reviews (for example, by new employees).[15]

lease outline drawing (LOD)   [LEASING/CONSTRUCTION] Material prepared for the tenant, showing the demised space and its relation to adjacent spaces and the center as a whole; electrical, plumbing, HVAC, and waste line entry points are identified, but existing partitions and fixtures are usually not shown.[17]

lease summary report   [ACCOUNTING/LEASING]   An abstract of information about the status of the leasable space in a center as well as pertinent information from each tenant's lease.[4]

leasehold value   [ACCOUNTING] The value of a tenant's interest in a lease, especially when the rent is below market and the lease has a long remaining term.[25]

leasing fees and commissions   [ACCOUNTING/LEASING] The expenses incurred for commissions paid to secure tenants for a center.[10]

ledger   [ACCOUNTING] *See* general ledger.

legal and audit expenses   [ACCOUNTING] The cost of legal services and accounting and audit services.[10]

lessee [LEASING/GENERAL] The tenant; one who rents or leases property from another.[3]

lessor [LEASING/GENERAL] The owner; one who rents or leases property to another.[3]

let [LEASING] To rent or lease.[3]

lethal-weapons policy [OPERATIONS/SECURITY] Guidelines by which security officers are to acquire, use, care for, and be trained in lethal weapons.[7]

letter of intent [LEASING/LEGAL] Generally a document submitted prior to a formal lease. It serves to delineate the intentions between the landlord and the tenant. Basic issues, including minimum rent, percentage rent, pass-through expenses, and other major points of negotiation, are outlined. Generally subject to execution of a complete contract.[7]

The expression of a desire to enter into a contract without actually doing so. [25]

letterpress [MARKETING] The process of printing directly from an inked, raised surface upon which the paper is impressed.[2]

leverage [FINANCE] The use of borrowed funds to complete an investment transaction. The higher the proportion of borrowed funds used to make the investment, the higher the leverage and the lower the proportion of equity funds.[7]

The level of debt against assets.[7]

The use of credit to finance a portion of the costs of purchasing or developing a real estate investment. Positive leverage occurs when the loan constant (interest rate) is lower than the capitalization rate (or lower than the projected IRR). REITs are low-leveraged, with an average industry-wide debt of 35 percent. [29]

liability [INSURANCE] An amount owed by one person (a debtor) to another (a creditor).[5]

A legal obligation or responsibility.[7]

Usually a financial obligation and the cost of meeting it.[7]

Those things that can be claimed against the business; what the business owes. *See* current liability and long-term liabilities.[7]

liability insurance [INSURANCE] *See* commercial general liability policy.

liability limit [INSURANCE] In the event of a loss, the maximum amount the insurer is required to pay.[7]

LIBOR [FINANCE] London Interbank Offered Rate. The interest rate offered on Eurodollar deposits traded between banks. There is a different LIBOR rate for each deposit maturity.[29]

lien [FINANCE] A charge, security, or encumbrance upon property for the payment of a debt.[3]

lifestyle data [RESEARCH] A clustering of socioeconomic information based on people who share similar lifestyle characteristics.[4]

LIFO [ACCOUNTING/FINANCE] *See* last in, first out.

lifts [OPERATIONS] The laying of a layer of asphalt on a prepared subgrade or another layer of asphalt.[7]

limited-time station (daytimer) [MARKETING] A radio station that is assigned a frequency for broadcasting during specific periods only, sharing its frequency with other stations.[2]

line [MARKETING] A unit for measuring space; one fourteenth of a column inch.[2]

line art [MARKETING] Illustrative material other than photographs.[4]

liquidated damages [FINANCE] Payments of an agreed upon amount for the breaching of a contract.[7]

liquidation [FINANCE/LEGAL] The sale of assets and the settlement of debts in the winding up of a business, estate, or other economic unit.[8]

liquidity [FINANCE] The ability to convert assets into cash.[7]

list price [RETAIL] The manufacturer's suggested retail price.[7]

local ad rate [MARKETING] The rate offered to advertisers who do not benefit from coverage beyond their own market area; it is substantially below national rates.[2]

A reduced rate offered by newspapers and broadcast stations to merchants and other local advertisers doing business in the area served by the medium and lower than that offered to national advertisers.[5]

local alarm [SECURITY] A detection device that, when activated, sounds a noise alarm.[7]

local tenant [LEASING/LEGAL] A retail tenant who operates one or more stores exclusively in a local market.[7]

lock-box structure [ACCOUNTING/FINANCE] A structure whereby the rental or debt-service payments are sent directly from the tenants or mortgagors to the trustee.[29]

logo (logotype) [MARKETING] *Also known as sig cut.* The name of a product, service, or business rendered in a consistent, distinctive style of lettering, frequently accompanied by a graphic symbol.[4]

A stylized characteristic symbol for sustained identification of a corporation, product, or service.[2]

LOI [LEASING/LEGAL] Letter of interest (or intent). A letter for a retailer expressing interest in leasing space in a project, but in no way obligates a prospective tenant; after an LOI is received, a shopping center is expected to provide rental rates and other terms and conditions to the lease agreement, which are then subject to due diligence by both parties.[19]

long-term lease [LEASING/GENERAL] A general term that may refer to a lease ten years or longer in term, or, in some areas, five years or longer.[18]

long-term liabilities [FINANCE] Those things owed after 12 months.[7]

loss [INSURANCE] The injury or damage sustained by the insured; in liability policies, it means the payments made by the insurer on behalf of the insured.[7]

loss control specialist [INSURANCE] A professional who evaluates fire protection systems, fire divisions or separations, seismic bracing, security features, interior construction, and a host of other factors that may have an effect on insurance and liability matters.[17]

loss leader [RETAIL] A selected item that is deliberately sold at less than cost in order to attract customers.[7]

low-end merchandise [RETAIL] Merchandise that has been sharply reduced from original prices, used for sidewalk, moonlight, midnight, and similar limited-period sale events.[2]

lump-sum contracts [OPERATIONS/CONSTRUCTION] These contracts are figured from completed plans and specifications by competing contractors who quantify and price the project. Usually submitted by sealed bid, the lowest price is the basis for award of the contract. A lump-sum contract is a "no-peek" contract—in other words, the developer has no right to see what the contractor's actual costs are.[11]

M

mace [SECURITY] A noxious combination of organic chemicals in spray form that is used to disable people. Chemical Mace is a trade name.

made-for-outlet goods [RETAIL] Also called *outlet-exclusive goods*, merchandise made especially to be sold in outlet stores, usually at a discounted price. These goods are generally basics, such as T-shirts, piece goods, or deliberate overruns of popular styles.[20]

mailer [MARKETING] A preprinted special advertising section with a cover page followed by ads relating to a specific center and event, delivered by mail.[2]

maintained markup [RETAIL] The difference between the net sales and the gross cost of merchandise sold. It is the margin on sales before making adjustments for cash discounts earned and alteration costs.[7]

maintenance [OPERATIONS] The upkeep of the various physical assets and common area of a shopping center.[7]

Maintenance involves the preservation of what is already there. For example, patching the parking lot and relamping the lights; painting wall surfaces and replacing deteriorated caulking; rodding the sewer line and changing the oil in the vehicles; and in general doing those things that prolong the economic life of the property in its present forms.[12]

maintenance and repair expenses [ACCOUNTING/OPERATIONS] Expenses related to the maintenance and repair of the shopping center. They may include the costs of payroll, employee benefits (taxes, workers' compensation, pension contributions, etc.), service contracts, and maintenance materials and supplies purchased for the center. They usually do not include major capital improvements or maintenance and repair services that are for the benefit of individual tenants and billed directly to the tenants.[10]

major tenant [GENERAL] The store that generates the greatest amount of customer patronage to a shopping center. The major tenant, sometimes referred to as the *key tenant* or the *anchor,* would be strong enough to stand alone and is effective in attracting patronage from beyond the primary zone of the trade area. Department stores, junior department stores, large variety stores, or supermarkets generally function as major tenants in regional, intermediate, and neighborhood shopping center developments respectively.[5]

makegood [MARKETING] The rerunning of an ad without charge by the medium because of a scheduling or other error committed by it.[2]

A replacement spot (or spots) for a regularly scheduled commercial which was not aired by the station or was aired with a technical problem. Makegoods should always have an audience equal to or larger than the spot being replaced (based on target audience delivery).[5]

mall [GENERAL] The typical mall is enclosed, with a climate-controlled walkway between two facing rows of stores. The term represents the most common design mode for regional and superregional centers and has become an informal term for these types of centers.[1]

mall manager [OPERATIONS/GENERAL] The person who supervises operations and maintenance of center common areas and parking lot, manages personnel, and acts in liaison with the owner/developer, individual tenants, and the marketing director.[2]

mall mayor [MARKETING/GENERAL] The merchant who is recognized by peers as an informal leader among the shopping center's tenants. This individual is likely to become the spokesperson for the group.[7]

management fee [ACCOUNTING/GENERAL] The fee charged by the fee manager or the owner to cover rental collection, administration, common area, maintenance, and tenant relations activities.[8]

A tenant and/or landlord charge. The management fee is calculated from a negotiated percentage of the gross collectible of a shopping center. The fee usually includes the CAM (common area maintenance) charge.[7]

The fee, whether a flat fee or a percentage of gross receipts, charged to the center for management services provided by the management company.[10]

management vision [DEVELOPMENT/GENERAL] A framework for a renovation project at the outset, subject to change based on market research; for example, the management vision could be to establish a high-end shopping center. The vision should be based on such factors as the financial goals for the project, the potential lender's requirements to fund it, the demographics and lifestyle characteristics of the customers whom a management wishes to attract, and what type of tenants are being sought.[17]

mandatory advertising   [MARKETING] Advertising requirements stipulated in a lease clause. They may include participation in an advertising fund or in center-sponsored cooperative advertising, tenant individual advertising (usually a stated percentage of gross annual sales), documentation of the mandatory advertising expenditures, and tenant reimbursement to the landlord of any shortfall.[4]

marginal cost of capital   [FINANCE] *See* risk premium.

markdown   [RETAIL] A reduction in the retail price of merchandise, primarily for clearance, special sales events, or to meet competition.[2]

A decrease from the original price of an item. The markdown percentage is usually stated as a percentage of the reduced selling price.[5]

A retail price reduction caused by the inability to sell goods at the original or subsequently determined retail price.[7]

market analysis   [RESEARCH] The process of determining the characteristics of the market and the measurements of its capacity to appeal to a community.[6]

market area   [RESEARCH] The area surrounding a shopping center from which the center draws its customers.[7]

market benchmarks   [RESEARCH] Comparisons of a center's market demographics with other markets in the U.S.[4]

market cap   [FINANCE] Closing price multiplied by the number of traded common shares outstanding, assuming the full conversion of all operating partnership units.[29]

market data   [RESEARCH] The demographic and economic characteristics of a center's market area (based on census data). *See* daytime business population data; lifestyle data; and psychographics.[4]

market-data approach   [RESEARCH] This appraisal technique, using actual market transactions, is based on the theory that the prices of equal, substitute properties establish value.[12]

market penetration   [RESEARCH] The percentage of the desired market reached by the proposed advertising schedule.[4]

market plan [MARKETING] Quite literally, a blueprint for the company's total marketing effort. It charts specific directions, objectives, strategies, and tactics for achieving optimum success in marketing efforts.[3]

A detailed document explaining all the steps and activities a shopping center will use to promote itself during a one-year period.[7]

market population [DEVELOPMENT/RESEARCH] The projected number of users on and near the site being renovated or otherwise changed, such as a food court.[17]

market potential [RESEARCH] The amount of expenditure and retail sales potential within the expanded or newly defined trade area; determined subjectively, based on hard market data (number of households and average household income), an understanding of consumer shopping behavior, and the economic realities of the competitive marketplace.[17]

market profile [RESEARCH] A demographic description of the people and households of the primary and secondary markets.[2]

market rent [LEASING/FINANCE] Properly, an amount based on sales potential of various types of retailers that together can do the optimum business in a particular center if it were properly leased by merchandise categories, and as compared to the total occupancy cost each retailer is able to pay and still make a profit. This is other than what is necessary to produce a desired return on investment or to cover development costs; the rate at which space would be leased if offered in a current competitive market based on similar sales and performance; sometimes used interchangeably with *budgeted rent* or *appraisal rent*.[15]

market research [RESEARCH] The initial and ongoing studies needed to make marketing decisions. A survey conducted for the developer before commitment to build and on a recurring basis for the marketing director, who disseminates pertinent information to tenants. Reports define demographics and psychographics of the market area.[2]

market research process [RESEARCH] The steps followed (in order) when conducting marketing research: 1. Identify information needs; 2. Determine a methodology; 3. Design a research data tool; 4. Collect the data; 5. Analyze the data; 6. Use the findings to make decisions; and 7. Repeat the process.[4]

market sales approach   [RESEARCH] An appraisal technique in which the market value estimate is predicated upon prices paid in actual market transactions and current listings. It is a process of correlation and analysis of similar recently sold properties. Also called the *market data* or *comparable value approach*.[7]

market segmentation   [RESEARCH] The designing and implementing of a product or service to meet the needs of a particular group.[2]

market share   [RESEARCH] The portion of trade-area retail potential attributable to proposed facilities, after consideration of their known market strength and relative position vis-à-vis comparable competition.[6]

market study   [RESEARCH] A comprehensive analysis of a center's consumer market. The customers, the demographics, and the competition are all components of a market study.[7]

market universe   [RESEARCH] A geographical area of statistical convenience but market representativeness that can be used as the base for statistical computations and derivations.[6]

market value   [FINANCE] The expected price if a reasonable time is allowed to find a purchaser and if both seller and prospective buyer are fully informed. Market value connotes what a property is actually worth, and market price what it might sell for.[7]

marketing   [MARKETING] Everything connected with sales, advertising, sales promotion, public relations and publicity, merchandising, distribution, and research.[5]

marketing direction   [MARKETING] Targeting a specific type of customer the center is trying to attract.[17]

marketing director   [MARKETING/GENERAL] The person responsible for all promotion activities, special events, and maintenance of budget parameters. Also responsible for ongoing market research as a planning tool, community relations, press contacts, and enforcement of lease terms relating to tenant participation or violations.[2]

marketing fund   [ACCOUNTING/MARKETING] A pool of marketing dollars, to which all tenants contribute, that is administered by the marketing director and an advisory board of tenants.[4]

An alternative to the merchants' association, a marketing fund requires contributions from each tenant; the recipient is not a merchants' association but the fund, which is controlled solely by the developer. Under this arrangement, some sort of advisory board is set up, composed of merchant representatives, and the developer consults with this board on the use of the promotional fund.[5]

The pooling and distribution of money paid by tenants for the overall marketing of the shopping center. The marketing fund is overseen by the center's marketing director and staff and is used for advertising and promotion activities.[7]

Established by a fee paid to the landlord, this is a pool of monies for which shopping center landlords are totally responsible. The fund has a tenant advisory board. A clause in the lease covers increases in the fee.[7]

marketing fund advisory board   [MARKETING] A group of tenants representing all aspects of the tenant mix that administers a marketing fund along with the marketing director.[4]

markup   [RETAIL] The difference between the retail selling price of the merchandise and the cost of the merchandise to the retailer.[7]

The difference between the cost price as billed (before deductions for cash discount) and the retail price at which the merchandise is originally offered.[5]

marriage mail   [MARKETING] Two or more messages mailed to a consumer under a single cover or as a package.[4]

masthead   [MARKETING] In magazines and newspapers, a listing of the publication's executive and editorial staff and their titles.[4]

mat   [MARKETING] Material from which an advertisement is printed.[2]

maximum milline rate   [MARKETING] The milline rate of a newspaper computed at its maximum, or highest, rate.[2]

mean   [RESEARCH] The arithmetic average of a series of numbers, calculated by adding up the numbers in the series and dividing the total by how many numbers there are in the series.[4]

The sum of a collection of measurements divided by the number of measurements.[6]

mechanical   [MARKETING] The final paste-up of the type and illustrative components of an ad.[4]

media   [MARKETING] In advertising, the means or instruments of communication: radio, television, newspapers, magazines, direct mail, and billboards.[4]

The vehicle—including radio, television, newspapers, magazines, and newsletters—through which public relations messages are transmitted.[4]

media alert　[MARKETING] A one-page outline of the basic facts of a story. It may also suggest story angles and photos available to illustrate them.[4]

media kit　[MARKETING] A packet of information issued to the media that supplies information about a particular event or activity and background information about the sponsoring organization.[4]

media plan　[MARKETING] An outline of the media determined to be most efficient for reaching a target market. It defines exactly which media will be used and when. The plan includes the media-buying budget.[4]

media representative　[MARKETING] The liaison for center merchants in cooperative promotions; associated with a publication or an electronic medium.[2]

median　[RESEARCH] The midpoint of a series of numbers. Half of the numbers are greater than the median, and half are less.[4]

The midpoint in a set of numbers, demonstrating there are the same number above and below the midpoint.[6]

membrane　[OPERATIONS] A component of a built-up roof system that is made up of roofing felts laminated with bitumen and top-coated.[3]

merchandise manager　[RETAIL] The executive in charge of the merchandise division of a store. In large stores, there are often divisional merchandise managers, each in charge of one of the major merchandise lines.[7]

merchandise mix　[LEASING] The variety and categories of merchandise offered by the retail tenants assembled in a particular shopping center.[7]

A merchandise mix is a group of products that are closely related because they satisfy a class of needs, are used together, or are sold to the same basic market targets. It is made up of a series of demand-related merchandise items, which are specific versions of a product that has a separate designation.[5]

merchandise plan　[LEASING] A forecast, usually by months for a six-month season, of the major elements that enter into gross margin. It normally includes the planning of sales, stocks, purchases, markups, and markdowns.[7]

merchandising　[LEASING/RETAIL] The planning involved in marketing the right merchandise in the right place, at the right time, in the right quantities, and at the right price.[7]

merchants' association [MARKETING/GENERAL] A merchants' association is a not-for-profit corporation organized to conduct merchandising programs, community events, shopping center decoration programs, advertising programs, and publicity programs, and to coordinate joint member cooperative advertising and marketing functions, events, and endeavors for the general benefit of the shopping center. The association acts as a clearinghouse for suggestions, ideas, and programming of merchandising events, and it serves as a quasi-court for handling complaints and differences of opinion.[5]

The tenant group organized to promote the center through cooperative advertising, public relations activity, and community involvement.[2]

An organization of merchants that works to advertise and promote a shopping center. It is a nonprofit, independent corporation.[7]

A not-for-profit, independent corporation with a board of directors who vote and sign checks. The members pay dues. Monthly meetings and an annual report are required.[7]

merchants' association articles of incorporation [MARKETING/LEGAL] Papers filed with the secretary of the state in which the center is located that declare the merchants' association's status as a not-for-profit organization and state the association's purpose.[4]

merchants' association by-laws [MARKETING/LEGAL] The basic rules of governance of a merchants' association.[4]

merchants' association dues [ACCOUNTING/MARKETING] The financial obligation of member tenants and landlord, fixed by a predetermined structure and used for centerwide promotion, special events, and community activities.[2]

metropolitan area [RESEARCH] A geographic area within a market that generally, but not always, corresponds to the U.S. Office of Management and Budget's Statistical Marketing Area (SMA).[4]

A group of whole counties surrounding a major city or twin cities of 50,000 population or more.[6]

metropolitan statistical area (MSA) [RESEARCH] A geographic unit composed of one or more counties consisting of a population of at least 50,000. Each county must have specific metropolitan characteristics.[4]

midnight sale [MARKETING/RETAIL] A centerwide, merchants' association–sponsored, low-end, off-price promotion, generally continuing until 11:00 P.M. or midnight; one night only.[2]

milline rate   [MARKETING] A unit for measuring newspaper advertising space rates as related to circulation. The formula for determining the rate is line rate x 1 million, divided by total circulation.[2]

minimum rent   [ACCOUNTING/LEASING/GENERAL]   The basic rent a tenant pays; usually expressed as a price per square foot.[7]

Rent that is not based on a tenant's sales.[7]

The specific dollar amount paid by a tenant for the amount of square footage leased.[7]

The basic rent that a tenant will pay the landlord each year, in twelve equal, consecutive installments, computed based on an amount of rent per square foot; also called *base rent*.[15]

misdemeanor   [SECURITY] An offense for which the sentence provided in the statute is less than one year in jail. Any crime which is not a felony is a misdemeanor.[3]

mix   [MARKETING/LEASING] A combination of media, tenants, or merchandise that provides choices for the consumer and balance to the shopping center.[2]

mixed-use centers   [DEVELOPMENT/GENERAL] These centers typically combine at least three revenue-producing uses from among retail, office, parking, restaurant, hotel, residential, and entertainment facilities. They may be built in suburban or urban areas. In downtown areas, where land costs are high, a multilevel or high-rise, single-mass design is commonly used to minimize the land area needed.[13]

mode   [RESEARCH] The number most frequently appearing in a set of numbers.[6]

modernization   [DEVELOPMENT] This change is generally considered as having to do with style and appearance rather than utility, such as a new pylon entrance sign or a remodeled building facade.[12]

modified bitumen   [OPERATIONS] A type of built-up roof. Basically, a modified bitumen membrane consists of a combination of roofing felts and bitumen that has been modified by the addition of synthetic rubber or plastic compounds.[7]

mom-and-pop store   [LEASING/RETAIL] A store whose owners own only that single store.[7]

moonlight sale   [RETAIL] *See* midnight sale. Hours usually end not later than 11:00 P.M.[2]

mortgage [FINANCE] The instrument in which the owner of a property pledges it as security toward the repayment of a loan.[29]

mortgage constant [FINANCE] The total annual payment of principal and interest (annual debt service) on a level-payment amortized mortgage, expressed as a percentage of the initial principal amount of the loan. It is used in mortgage-equity analysis as well as in estimating cash flows generated by income-producing real estate.[7]

mortgage, wraparound [FINANCE] The owner takes a second mortgage that encompasses the first mortgage. It is a method of refinancing often used when property value has increased significantly and the owner wants to obtain extra funds based on the property's current market value. When a wraparound is used, the borrower avoids losing the benefit of a favorable (lower) interest rate on the original loan even though the new, second mortgage money is borrowed at a higher rate.[12]

motion detector [SECURITY] A device that detects the physical movements of an intruder in a protected area.[7]

MSA [RESEARCH] *See* metropolitan statistical area.

multiple percentage rate [ACCOUNTING/LEASING] A lease agreement in which the percentage rent rate changes at various increments of sales.[7]

multiple prime contracts [CONSTRUCTION] In a general contract the developer enters into an agreement with a general contractor who, in turn, enters into subcontracts with trade contractors for masonry, concrete, carpentry, etc.

In a multiple prime contract, which is used most often in public works, the owner enters into separate prime contracts with various trade contractors.[11]

multiplex cinema [RETAIL/GENERAL] A facility offering several movie screens, often with a wide range in the number of seats in each theater and showing a variety of movies to appeal to different customers; typically the focus of a type of shopping center called an entertainment complex.[17]

mystery shoppers [MARKETING] *See* secret shoppers.

N

named insured   [INSURANCE] The person or business entity designated on a policy as being insured.[7]

named-peril insurance   [INSURANCE] Coverage that specifies the perils that it covers.[7]

national rate   [MARKETING] The rate offered to national advertisers (many markets). Used by both print and electronic media, and substantially more costly than a local rate.[2]

national tenant   [LEASING/DEVELOPMENT] A retailer who operates a chain of stores on a nationwide basis.[7]

natural breakpoint   [LEASING/ACCOUNTING] *See* breakpoint.

natural disaster   [LEGAL] An emergency created by an act of God.[7]

negligence   [INSURANCE] The act of being extremely careless. The failure to use such care as a reasonably prudent and careful person would use under similar circumstances. If found negligent in a court of law, a center can be held liable for the actions of a guard or a criminal.[7]

negligent hiring   [OPERATIONS/INSURANCE] Careless hiring on the part of a shopping center that directly or indirectly causes a crime or an accident. If a center is guilty of negligently hiring an employee, it may be held liable for all negative actions by that employee.[7]

negligent retention   [OPERATIONS/INSURANCE] Retaining the services of an employee despite a poor work record. The center may be held liable for an employee's action if it is determined that the employee should have been terminated prior to an incident or accident.[7]

negligent security training   [SECURITY] The careless training or lack of training of an employee for security work. If it is found in a court of law that a center did not adequately train a security officer who causes an accident or fails to perform adequately, the shopping center may be held liable.[7]

negotiated bid   [OPERATIONS/CONSTRUCTION] An approach to selecting the contractor for a project, based on information in an initial, incomplete phase of a design, which results in predetermined parameters of an eventual contract.[17]

negotiated contract [OPERATIONS/CONSTRUCTION] A contract arranged on some type of fee basis plus costs with a cap, or guaranteed maximum cost. The fee covers the contractor's indirect (off-site) overhead and profit, while the costs cover all other elements, such as labor, material, subcontracts, and jobsite supervision.[11]

negotiated inducements [LEASING] Any incentives offered by a landlord to persuade a tenant to commit to a lease. As known factors that will definitely occur, such as tenant improvement construction allowances or free rent periods, these are quantifiable in terms of amount and timing.[15]

neighborhood centers [GENERAL] Designed to provide convenience shopping for the day-to-day needs of the immediate neighborhood, these centers are usually anchored by a supermarket supported by stores offering drugs, sundries, snacks, and personal services. The majority of neighborhood centers range from 30,000 to 100,000 square feet of GLA (gross leasable area) and are sited on three to ten acres.[12]

Shopping complexes built around a supermarket as the principal tenant and having a typical gross leasable area of 50,000 square feet.[6]

net [ACCOUNTING] What remains after specified deductions from the gross amount.[7]

net income [ACCOUNTING] *See* income, net.

net lease [ACCOUNTING/LEASING] A lease in which the tenant agrees to pay rent and its proportionate share of the center's ongoing expenses, such as taxes, insurance, and property repairs and maintenance.[15]

net operating income [ACCOUNTING] The income after deducting from gross income the operating expenses, including property taxes, insurance, utilities, management fees, heating and cooling expenses, repairs and maintenance, and replacement of equipment.[7]

net present value (NPV) [FINANCE] A method of calculating present value for multiple payments made in different future years and bringing together all of these amounts into today's dollars. A higher discount rate means a smaller NPV.[15]

net price [RETAIL] Sometimes called retailer's cost price. The amount a retailer must pay for a particular item.[7]

net profit [ACCOUNTING/RETAIL] The amount of money left after all expenses have been paid.[4]

The profit over a specified period of a corporation or other business after deducting operating costs and income deductions; equals net income.[6]

net profit projection   [RETAIL/ACCOUNTING] A statement of a tenant's financial goals, calculated by subtracting the cost of merchandise, payroll, rental fees, advertising, and other expenses from projected sales to determine earnings before taxes. Net profit is then determined by subtracting taxes.[16]

net sales   [RETAIL] Gross sales less returns and allowances, freight-out, and often cash discounts allowed. In recent years the trend has been to report as net sales the net amount finally received from the customer.[5]

net worth   [ACCOUNTING] What the owner actually owns in the business.[7]

news conference   [MARKETING] A special meeting to release important information simultaneously to all media.[4]

news release   [MARKETING] *See* release.

nonanchors   [LEASING] Stores or establishments that do not serve as primary traffic generators (generally, tenants), excluding any freestanding units.[10]

noncash charges   [ACCOUNTING] Depreciation and amortization; the amounts recorded in these accounts represent economic value received in the current year from an asset, not expenditures in the current accounting period.[15]

noncash expenses   [ACCOUNTING] Expenses that are placed in the budget for future billing purposes but are not paid out of the funds held by the manager.[8]

noncurrent liabilities   [ACCOUNTING/FINANCE] Debts that fall due beyond one year; also called *long-term liabilities*.[15]

nondisturbance covenant   [LEASING/LEGAL] A clause in the lease that usually gives a tenant assurance of continuous operation of its store in the event of the landlord's foreclosure.[7]

nonlethal weapons   [SECURITY] Weapons used by center security that, in normal use, cannot kill a human being.[7]

nonoperating tenants   [LEASING/LEGAL] Rent-paying tenants who discontinue their retail operations. A tenant that closes its retail store but continues to pay rent and abide by other terms of the lease.[23]

nonpreemptible spots   [MARKETING] This refers to the highest rate charged by a station for a commercial, frequently called a "Section I" rate. In negotiation, spots at lower rates may be classified nonpreemptible as a concession by the station.[8]

nonrecourse loans   [FINANCE] A type of loan, preferred by borrowers, in which the lender can look only to the sale of a property as the source of repayment of a loan, not to the borrower's other assets, if the loan is not repaid.[15]

nonretail tenants   [LEASING] Shopping center tenants, primarily service-oriented tenants, who do not fit into the traditional category of retailers; a tenant selling services, not goods.[7]

notice to quit   [LEGAL] A notice by a landlord to a tenant to vacate rented property. There are two types: for nonpayment of rent or a second type for any reason. Usually the notice for nonpayment allows less time to vacate.[18]

NPV   [FINANCE] *See* net present value.

O

occupancy area [GENERAL] The total square footage of a center, including all vacant spaces.[10]

occupancy cost [ACCOUNTING/LEASING/RETAIL] The sum of a tenant's fixed rent, percentage rent, and add-ons. Also called total rent.[4]

occupancy cost ratio [ACCOUNTING/LEASING/RETAIL] A comparison of a retailer's annual sales volume to its annual occupancy costs (including base and percentage rent, real estate taxes, common area maintenance (CAM), building insurance, and marketing/promotion funds), expressed as a percentage.[15]

occupancy rate [ACCOUNTING/LEASING/GENERAL] The ratio of the space rented to the total amount of space available for rent.[25]

occurrence [OPERATIONS/SECURITY/INSURANCE] Broadens the definition of "accident" to include incidents that occur over a period of time.[7]

OES [MARKETING] *See* optimum effective scheduling.

office equipment expenses [ACCOUNTING/OPERATIONS] The cost of renting or servicing office equipment such as copiers, personal computers, and other office equipment (sometimes excluding telephones).[10]

off-price advertising [RETAIL/MARKETING] Promotes price-reduced merchandise during a specific sale period.[2]

off-price centers [GENERAL] Not to be confused with outlet centers, off-price centers sell branded merchandise that can be found in conventional specialty and department stores at higher prices. Usually the merchandise is first quality. Some manufacturers require that their merchandise be sold without labels in off-price centers.[12]

off-price retailing [GENERAL] The sale of branded merchandise at reduced prices.[19]

offset [ACCOUNTING] A reduction in the cost of percentage rent when a tenant meets a prearranged goal in another area, usually sales.[7]

A deduction of specified expenses or investments from all or a portion of percentage rent.[7]

offset printing [MARKETING] A process in which an inked impression from a plate is made on a rubber-blanketed cylinder and then transferred to the paper being printed.[2]

on the break [MARKETING] *See* break.

one-line budget [ACCOUNTING] An abbreviated budget showing only the net balance of probable income less probable expenses.[8]

on-site payroll and benefits [ACCOUNTING] All payroll and associated employee benefits related to mall personnel directly involved in the management of the shopping center. This includes the manager, assistant manager, secretary, bookkeeper, and other on-site management staff. This does not include the administrative costs attributable to marketing.[10]

open and operate provision [LEGAL/LEASING] A lease provision requiring the tenant to commence operations in the premises being rented, or to maintain continuous operations there. Also known as *operating covenant*.[23]

open rate [MARKETING] An all-media term. The line, inch, or time cost paid by advertisers without contracts or center rate availability.[2]

open-to-buy [RETAIL] Spendable dollars remaining in the buying plan for a special merchandise category, for a specific period.[2]

The amount of merchandise that may be ordered for delivery during a control period. It is the difference between the planned purchases and the commitments already made for the period.[5]

open windows [MARKETING/OPERATIONS] Display areas fronting the mall, with no glass enclosure or barriers. Used in enclosed malls only. Fully exposes the store interior to mall passersby.[2]

opening contribution [MARKETING/ACCOUNTING/LEASING] Tenant's one-time contribution to the marketing fund for a center's grand opening or grand reopening.[24]

operating budget [ACCOUNTING] An outline of how much income a shopping center has and how that income will be spent.[7]

Includes all income other than sale of capital assets, offset by all items of expense other than depreciation and interest on debt and payments on debt principal or added investment.[12]

operating cost ratio   [ACCOUNTING] The complement of the operating margin, frequently used by analysts; the two add up to 100 percent.[15]

operating expenses   [ACCOUNTING] Generally speaking, all expenses, occurring periodically, that are necessary to produce net income before depreciation. Under some conditions these expenses are placed in two categories: operating expenses and fixed charges.[7]

Monies needed to operate a business, as distinct from outlays to finance the business.[7]

operating margin   [RETAIL] A ratio measuring the operational efficiency of a company, this is calculated by dividing operating income by net sales; the result describes what percentage of every dollar of sales was retained as profit from operations.[15]

operating statement   [ACCOUNTING] A management statement that provides net sales, costs, and expenses and net operating profit or loss for a fixed period.[7]

A financial statement showing income and expenses by specific category and for a specific time frame.[8]

operating year   [ACCOUNTING/LEGAL] Usually a calendar year of January 1st through December 31st. Estimates and increases in landlord's operating costs run on this cycle as in a fiscal year.[24]

optimum effective scheduling (OES)   [MARKETING] A scheduling technique, based on a series of mathematical calculations, designed to deliver a minimum of 50 percent of a radio station's weekly cume an average of three or more times.[4]

orbit   [MARKETING] In television, a type of modified run of station (ROS) schedule, where spots will rotate within a given number of adjacencies, as Prime Time orbit. Example: Monday, 8:30 P.M.; Tuesday, 9:00 P.M.; Friday, 10:30 P.M. and then repeat.[5]

OTB   [RETAIL/RESEARCH] *See* open-to-buy.

OTO (one time only)   [MARKETING] Applies to a spot that is bought to run only once.[5]

outboard   [RESEARCH] That portion of a trade area that lies on the side of a shopping center away from the central city district. The population in this section is normally more effective in patronizing the shopping center than is the population on the inboard side, since its normal traffic movements are oriented in the direction of the central city area.[6]

outlet centers [GENERAL] Usually located in a rural area or occasionally in a tourist location, outlet centers consist mostly of manufacturers' outlet stores selling their own brands at a discount. An outlet center typically is not anchored. A strip configuration is most common, although some are enclosed malls, and others can be arranged in a "village" cluster.[1]

outlet retailer [RETAIL] A retail unit owned and operated by the manufacturer of branded goods; a vertical lifestyle retailer, or a company operating as the exclusive brand licensee; retailers operating primarily in outlet centers.[20]

outlot tenant [DEVELOPMENT/GENERAL] *See* pad tenant.

outparcels [DEVELOPMENT/GENERAL] Unused portions of a shopping center's site that constitute the perimeter areas, not including the center facility or parking lot, and that may be used or developed for similar or nonsimilar purposes.[7]

outposting [MARKETING/LEASING] The practice of placing a long-term in-line tenant in a cart, kiosk, or temporary in-line location to help the tenant market a new or special product line, for example.[16]

overage rent [LEASING/ACCOUNTING] Percentage rent (beyond base minimum rent) paid on gross sales in excess of a stated breakpoint for that tenant.[15]

overages [LEASING/ACCOUNTING] *See* overage rent.

overhead [ACCOUNTING] A synonym for fixed expenses.[4]

overstocks [RETAIL] Manufacturers' surplus items after sales to wholesale accounts (also called overruns).[20]

owner's protection coverage [INSURANCE] Insurance that covers the residual liability of the owner by picking up claims falling outside the scope of the contractor's programs.[17]

P

package [MARKETING] A group of television or radio spots offered for sale together at a given price. A package price is generally lower than the aggregate cost of the spots if bought individually.[5]

pad [DEVELOPMENT/GENERAL] The exact parcel of land on which a department store's building stands.[12]

pad tenant [LEASING/GENERAL] A tenant, usually free-standing, located on a separate parcel at the front of a shopping center. Also called an *outlot tenant.*[6]

paint unit [MARKETING] *See* bulletin.[4]

parking area [OPERATIONS/DEVELOPMENT] The space in a shopping center devoted to parking, including aisles, walks, islands, minor landscaping, and other features incidental to parking.[6]

parking lot cleaning/sweeping/repair expenses [OPERATIONS] All costs (payroll, benefits, materials, service contracts, and supplies) incurred in the striping, repairing of potholes, cleaning, and sweeping of the parking lot, sidewalks, and service courts. They also include all expenses incurred in the maintenance and repair of the parking lot sweeping equipment.[10]

parking ratio [DEVELOPMENT] The relationship of space used for parking and necessary vehicular and pedestrian movement to land area covered by buildings or space within the buildings. This relationship can be expressed in the number of car spaces per 1,000 square feet of rentable area.[6]

pass-along reader [MARKETING] One who is exposed to a publication that neither he nor any member of his household received by purchase or by request, as in the case of nonpaid publications. Readers from purchase or request households are called primary readers. The total audience of the publication is the sum of primary and pass-along readers.[5]

pass-through expenses [ACCOUNTING] A tenant's portion of expenses composed of common area maintenance, taxes, insurance, and any other expenses determined by the landlord to be paid by the tenant.[7]

patching [OPERATIONS] A procedure used in both roof and asphalt repair. In both cases, it involves repairing a tear, hole, or other type of defect by filling it with an appropriate compound.[7]

pending nonrenewal [MARKETING] *See* PNR.

penetration ratio [RESEARCH] The rate at which stores obtain sales from within a trade area or sector relative to the potential generated. Usually used for existing facilities.[6]

per capita [RESEARCH] A means of expressing total municipal expenditures or income by dividing them by the total user or resident population.[6]

per capita income [RESEARCH] *See* income, per capita.

per capita retail sales [RESEARCH] Total sales for retail categories as defined from a universe such as a metropolitan area, divided by the population of that area and corrected for export/import.[6]

per inquiry (PI) [MARKETING] A method used in direct-response radio and television advertising. Orders are the result of a commercial and go directly to the station; the advertiser pays the station on a per inquiry (or per order) basis.[2]

percentage rent [ACCOUNTING/LEASING/GENERAL] A percentage of the tenant's total annual sales paid in addition to fixed rent. This additional rent is normally paid after a predetermined sales level has been achieved. The percentage factor is then applied to all sales over the present level (breakpoint).[4]

The payment by a tenant as rent of a specified percentage of the gross income from sales made upon the premises. Developers in shopping centers customarily charge a minimum rent plus a percentage rent when sales exceed a certain volume.[6]

Percentage rent is a function of sales activity. A tenant's sales during a lease year are multiplied by the percentage rent rate(s); any excess over the minimum rent is percentage rent.[7]

Extra rent paid to a landlord if a tenant's sales figures exceed a prearranged figure.[7]

perils [OPERATIONS/INSURANCE] Inherent dangers, such as windstorms or explosions, that can cause a loss or an injury.[7]

perimeter protection [SECURITY] Devices designed to protect the exterior openings of a shopping center; for example, door locks and window bars.[7]

permitted use   [LEGAL/LEASING] What tenant is permitted to sell, to insure control of the tenant mix of the shopping center. (The qualifying words "and related items" should be avoided so as not to dilute the tenant mix or violate any other tenant's exclusives.)[24]

personal guarantee   [FINANCE/LEASING/ACCOUNTING] A lease provision for undercapitalized tenant companies with limited assets that obliges the tenant to use the personal assets of an officer of the tenant company or a related party as a secondary means to meet financial obligations to the landlord under the lease. For loans *see* recourse basis.

personal injury   [INSURANCE] A nonstandard part of liability coverage insuring the policyholder, on a named-perils basis, against such things as libel, slander, and unlawful detention.[7]

photo opportunity   [MARKETING] An occasion for the media to take a photograph.[4]

pica   [MARKETING] A print media measurement term; one-sixth of an inch, or 6 picas to an inch.[2]

piece goods   [RETAIL] The practice of combining a style from one season with leftover fabric from another season to create a new item that uses up excess materials.[20]

piggyback   [MARKETING] The broadcasting of two separate products side by side within the same commercial.[2]

   In broadcast, refers to the practice of combining completely separate commercials for two different products (made by the same advertiser) within a single announcement.[5]

pitch   [MARKETING] To present a story idea to an editor.[4]

plainclothes officers   [SECURITY] Police officers or security staff allowed to patrol in normal, everyday clothing.[7]

plies   [OPERATIONS] The layers of felts and bitumen formed during the creation of a built-up roof.[7]

plot plan   [DEVELOPMENT/GENERAL] The blueprint of a center showing the location and square footage of all tenants, as well as surface facilities.[2]

ply   [OPERATIONS] A single layer or thickness of roofing material. Built-up roofs may be three-ply, four-ply, etc., according to the number of layers of felt used to build the membrane.[8]

PNR (pending nonrenewal)   [MARKETING] Applies to the purchase of a spot pending the nonrenewal of the contract by the advertiser who already owns that spot (PNR orders are generally used only on the better, higher-rated spots of a station).[5]

point-of-origin survey [RESEARCH] A customer survey designed to determine what the primary trading area of a retail facility is by asking customers their home address. These addresses are pinpointed on a street map, allowing the researcher to delineate the trading area of the retail facility. Generally speaking, a minimum sample size of 300 is required to obtain a reasonable degree of accuracy.[6]

point size [MARKETING] The measure of size in which a typeface can be set.[4]

policy [INSURANCE] The written insurance contract.[7]

policyholder [INSURANCE] The person or company having an insurance contract.[7]

ponding. [OPERATIONS] Also known as *ponds See* birdbath.

poster [MARKETING] An outdoor advertising unit, usually 12' x 25', on which a message (printed on paper sheets) is displayed.[4]

posting [ACCOUNTING] The bookkeeping process of transcribing journal entry information to the ledger accounts.[5]

pothole [OPERATIONS] The commonest type of hole in asphalt pavements. It occurs when a small surface break is allowed to develop until it involves a larger area; also called *chuckhole.*[3]

Ever-widening craters that begin as small cracks that are allowed to develop until they involve a large area.[14]

power center [GENERAL] A center dominated by several large anchors, including discount department stores, off-price stores, warehouse clubs, or "category killers," i.e., stores that offer a tremendous selection in a particular merchandise category at low prices. The center typically consists of several freestanding (unconnected) anchors and only a minimum amount of small specialty tenants.[1]

preaudit [ACCOUNTING] A miniaudit professionally conducted 90 days prior to year-end, in advance of a complete annual audit.[4]

preempt [MARKETING] As an electronic media term, time sold at a lower rate and subject to resale by the station if a higher rate is offered.[2]

preemptible spots [MARKETING] Commercial positions sold at lower rates until they can be "recaptured," at the station's discretion, for an advertiser who is willing to pay the full rate. When this occurs, the first advertiser is given the option of paying the higher rate to keep the spot. Preemptible spots are often referred to as *Section II* spots (preemptible on 2 weeks' notice) or *Section III* spots (preemptible immediately). Section III is cheaper than Section II.[5]

preferred positioning [MARKETING] A print media term referring to the desirable positioning of an ad—that is, right-hand pages 3 or 5 or preceding a centerfold.[2]

premium [INSURANCE] The amount paid for an insurance policy.[7]

The fee paid to an insurance company as an inducement for assuming part of the insured's risk.[7]

prepaid expenses [ACCOUNTING] Advance payments to suppliers. Examples include prepaid rent and insurance. They belong in current assets, because if they were not present, more cash would be needed to conduct current operations.[15]

present value (PV) [FINANCE] Unlike future value (FV), this is a calculation that relies on the discount rate to determine what the present value of a known future amount of money should be.[15]

primary market [RESEARCH] The geographic market from which a center's predominant shoppers and/or sales come. *See* secondary market.4

A geographic term used to define the immediate trading area of a shopping center.[2]

primary research [RESEARCH] The process of gathering original information because existing data on an issue are not available. *See* secondary research.[4]

primary trading area [RESEARCH] The geographic area around a particular retail facility from which approximately 60 percent to 70 percent of the facility's customers come. The geographic radii and driving times to the primary zone vary among center types.[6]

prime rate [FINANCE] The base rate on corporate loans posted by at least 75 percent of the nation's 30 largest banks.

prime time [MARKETING] A television term denoting the hours television viewing is at its peak. Usually 7:30 P.M. to 11:00 P.M., local time, or not less than three continuous hours per broadcast day. The time frame will vary in different locales and with different demographics.[2]

private placement [LEGAL/FINANCE] The sale of securities to a small group of investors (generally 35 or fewer) that is exempt from U.S. Securities and Exchange Commission (SEC) registration requirements. The investors execute an investment letter stating that the securities are being purchased for investment without a view toward distribution.[20]

pro forma [FINANCE] The developer's estimate of all costs of planning, developing, building, and operating the center. Then he develops estimates of income, primarily from rents to be paid by tenants. From these estimated expenses and income, the developer computes the anticipated net income for the shopping center. From that item, the projected value of the completed, operating shopping center may be calculated through application of a capitalization rate.[12]

pro rata share [ACCOUNTING] The assessment of expenses on a proportional basis between landlord and tenant.[7]

probability distribution [FINANCE] A compilation of all potential outcomes of a transaction, along with the probability, or degree of certainty, that each will occur—ranging from zero, or no possibility, to one, or complete certainty. The sum of all values in such a distribution must equal one.[15]

process color [MARKETING] In printing, a computer process that layers in colors and blends them at the time of printing.[4]

professional fee [CONSTRUCTION/GENERAL] An amount covering the contractor's fixed overhead costs and profit for the project; generally presented as a percentage of the construction costs, but sometimes converted to a fixed lump sum amount.[17]

profit [ACCOUNTING] A general term for the excess of revenue, proceeds, or selling price over related costs.[5]

profit and loss statement [ACCOUNTING] A financial statement showing revenues earned by a business, the expenses incurred in earning the revenues, and the resulting net income or net loss; also called operating statement, variance report, income statement, or statement of income and expenses.[5]

project [GENERAL] A shopping center.[20]

project delivery approaches [CONSTRUCTION/GENERAL] Methods by which a project manager forms the team, assigns responsibilities, writes contractual agreements, purchases needed materials, and ensures effective owner management throughout. The three basic approaches are traditional, in which all design and construction activities are sequential; fast track, in which those activities overlap so that construction begins before design is complete; and design/build, in which the owner selects a single design and construction entity, contractually integrating responsibility for both activities.[17]

project management [CONSTRUCTION] The organized, systematic approach toward planning, organizing, and managing the process of design and construction. A project manager operates as an agent on behalf of the owner.[17]

promotion [MARKETING] An activity that benefits the center's business purpose. In terms of effect, promotion is intended to directly stimulate shopper traffic and subsequently sales.[12]

promotion fund contribution [ACCOUNTING/MARKETING/LEASING] Tenant's contribution toward the marketing fund, often calculated using a sum of money multiplied by the number of square feet contained in tenant's floor area.[24]

promotional license agreement [MARKETING/LEGAL] A written agreement between the landlord and an individual or organization staging an event or activity in the shopping center common area that details requirements for insurance, payment, and all other indemnity and limits the landlord's liability resulting from events hosted by outside groups. *See* hold-harmless agreement.[4]

promotions [MARKETING] Also known as *special events expenses*. The cost of producing special events and promotional activities within the center, except at Christmastime. They include labor, decorations, signs, point-of-purchase materials, special entertainments, etc., attributable to such events.[10]

proof [MARKETING] A printed copy of a publication-set ad, submitted to the advertiser for corrections or approval prior to publication.[2]

Copies of an ad for review at different stages in its progress. *See* blue line; color key.[4]

property damage [INSURANCE] Part of liability coverage defined as direct damage to physical property and loss of use thereof.[7]

property insurance   [INSURANCE] First-party insurance covering the insured for damage to his or her personal or real property or the loss of its use.[7]

property, plant, and equipment   [ACCOUNTING/OPERATIONS] *See* tangible assets.

proprietary security   [SECURITY] In-house security developed, managed, and maintained by a center's manager or landlord.[7]

protected premises   [SECURITY] A shopping center that has had an alarm system installed.[7]

PruneYard court case   [LEGAL] In matters involving political petitions, one landmark decision by the United States Supreme Court, *PruneYard Shopping Center v. Robins,* has had far-reaching effects on shopping centers. Decided in 1980, the PruneYard decision, as it is known, held that the state (California) can require public access to a shopping center for political petitioning under reasonable rules and regulations without violating the shopping center owner's constitutional rights.[12]

PSAs   [MARKETING] *See* public service announcements.

psychographics   [RESEARCH] The motivating forces that influence shopping patterns and consumer behavior.[2]

Information based on categorization of consumer values, motivation, how people are influenced, what they spend their money on, and the psychological attributes they exhibit in terms of shopping behavior.[4]

An interpretation of lifestyle issues: how people are influenced and what they spend their money on.[7]

Factors about lifestyle that influence how and on what people spend their money.[4]

psychological testing   [LEGAL] An examination performed by a psychologist to determine the emotional stability of a person.[7]

public relations   [MARKETING] The establishment and maintenance of goodwill, promulgated by participation and concern for communitywide activities.[2]

public service announcements (PSAs)   [MARKETING] Free television or radio promotions of the programs and activities or services of government agencies, nonprofit organizations, and others that serve the interests of the community.[4]

publicity   [MARKETING] Newsworthy information that, when released to the media, will be published or broadcast as news. It is used as free advertising.[7]

The use of selected media to carry messages and stories without cost.[4]

The dissemination of news and information concerning a person or organization through channels of communication such as newspapers, magazines, television, and radio, the use of which is not paid for by the publicity seeker.[5]

publicity release   [MARKETING] Information with news value distributed to the media for purposes of favorably influencing consumers.[2]

pub-set   [MARKETING] An ad prepared by a publication when submitted as copy and layout.[2]

put to bed   [MARKETING] To close an issue of a publication, after which time no additional material may be inserted.[4]

PV   [FINANCE] *See* present value.

Q

quick assets   [ACCOUNTING/RETAIL/FINANCE] What is available to cover a sudden emergency—in other words, readily available cash; determined by taking current assets and deducting inventories, prepaid expenses, and any other illiquid current assets (ones that cannot be readily converted to cash).[15]

quick ratio   [ACCOUNTING/FINANCE] A ratio determined by dividing quick assets by current liabilities; the result measures the adequacy of available working capital.[15]

quiet enjoyment clause   [LEGAL] A lease clause that gives a tenant assurance that the landlord has authority to enter into a binding lease.[7]

quote rates   [LEASING] Typically expressed in dollars per square foot of a tenant's or prospective tenant's proportionate share of common area maintenance (CAM), real estate taxes, and other ongoing shopping center charges based on budgeted expense and budgeted occupancy.[15]

R

racetrack design [DEVELOPMENT] The design of a shopping center in which the merchants are arranged around both sides of a large oval, sometimes with a food court in the middle.[20]

radio A time [MARKETING] Monday through Friday, 6:30 P.M. to sign-off, and Saturday and Sunday all day.[2]

radio AA time [MARKETING] Monday through Friday, 9:00 A.M. to 4:30 P.M.[2]

radio AAA time [MARKETING] Monday through Friday, 6:00 A.M. to 8:00 A.M. and 4:30 P.M. to 6:30 P.M.[2]

radius restriction [LEASING/GENERAL] *See* competing business.

radius restriction clause [LEASING/LEGAL] A clause inserted into a shopping center retail lease establishing the distance from the center that the retailer may operate another, similar store.[7]

A specific trade radius in which a tenant may not operate another business, usually of the same type or name.[7]

rate card [MARKETING] A published list of advertising rates for any given medium.[2]

rate holder [MARKETING] The minimum-size ad that must appear during a given period if the advertiser is to secure a certain time or quantity discount.[2]

rate of retention [LEASING] The rate at which existing tenants renew their leases in their existing spaces.[15]

rate of return on assets [FINANCE] This measure determines the income generated by the investment compared to the cost of the investment stated as a percentage. This indicator can be compared to other possible investments or against some minimum threshold rate set by the investor.[26]

rates and data book [MARKETING] A publication that lists all pertinent information relating to newspapers published in the United States.[2]

rating [MARKETING] The estimated size of an audience expressed as a percentage of the specified universe.[4]

The percentage of a given universe who watch (listen to) a given station at a given time. A 10 rating means that 10 percent of the people universe (or household universe) were watching the show. Ratings can be added together. (*See* gross rating points.) However, since there is never a time when 100 percent of the homes have their TV sets turned on, ratings in a time period (quarter hour) never add up to 100.[5]

rating point   [MARKETING] One percent of the homes in the measured area whose sets are tuned to a specific station: used for making comparisons of stations.[2]

raveling   [OPERATIONS] The undoing of the texture of a pavement, typically through the loss of aggregate from the surface or the stripping of the asphalt cement from the aggregate; also called abrasion.[3]

A rough, pockmarked surface due to the undoing of the pavement through loss of aggregate from the surface or through stripping of the asphalt cement from the aggregate. The wheels of passing traffic break free pavement fragments.[14]

reach   [MARKETING] The number of people who read, watch, or listen to a newspaper, magazine, television program, or radio program.[4]

The total audience a medium actually covers.[2]

The estimated number of persons or households in the audience likely to be exposed to a commercial message at least one time in a designated time period.[4]

reach and frequency   [MARKETING] Reach is a measure of the net percentage of homes (or viewers) reached by a schedule during a given period of time; frequency is the average number of times each home (or individual) that is reached saw that commercial. Reach and frequency are functions of the gross rating points of a schedule. (Reach x Frequency = Gross Rating Points.)[5]

real income   [RESEARCH] *See* income, real.

recapture   [ACCOUNTING] A right, usually held by major tenants, to deduct such items as common area maintenance or insurance paid from percentage rents that may be owing.[6]

recapture rate   [FINANCE] The annual rate at which capital investment is returned to an investor over a specified period of time; the annual amount, apart from interest or return on interest (compound interest), that can be recaptured from an investment, divided by the original investment. Also called capital recovery rate.[7]

receipt of goods (ROG) terms   [RETAIL] Cash discounts that begin when merchandise reaches the store.[5]

receivable collection   [RETAIL/ACCOUNTING] A ratio determined by dividing average accounts receivable by net sales over 365 days.[15]

recoating   [OPERATIONS] A procedure in both roof and parking lot maintenance in which a deteriorated surface is rejuvenated by a coat of, usually, a petroleum-based product.[7]

reconfiguration   [DEVELOPMENT] Changing the layout of the various stores and the common area connecting them, to accommodate a new anchor, compensate for the loss of an anchor, improve the parking lot, add a second level, or change the shopping center's use or image. Neighborhood and community centers, sometimes referred to as *strip malls,* are usually configured in a straight line or L shape; regional and superregional centers, sometimes referred to as *regional malls,* traditionally are composed of at least two facing strips of retail stores with anchors on each end, sometimes in a cross or "X" pattern in larger centers, connected by an open or enclosed common area.[17]

recourse basis   [FINANCE] A type of loan, preferred by lenders, that obliges the borrower to use personal assets as a secondary means to repay a loan, if the proceeds from a sale of the property are not sufficient to cover the amount owed on the loan; sometimes referred to as a *personal guarantee.*[15]

re-covering   [OPERATIONS] The placing of a new roof over an existing roof. This procedure may be done one time without the tearing-off of an existing roof membrane. Local codes will dictate reroofing policies.[7]

recovery ratio   [ACCOUNTING] The relationship between related revenue and expense.

redevelopment   [DEVELOPMENT] Usually a comprehensive action that may include extensive leasing activity, renovation, expansion, and/or reconfiguration, but that typically substantially changes the leasing and marketing direction of an existing shopping center.[17]

reflection crack   [OPERATIONS] A crack pattern on the surface caused by cracking in the pavement underneath the surface, which is due to expansion and contraction.[3]

A surface cracks without a distinctive pattern that reproduces cracking of a similar pattern in the subsurface pavement layers. The undersurface cracks open owing to expansion and contraction.[14]

regional center [GENERAL] This center type provides general merchandise (a large percentage of which is apparel) and services in full depth and variety. Its main attractions are its anchors: traditional, mass merchant or discount department stores, or fashion specialty stores. A typical regional center is usually enclosed, with an inward orientation of the stores connected by a common walkway, and parking surrounds the outside perimeter.[1]

regional tenant [GENERAL/RETAIL] A retailer who operates stores in a particular region of the country.[7]

reinvestment rate [FINANCE] The rate at which an investment will grow each year, analogous to the interest rate on a bank account; used to determine future value.[15]

REIT [FINANCE/LEGAL] (U.S. and Canada.) An acronym for a *r*eal *e*state *i*nvestment *t*rust, a form of ownership of shopping centers and other properties. A business trust or corporation that combines the capital of many investors to acquire or provide financing for real estate. Under U.S. law, a corporation that qualifies for REIT status is not required to pay corporate income tax if it distributes (most) of its taxable income to shareholders.[15]

relative draw analysis [RESEARCH] A technique used to understand the demographic and geographic strengths and weaknesses in a center's draw.[4]

release [MARKETING] A manuscript sent to the media to announce information or convey a story.[4]

relocation clause [LEGAL/LEASING] A lease clause that gives a landlord the ability to move the tenant to another location within the shopping center premises.[7]

renewal option [LEGAL/LEASING] An agreement at the time of the original lease as to the terms of a tenant's extension of lease term.[7]

renovation [DEVELOPMENT] Improvements or modifications of existing features of a shopping center, such as new ceiling, floor and wall surfaces, the addition of skylights or fountains, the redesign or addition of rest rooms and other amenities, landscaping, furnishings, upgraded lighting, and resurfacing of parking spaces.[17]

rent leveling [ACCOUNTING/LEASING] Sometimes referred to as straight-line rent. A purely accounting process by which average rent is recognized as income in each year throughout a lease, regardless of the actual schedule of payments. Renovation is usually undertaken as part of a redevelopment. *See* redevelopment.[15]

rent roll or **rent schedule**   [LEASING/ACCOUNTING] A summary schedule listing of all spaces in a shopping center, vacant as well as occupied, for quick reference and full disclosure. Information listed here includes tenant names by retail category, size of each store, fixed minimum annual rent, the term of each lease (including commencement and expiration dates), the annual percentage rent breakpoint for each tenant, and the percentage rent rate(s), as well as other information.[15]

rent/sales index   [ACCOUNTING/LEASING] A measure that helps determine whether a store's rent is in proportion to the sales it generates. It is calculated by dividing the percentage of rent by the percentage of sales.[4]

rent steps   [LEASING/ACCOUNTING] The scheduled increases in rent that are specified in a tenant's lease, and budgeted in the appropriate month.[15]

rent-to-sales ratio   [ACCOUNTING/LEASING] A tenant's total occupancy costs divided by its total sales, expressed as a percentage. The ratio is an indicator of a tenant's financial viability.[4]

rental area   [LEASING] The square footage of a building that can actually be rented. (Halls, lobbies, elevator shafts, maintenance rooms, and lavatories are excluded.)[5]

That part of gross floor area used exclusively by individual tenants and on which rent can be obtained.[6]

rental year   [ACCOUNTING] The method in determining the rental years for step increases in rent.[24]

replacement   [OPERATIONS] In a strict sense, it implies removing some portion of the property and restoring the missing part on a like-for-like basis.[13]

replacement cost   [OPERATIONS/CONSTRUCTION] Today's cost of construction, without considering depreciation.[7]

replacement value   [INSURANCE] The basis for loss payment can, by endorsement (specifying changes in or additions to the policy) and additional premium, be changed from actual cash value (replacement cost less depreciation) to replacement value, which is the full cost of replacement as of that date. This change adds to the annual expense of insurance.[12]

reports [OPERATIONS/SECURITY] Written documentation, based on investigation, describing events that took place during an incident.[7]

repositioning [DEVELOPMENT] *See* redevelopment.

representative (rep) [MARKETING] The salesperson or contact for any medium.[2]

request for proposal (RFP) [CONSTRUCTION/OPERATIONS] Information sought from architects or other contractors for contracts being considered for a project.[17]

reserve for replacement [ACCOUNTING] Monies put up by the owner or collected from tenants to be used for large repairs or replacements in the future.[8]

residual analysis [RESEARCH/DEVELOPMENT] An analytical procedure in which the potential for a store or a shopping center is derived on the basis of sales volume estimated to be available, based on population, income, and expenditure characteristics of the population, and allowing for the effects of present and future competing stores to obtain their operating sales volumes.[6]

retail [GENERAL] The price at which goods are offered for sale.[7]

retail expenditures [RESEARCH] Spending for retail by trade area residents adjusted for income differences in relation to market universe retail sales, adjusted by the elasticity factor (= per capita retail expenditure). Projected into the future at a rate reflecting an increased standard of living (excluding inflation), generally 1.5 percent to 1.7 percent per annum simple. Multiplied by projected population, it yields total retail potential, i.e., expenditures incurred by trade area residents in existing stores, at home and elsewhere, and potentially in proposed facilities.[6]

retailer survey [MARKETING/RESEARCH] A study of retailers' opinions and expectations about the shopping center, often from a renovation or redevelopment.[17]

retailer's cost price [RETAIL] *See* net price.

retailing [GENERAL] The business activities concerned with selling goods to ultimate consumers.[5]

retained earnings [ACCOUNTING] Accumulated income less distribution to stockholders and transfers to paid-in capital accounts.[3]

This represents the profit or loss held in a company, based on accumulated income minus whatever is distributed to stockholders or transferred to capital accounts; also referred to as *retained income*.[15]

retained income   [ACCOUNTING] *See* retained earnings.

return on assets   [FINANCE] A ratio calculated by dividing net income by average total assets.[15]

return-on-equity (ROE) ratio   [FINANCE] A measurement of profitability, often used in conjunction with return on investment (ROI), and calculated by dividing net income by the average equity of a two-year period; this ratio helps an investor determine if a business would make an attractive investment.[15]

return on investment (ROI) analysis   [FINANCE] A formula used to determine the relative worth of an asset. There are many different kinds of analyses: they're usually used to determine if an asset should be repaired or replaced.[7]

return on sales   [RETAIL] A ratio determined by dividing net income by net sales.[15]

revenue growth   [RETAIL] A ratio determined by dividing the difference between this year's net sales and last year's net sales by the amount of last year's net sales.[15]

revenues   [ACCOUNTING] What a company receives for its products or services; for a shopping center, its rents and other charges paid by tenants, plus ancillary income generated from other sources.[15]

reverse allowance   [ACCOUNTING/LEASING] The tenant pays a specific amount of money over any minimum and percentage rents for the landlord's cost of building the space.[7]

rider   [INSURANCE/LEGAL] An amendment or addition to a document of record.[3]

right of subrogation   [INSURANCE/LEGAL] Ordinarily, an insurance company that pays its insured for a loss has the right of action against a third party who may have been responsible for the loss. This right of action is called the right of subrogation.[12]

ring road   [GENERAL] Road that completely encircles a shopping center.[17]

ripple   [OPERATIONS] A form of plastic movement at points where traffic stops and starts.[3]

risk   [INSURANCE] The peril insured against; the chance of loss.[7]

risk management   [INSURANCE] The branch of management that is concerned with protecting a business against the risks of accidental loss.[7]

risk premium [FINANCE/INSURANCE] The difference between a discount rate and a risk-free, or safe, rate of return such as that of a U.S. Treasury note; this factor, often referred to as the *marginal cost of capital*, compensates the investor for inherent market risks, business risks, portfolio management, and loss of liquidity.[15]

Risk Retention Act companies [INSURANCE] This 1986 federal act permitted industries to jointly set up insurance vehicles that were licensed in a single state and then to write business in other states.[7]

RMU [LEASING] Retail merchandising unit. *See* cart.

robbery [SECURITY] Forcibly taking property directly from another person.[7]

ROE [RETAIL] *See* return-on-equity ratio.

ROG [RETAIL] *See* receipt of goods (ROG) terms.

ROI [FINANCE] *See* return on investment.

roof cement [OPERATIONS] A cement normally used for minor repairs of a roof, such as nonrecurring leaks. It may be asphalt, a pitch-based plastic, or a flashing, and must be compatible with the original materials.[3]

roof deck [OPERATIONS] The prepared subsurface of a roof on which a membrance is laid.[7]

roof repair [OPERATIONS] The cost of routine maintenance and repairs to the roof of a center. It does not include the cost of major capital improvements.[10]

ROP [MARKETING] *See* run of paper.

ROR [RETAIL] *See* rate of return on assets.

ROS [MARKETING] *See* run of station.

run of paper (ROP) [MARKETING] The placement of a newspaper ad in any portion as determined by the publication.[2]

run of placement (ROP) color [MARKETING] In printing, this is a random placement of one or two colors in an ad, usually determined by the media representative.[4]

run of station (ROS) [MARKETING] Spot commercials bought for placement anywhere within a station's schedule (at its discretion). The ROS rate is generally the lowest offered by a station.[5]

Preemptible spot commercials bought for airing within a station's schedule, timed at the station's discretion.[2]

S

sales [RETAIL] The amounts received by or accrued to the store in exchange for merchandise sold to customers during an accounting period.[4]

sales analysis report [ACCOUNTING] A report of actual sales and percentage of change over a given time. It also shows sales per square foot for each tenant or merchandise category.[4]

sales area [RETAIL] Rentable area minus storage space. The proportion of rentable store area devoted to sales varies among store types and among stores of the same type, so that calculations of sales or rent are more uniform if made on the basis of total store area.[6]

sales benchmarks [RESEARCH] Allows comparisons of the center to other shopping centers in terms of sales, rent, and other statistics.[4]

sales breakpoint [LEASING/ACCOUNTING] *See* breakpoint.

sales contribution [RESEARCH] An estimate of how much of a center's sales come from a geographic or a demographic group. Sales contribution is a component of a center's share of market calculation.[4]

sales efficiency ratio [RESEARCH] A comparison, expressed as a ratio, of the percentage of a merchandise category's total square footage to its percentage of gross sales. The ratio is an indicator of category productivity.[4]

sales per square foot [ACCOUNTING/LEASING/RESEARCH] Total annual sales divided by the total number of square feet of rentable area.[6]

sales potential [RESEARCH] Estimates of how much money the people who live in a market will spend on consumer goods and services.[4]

Total retail spending by trade area residents, usually stated in terms of store type. This potential is the product of the multiplication of population and per capita expenditures. The sales potential provides the support base for the planned new facilities as well as for existing competitive facilities both within and beyond the trade area.[6]

sales projection [ACCOUNTING/RETAIL/LEASING/RESEARCH] A tenant's estimate of monthly sales and total annual sales for the balance of the lease.[16]

sales/rent report [ACCOUNTING] Information that helps evaluate the sales performance of a center and its stores. It is considered the center's "report card" and is an ongoing measure of productivity.[4]

sample size [RESEARCH] The determination of how many shoppers or market residents will be included in a shopper intercept or telephone survey.[4]

sans serif [MARKETING] A typeface in which the letters have no serifs. *See* serifs.[4]

saturation [MARKETING] A media pattern of wide coverage and high frequency during a concentrated time period, designed to achieve maximum impact, coverage, or both.[2]

scatter plan [MARKETING] The use of announcements over a variety of stations and time segments to reach as many people as possible in a market.[2]

screen halftones [MARKETING] Photographic illustrations in an ad whose image results from a percentage application of ink.[4]

scupper [OPERATIONS] A hole in a parapet wall of a roof that allows water to flow into the roof drain. A scupper also acts as an overflow precaution in case of a gutter blockage.[7]

sealers [OPERATIONS] Liquid coatings used to protect asphalt parking lots and roadways.[7]

search procedure [OPERATIONS] Step-by-step instruction on how to search an entire shopping center.[7]

seasonality index [RESEARCH] A table of percentages of total annual sales generated at a shopping center during each selling season (holiday, winter clearance, spring, and so on).[4]

second stage [FINANCE] Working capital for the initial expansion of a company that is producing and shipping and has growing accounts receivable and inventories. Although the company has clearly made progress, it may not yet be showing a profit.[20]

secondary market [RESEARCH] The geographic market located outside the primary market from which a center obtains shoppers or sales. *See* primary market; inflow market.[4]

A geographic term used to designate areas outside the primary market, the fringes of the market and beyond.[2]

secondary public offering [FINANCE] A public offering of securities to raise capital subsequent to an initial public offering. A secondary public offering can be either an issuer offering or an offering by a group that has purchased the issuer's securities in the public markets.[20]

secondary purchase [FINANCE/RETAIL] Purchase of a stock in a company from a shareholder, rather than purchasing stock directly from the company.[20]

secondary research [RESEARCH] Information that has already been gathered by another party and is available. *See* primary research.[4]

secondary zone [RESEARCH] The portion of a trade area that supplies additional support to a shopping center beyond that obtained from the primary zone. Secondary zone patronage for a shopping center is primarily generated by the comparison shopping stores in the center; convenience shopping is primarily done by secondary zone residents at other neighborhood centers closer to home.[6]

seconds [RETAIL] Significant flaws in retail goods that are more serious than those of irregulars. Product may be misshapen, mismatched, stained, dented.[19]

secret shoppers [MARKETING] A process by which individual stores are evaluated in terms of sales staff, merchandise techniques, store appearance, and other issues. Also called *mystery shoppers*.[4]

sector [RESEARCH] A smaller geographic division of a primary or secondary trade area. Sectors are based on geographic and demographic characteristics. They allow the trade area to be analyzed in greater detail.[6]

sector analysis [RESEARCH] Research into segments of a trade area to determine population, socioeconomic characteristics, rate of sales penetration, and sector market shares. Usually for focus advertising.[6]

securitization [FINANCE] The process of converting an illiquid asset, such as a mortgage loan, into a tradable form, such as mortgage-backed securities.[29]

security [SECURITY] To the owner, security connotes the preservation of the buildings representing his investment and the maintenance of peace and order, the absence of which will deter shoppers. To the tenant, security revolves around protection of his merchandise and employees, plus that same interest in a peaceful environment for his customers. To the shopper, security has to do with personal safety and the safety of property while in the center or traveling to and from it.[12]

security chain of command   [SECURITY] The ordering of a security force by rank or importance.[7]

security expenses   [ACCOUNTING/SECURITY] This major category includes costs associated with security at the center. These include payroll and employee benefits of center-employed security personnel, the costs of contracted security services, equipment, uniforms, and supplies attributable to the security function.[10]

security revenue   [ACCOUNTING/SECURITY] Receipts from tenants to recover the cost of center security services.[10]

selectivity   [MARKETING] In advertising, the ability to choose one medium or even one feature of a medium (ZIP code or family income) to suit an advertiser's needs.[4]

self-managed REIT   [FINANCE] A REIT whose employees are responsible for performing property management functions.[29]

series discounts   [RETAIL] A number of discounts offered by the manufacturer to the retailer.[7]

serifs   [MARKETING] The short lines stemming from the end strokes of printed letters.[4]

SET   [E-COMMERCE] An e-commerce acronym for *secure electronic transaction*, a standard that enables secure credit card transactions on the Internet.[27]

share   [MARKETING] Of all the homes that have their television sets turned on at a given moment, the percentage tuned to a given station. Shares for a given quarter hour add up to 100; rating points do not.[5]

A station's or program's portion of the total listening or viewing audience expressed as a percentage of the total potential audience.[4]

share of market   [RESEARCH] An estimate of the percentage of a geographic market's sales potential that a center receives in sales.[4]

share-of-the-market analysis   [RESEARCH] An analytical technique in which it is assumed that strong stores, capably and aggressively merchandised, will obtain their representative share of the total market in that category, notwithstanding the existence of competing units. Stores that have an identifiable name appeal and impact on shopping habits, such as department stores, are strong enough to attract a certain share of total business under normal operating conditions.[6]

shopper intercept survey [RESEARCH] A tool used to gather information about a center's shoppers and shopping patterns.[4]

A survey conducted by stopping shoppers at the center.[4]

shopping attitudes [MARKETING/RESEARCH] Motivations for selecting favorite shopping destinations, including tenant mix, convenience, ambience, quality, price/value, parking, and other factors, as well as what customers like most and least about the present retail options. One of the most important groups of questions in field surveys of customers.[17]

shopping behavior [MARKETING/RESEARCH] Factors explored in field surveys of actual and potential shoppers, such as reasons for visiting the center, which other centers have been visited, how often such visits take place, what types of items are sought and purchased, and the type of transportation used to make the visit.[17]

shopping center [GENERAL] A group of retail and other commercial establishments that is planned, developed, owned, and managed as a single property. On-site parking is provided. The center's size and orientation are generally determined by the market characteristics of the trade area served by the center. The two main configurations of shopping centers are malls and open-air strip centers.[1]

shopping goods [GENERAL] Goods from variety, department, and general merchandise stores: toys, hobbies, sporting goods, small appliances, household, textile, garden and lawn supplies, luggage and leather, music, books, housewares, children's apparel, candy, radios, and televisions.[6]

shopping patterns [RESEARCH] Various types of behavior a consumer exhibits in a shopping center which are measured with consumer data tools. Shopping patterns might include the following: shopper origin, next destination, mode of transportation, primary purpose of center visit, shopping frequency, amount spent, time spent shopping, stores visited/purchased in, and buyer conversion.[4]

short rate [MARKETING] A print media term which means that the paper charges a higher rate if the advertiser does not fulfill its contract.[2]

short-term debt [ACCOUNTING/FINANCE] *See* current liabilities.

short-term lease   [LEASING] *See* long-term lease.[5]

shrinkage   [RETAIL] The difference between merchandise on hand shown by a physical inventory and that shown as "book value." It may be due to theft, internal or external fraud, record distortion, waste, sabotage, general laxity, or careless operation.[5]

shrinkage cracks   [OPERATIONS] Cracks usually having sharp corners or angles and identifiable by their tendency to run in any direction.[3]

sidewalk sale   [MARKETING] A centerwide, merchants' association-sponsored, off-price, low-end promotion; merchandise is displayed from common areas fronting each store.[2]

sig cut   [MARKETING] *See* logo.[2]

single-family house   [RESEARCH] A single detached structure of one unit.[6]

single ply   [OPERATIONS] A type of roof made from a single layer of specially reinforced rubber or plastic.[7]

site   [DEVELOPMENT] A specific tract of land proposed for center development, exhibiting qualities of size, shape, location plus accessibility, and zoning, and suited for the development of a center.[6]

site-specific demand analysis   [DEVELOPMENT/RESEARCH] A study to determine demand when only a particular area of a center, such as a food court, is being renovated or otherwise changed. This includes determining the projected number of uses (market population), number of seats needed based on people demand, and amount of square footage needed based on number of seats.[17]

slab   [OPERATIONS] The base on which roofing insulation is laid.[13]

sleepers   [OPERATIONS] Part of a bracing system that keeps HVAC (heating, ventilation, and air-conditioning) units anchored and off the roof and limits vibrations to the premises.[7]

slightly imperfect   [RETAIL] Refers to garments, with unnoticeable flaws, sold to consumers below market retail prices.[19]

slip and fall litigation   [INSURANCE] The type of lawsuit brought against a shopping center when a consumer is hurt by slipping on a defective surface.[7]

slippage cracks   [OPERATIONS] Crescent-shaped cracks that usually appear in the direction of greatest traffic thrust because of a lack of bonding between the top layer of the pavement and the layer beneath. The top layer literally slips over the lower layer.[14]

Generally crescent-shaped cracks usually found in the direction where traffic thrust is greatest.[3]

slurry   [OPERATIONS] A type of asphalt sealer. There are different types, and usage depends on the kind of roadway and desired protection.[7]

small town rural   [RESEARCH] A town outside of a U.S. metropolitan statistical area or outside of the suburbs of an urban core Canadian city.[10]

S/MIME   [E-COMMERCE] An e-commerce term, short for Secure/MIME, which is a version of the MIME protocol that supports encryption of electronic messages. It is expected that S/MIME will be widely implemented to make it possible for people to send secure e-mail messages to one another, even if they are using different e-mail services.[27]

SMSA   [RESEARCH] *See* standard metropolitan statistical area.

snipe   [MARKETING] A copy strip added over an outdoor poster or board containing special information.[2]

snow removal expenses   [OPERATIONS] The cost of snow removal from the building roof and parking lot and salting or sanding of the parking lot. It includes manpower, equipment, and material provided by an outside contractor or by the center.[10]

sodium light   [RESEARCH] A lamp in which light is produced by an electrical current passed through sodium vapor. Available in both high- and low-pressure applications.[7]

soft costs   [ARCHITECTURE/CONSTRUCTION] Architectural fees, interest on loans, payroll, and indirect expenses in a redevelopment project.[15]

soft goods   [RETAIL] Merchandise, also known as softlines, of nondurable character, such as wearing apparel, domestics (including linen, towels, and bedding), and yard goods.[6]

source of sales   [MARKETING/RESEARCH] Data that provides information about such factors as the geographic location and types of consumers from which a project's sales are expected to be derived.[17]

space deadline   [MARKETING] The lead time required by a publication to reserve advertising space for a specific date.[2]

special event   [MARKETING] A centerwide, merchants' association–sponsored promotion aimed at generating increased customer traffic. *See* promotions *or* special events expenses[2]

special marketing assessment [ACCOUNTING/MARKETING] A supplemental marketing contribution.[4]

specialty leasing program [LEASING] A program for establishing temporary tenants either in-line or on the common area of a shopping center, also known as *temporary tenant programs.*[16]

specific performance clause [LEGAL] In a lease, the clause that gives one party the right to cause another party to comply with the lease.[7]

split run [MARKETING] A facility available in newspapers and periodicals whereby the advertiser alternates different advertising copy in every other copy of the same issue. This makes it possible to compare coupon returns from two different advertisements published under identical conditions.[5]

spot [MARKETING] A commercial announcement; also denotes schedules placed locally, as opposed to national network buys.[5]

spot color [MARKETING] An application of color to one or two places in an ad.[4]

sprinkler contribution rate [ACCOUNTING/LEASING] Tenant's contribution to the maintenance of the fire-protection sprinkler system.[24]

SSL [E-COMMERCE] An e-commerce term, short for *s*ecure *s*ockets *l*ayer, a protocol developed by Netscape for transmitting private documents via the Internet. SSL works by using a private key to encrypt data that is transferred over the SSL connection. Both Netscape Navigator and Microsoft Internet Explorer support SSL, and many Web sites use the protocol to obtain confidential user information, such as credit card numbers. By convention, Web pages that require an SSL connection start with *https:* instead of *http:*.[27]

staggered schedule [MARKETING] A schedule of space to be used in two or more periodicals, arranged so that the insertions alternate.[2]

standard inspection [OPERATIONS] A daily, weekly, or monthly examination of mechanical systems or other shopping center assets.[7]

standard metropolitan statistical area (SMSA) [RESEARCH] A statistical unit defined by the Census Bureau as a county or a group of contiguous counties that contains at least one city of 50,000 inhabitants or more, or "twin cities" with a combined population of at least 50,000. In addition to the county or counties containing such a city or cities, contiguous counties are included in an SMSA if, according to certain criteria, they are socially and economically integrated with the central city. In the New England states, SMSAs consist of towns and cities instead of counties.[6]

standard operating procedure   [OPERATIONS] A course of action that states precisely how a particular system of maintenance policy is to be conducted.[7]

standard operating procedures manual   [OPERATIONS] A booklet that outlines a center's maintenance policy.[7]

statement of cash flows   [ACCOUNTING] The portion of a financial statement that reports on cash receipts and cash payments, it reveals the relationship of net income, shown on the operating statement, to changes in cash balances.[15]

statement of changes in financial position   [ACCOUNTING/FINANCE] A description of changes on a balance sheet from one accounting period to another; a measurement of the resources provided during an accounting period and the uses to which they were put.[15]

statement of retained earnings   [ACCOUNTING/FINANCE] Reconciles the balance of retained earnings from the beginning of the year to the end.[15]

step-down rents   [ACCOUNTING/LEASING] Rents that are structured so that percentages paid on total sales by a tenant decrease as sales grow.[7]

step-up rents   [ACCOUNTING/LEASING] Rents that are structured so that they increase at specific times during the life of a lease.[7]

stock turnover   [RETAIL] The degree of balance between a retailer's inventory and sales and the speed with which its merchandise moves into and out of a department or store.[7]

The number of times inventory turns over in a given period of time. It is calculated by dividing average inventory at retail into the net sales for the year. Average yearly inventory is the sum of the retail inventories at the end of each month added to the initial opening inventory and divided by 13, the number of inventories used.[5]

straightlining   [FINANCE/ACCOUNTING] Averaging the tenant's rent payments (usually for commercial, not residential properties) over the lease's life (i.e., rental revenues are overestimated in the early years and underestimated in the later years). REIT's straightline rents because generally accepted accounting principles (or GAAP) require it.[29]

straight-line depreciation [ACCOUNTING/FINANCE] A method of depreciation in which an expense is recognized in equal amounts over the useful life of the asset.[15]

straight-line rents [ACCOUNTING/LEASING] The amounts recorded to amortize rents evenly over the term of a lease regardless of the actual schedule of payments. *See* rent leveling.[15]

strip center [GENERAL] A strip center consists of an attached row of at least three retail stores, managed as a coherent retail entity, with on-site parking in front of the stores. GLA (gross leasable area) for the center must be at least 10,000 sq. ft. Open canopies may connect the storefronts, but a strip center does not have enclosed walkways or malls linking the stores. A strip center may be configured in a straight line, or have an "L" or "U" shape.[10]

A straight line of stores with parking in front and a service lane in the rear. The anchor store, commonly a supermarket in small strip centers, is placed either at one end or in the center of the strip. A strip center is usually a small neighborhood center, and the terms have come to be used interchangeably, although a strip may also be a large center.[12]

stun gun [SECURITY] A small handheld device that momentarily incapacitates an intruder through the use of an electrical current or charge. Illegal in many states.[7]

subcontractors [OPERATIONS/CONSTRUCTION] Sources of skilled labor from specialized trades such as mechanical, electrical, fire protection, carpentry, painting, HVAC (heating, ventilation, and air-conditioning), and floor and ceiling fixtures.[11]

subgrade [OPERATIONS] The prepared surface on which asphalt is laid.[7]

sublease [LEASING/LEGAL] The renting or leasing of premises by a tenant to a third party, but with some portion or interest in them still being retained. Either all or part of the premises may be subleased, for either the whole term of the original lease or a portion of it. However, if the tenant relinquishes his or her entire interest, it is no longer considered a sublease but an assignment.[3]

The original tenant remains liable for the lease while a new tenant assumes occupancy.[7]

submission date [CONSTRUCTION] The date by which tenant is required to submit its initial architectural and construction plans to landlord.[24]

subordinated bonds or **debentures** [FINANCE] These are junior (second in priority) to the other creditors in exercising claims against assets.[15]

subordination [FINANCE/LEGAL] The process of sharing the risk of credit losses disproportionately among two or more classes or "tranches" of securities.[29]

subordination clause [FINANCE/LEGAL] Defines whether tenant or landlord obligations are recognized first in the case of foreclosure or sale of the property.[7]

subrogation [INSURANCE] The right of an insurance company to recover its loss from the responsible party after paying the policyholder's claim.[7]

substrate [OPERATIONS] The base on which roofing insulation is laid.[13]

suburban center [GENERAL] A center located in a less-dense city or town that surrounds either the central city of a U.S. metropolitan statistical area or the urban core of a Canadian city.[10]

suburban share [RESEARCH] The portion of retail expenditures by the population in a trade area that is retained in stores outside of the downtown business district. The designation does not refer to political boundaries and is not meant to limit the term to those stores outside the city limits. The range of suburban shares for different retail categories varies from department stores, which register a substantial portion of their sales downtown, to food stores, in which nearly all sales are transacted in sections other than the central business district.[6]

superregional center [GENERAL] Similar to a regional center, but because of its larger size, a superregional center has more anchors, a deeper selection of merchandise, and draws from a larger population base. As with regional centers, the typical configuration is as an enclosed mall, frequently with multilevels.[1]

supervision   fee [ACCOUNTING/OPERATIONS/CONSTRUCTION] A fee added to common area costs to cover the owner's cost of supervising the contractors and bidding necessary work. Generally stated as a percentage of the actual costs.[8]

surety bonds [INSURANCE] Payment and performance bonds usually used on significant construction jobs.[7]

Stand behind the general contractor's obligations to the owner under the terms and conditions of the contract. Generally such surety bonds cost ½ percent to 1 percent of the total contract amount.[11]

T

TAP [MARKETING] *See* total audience plan.

TF [MARKETING] *See* till forbid.

T-shaped center [DEVELOPMENT/GENERAL] A center designed to accommodate three anchor stores, the T type has parking on all sides, with service provided through a tunnel or shielded service bays or a combination of both. T centers may be open or enclosed. Note that one anchor is not visible from the front entrances of the other two. Some authorities consider this a disadvantage in that shoppers may not be drawn to all parts of the center. Other authorities, however, consider this an advantage in that each anchor store provides an attraction helpful to the satellite stores in its vicinity.[12]

T-stand [RETAIL] A type of merchandising fixture commonly used to display apparel, with either straight or waterfall arms.[16]

tall-wall mall stall [LEASING/RETAIL] A merchandising unit used by temporary tenants that is built out from an empty wall, usually measuring from six to ten feet deep by ten feet or more in length.[16]

tangible assets [ACCOUNTING/FINANCIAL] Physical items that can be seen and touched, such as property, plant, and equipment; usually called fixed assets.[15]

target audience [MARKETING] The consumers the advertiser wants to reach.[4]

The particular demographic group that an advertiser most wants to reach with advertising messages.[5]

tear-off [OPERATIONS] A roofing and asphalt procedure in which an old membrane or surface is removed as a prelude to replacement with a new product.[7]

tear sheet [MARKETING] A printed, dated copy of an ad as it appeared; generally submitted with the invoice as proof of publication.[2]

teaser ads [MARKETING] Small ads, run in advance of a major effort, to arouse interest in a forthcoming campaign.[2]

telephone survey [RESEARCH] A tool used to measure the competitive shopping patterns and perceptions among residents of a center's market area.[4]

temporary tenant [LEASING] Retailers that lease space for periods of usually less than a year. They are housed in merchandising units such as carts, kiosks, and tall-wall mall stalls, most often located in the shopping center's common areas, vacant in-line spaces, parking lots, and peripheral areas.[16]

temporary tenant program [LEASING] *See* specialty leasing program.

tenant [GENERAL] A party who leases real property from the owner of the property (or of a leasehold interest in the property) for value considerations.[3]

tenant allowance (TA) [LEASING/FINANCE] A provision sometimes made by landlords to build a tenant space or provide rent concessions, even free rent, for a period of time to induce the tenant to lease. *See* tenant improvement allowance.[17]

tenant evaluation [MARKETING/LEASING] A tool used to analyze the individual stores in a center in terms of their sales staff, variety and selection of merchandise, merchandising techniques, and store appearance.[4]

tenant improvement allowances [LEASING] Provisions in a lease in which the landlord agrees to pay for certain changes to enhance a tenant's space.[15]

tenant improvements [LEASING] Building improvements that enhance a tenant's space. May be paid for by either landlord or tenant and induce the tenant to lease. *See* tenant allowance.[8]

tenant mix [LEASING] The distribution of store types within a retail complex.[4]

The types and price levels of retail and service businesses within a shopping center.[7]

tenant representatives or **tenant reps** [LEASING] Brokers commissioned to handle leasing for and by retail tenants.[23]

tenant roster [ACCOUNTING/LEASING] The tenant roster is a master record. It lists such basic information as each tenant's name, the space number occupied, and the type of business being operated. It also lists key details in the tenants' leases, such as the square footage occupied, the rent per square foot and the total monthly rent, the lease date (which could be either the date it is prepared or the date it is signed), the commencement and expiration dates of the lease, and any special provisions.[9]

tenant trade name [LEASING/RETAIL] The name under which a tenant is doing business. Tenant signage should reflect this name, as contrasted with the name of the corporate entity that owns the tenant.[24]

tenant's floor area [ACCOUNTING/LEASING] The total square footage of tenant's premises. This total is used in determining the tenant's proportionate share of costs associated with the shopping center and used to quote annual rent per square foot.[24]

10K [FINANCE/LEGAL] (U.S.) The required annual filing of a publicly owned and traded company's financial statement, and all supporting schedules, with the Securities and Exchange Commission (SEC) for public disclosure.[15]

10Q [FINANCE/LEGAL] (U.S.) The required filing by a publicly owned and traded company of a quarterly financial statement with the Securities and Exchange Commission (SEC) for public disclosure.[15]

term [FINANCE/LEGAL/LEASING] The length of a loan; the length of a lease.[15]

termination [GENERAL] 1. Interruption of the lease before the term expires.[7] 2. The firing of an employee.[7]

tertiary zone [RESEARCH] An outlying segment of the trade area that can be identified in certain circumstances as contributing a recognizable share of sales volume to a shopping center. This zone is designated when there appears to be a tributary area extending beyond the normal limits of the secondary zone, usually in a specific direction.[6]

theme/festival center [GENERAL] This center typically employs a unifying theme that is carried out by the individual shops in their architectural design and, to an extent, in their merchandise. The biggest appeal of this center is to tourists; it can be anchored by restaurants and entertainment facilities. The center is generally located in an urban area, tends to be adapted from an older, sometimes historic, building, and can be part of a mixed-use project.[1]

third-party insurance [INSURANCE] This insurance protects the insured against liability arising out of property or bodily damage to others caused by another party.[7]

three-party agreement [DEVELOPMENT] A three-party agreement between the developer (owner), architect/engineer, and general contractor is the traditional method of contracting. In this case, the developer works closely with the architect/engineer to plan and design the project. The developer explains the concept and the architect/engineer executes the plans and specifications accordingly. These plans and specifications are then submitted to competing contractors who estimate the cost and time it will take to complete the project.[11]

till forbid (TF)   [MARKETING] An order to a station to run a spot at the designated time until further notice, or until the client orders them to stop.[5]

time value of money   [FINANCE] The concept underlying compound interest: that a dollar received today is worth more than a dollar in the future, due to opportunity cost, inflation, and certainty of payment.[7]

The concept that the same amount of money is better to have now than at some future date, because now that amount can be invested or used immediately.[15]

tonnage   [OPERATIONS] A measurement that determines the strength of an HVAC (heating, ventilation, and air-conditioning) system. Also used as a determinant to gauge air requirements for a tenant space. One ten of air is equivalent to 12,000 BTUs (British thermal units.)[7]

total audience plan (TAP)   [MARKETING] A radio term for an ROS (run of station) schedule. TAP Plans generally specify the number of commercials to be aired in each daypart.[5]

total income   [RESEARCH] *See* income, total.

total market coverage   [MARKETING] A program offered by some newspapers that combines newspaper insertion with direct mail or direct delivery to saturate a geographic area.[4]

total personal income   [RESEARCH] *See* income, total personal.

total rent   [ACCOUNTING/LEASING] The minimum and percentage rent paid by a tenant, coupled with any extra charges that the tenant must pay.[7]

total survey area   [MARKETING/RESEARCH] A geographic area designated by rating services composed of all the counties in which approximately 98 percent of the area's home market station's viewing or listening occurs.[4]

The geographic area sampled in a rating survey. The total survey area is determined by the amount of viewing or listening done to stations in the market being measured. The total survey area of a market is larger and contains more counties than the ADI (area of dominant influence) of the metro area. Total survey areas are not mutually exclusive, as are ADIs.[5]

trade area   [RESEARCH] The geographic area from which a center draws its shoppers. Limits that define a trade area may be distance, natural barriers such as rivers, or man-made obstructions such as a highway that is difficult to cross.[7]

The geographic area from which the sustaining patronage for steady support of a shopping center is obtained. The extent of the trade area is governed in each instance by a number of factors, including the matter of the center itself, its accessibility, the extent of physical barriers, the location of competing facilities, and limitations of driving time and distance.[6]

The territory from which 85 percent to 90 percent of retail trade will come on a continuing basis.[12]

trade area zones   [RESEARCH] Those segments into which a trade area is normally divided in order to better illustrate variations in the probable impact of proposed shopping centers as regards distance, travel time, and competitive facilities. Most frequently, trade areas are divided into primary and secondary zones. In addition, a tertiary zone is sometimes indicated.[6]

trade discount   [RETAIL] The manufacturer's or supplier's discount from the suggested list price; it is expressed as a percentage.[7]

trade fixture   [LEASING/RETAIL] An item specific to a tenant's business, usually not attached to the walls or floor; usually removed at lease expiration.[7]

trade name   [GENERAL/RETAIL] The name under which a tenant operates a business.[7]

traffic   [RESEARCH] The number or volume of shoppers who visit a shopping center during a specified period of time.[7]

traffic count   [RESEARCH] Research, based on counting the number of shoppers (or vehicles) in a given period and place, to estimate how much traffic is in a center on a daily, weekly, or monthly basis.[17]

traffic estimates   [RESEARCH] *See* traffic count.

traffic-building device   [MARKETING] A center-sponsored promotional activity designed to stimulate customer traffic.[2]

training record   [OPERATIONS/SECURITY] Written documents that show how a security officer was trained.[22]

transactions   [ACCOUNTING/E-COMMERCE] A transfer of value to or from a company, the most basic kinds being sales and purchases.[15]

transfer   [RETAIL] The sales volume transferred from the parent store or other branch units to a newly opened unit of the same store.[6]

trial balance [ACCOUNTING] A list of all open accounts in a general ledger, with their balances, used in the preparation of financial statements; when it is complete, debits and credits will prove equal.[15]

triangle-shaped center [DEVELOPMENT/GENERAL] Similar in many respects to the T-shaped center but with the added factor of providing visibility of all anchor stores from the front of each. A triangular design is likely to be somewhat wasteful of land, but it may be the optimum design for sites that are not rectangular. Designed to accommodate three anchors, the triangle center may have two levels, with parking around its perimeter. In most cases, when a center has two levels without a parking structure, it is designed with graded parking lots to allow entry at each level.[12]

triple net lease [ACCOUNTING/LEASING] A lease in which 100 percent of all taxes, insurance, and maintenance associated with a shopping center is paid by the tenant.[7]

turn key [LEASING] The landlord builds and finishes out a retail space; the tenant shows up with merchandise and is ready for business.[7]

two-party design/construct agreement [DEVELOPMENT] The developer works with a company that provides architectural/engineering *and* construction services. Under most state laws, a contractor cannot furnish these services unless he has *licensed* architects and engineers on staff.[11]

U

U-shaped center   [DEVELOPMENT/GENERAL] A strip center with two lines of stores placed at right angles to the strip, forming a U, with parking in front of the stores and service lanes behind them. U-shaped centers usually have more store space than L-shaped strips and consequently tend to be community-type rather than neighborhood-type centers. Because of their size, they may have as many as three anchors, one at each end and one in the middle, with the major anchor generally located in the middle.[12]

umbrella excess liability   [INSURANCE] A form of insurance that protects against losses in excess of amounts covered by other liability insurance policies. It is used to protect against catastrophic losses.[7]

underwriting   [FINANCE/INSURANCE] An investment banking firm acting as underwriter sells securities from the issuing corporation to the public. A group of firms may form a syndicate to pool the risk and assure successful distribution of the issue. There are two types of underwriting arrangements: best efforts and firm commitment. With best efforts, the underwriters have the option to buy and authority to sell securities, or if unsuccessful, may cancel the issue and forgo any fees. This arrangement is more common with speculative securities and with new companies. With a firm commitment, the underwriters purchase outright the securities being offered by the issuer.[20]

unnatural breakpoint   [LEASING/ACCOUNTING] A set sales hurdle, negotiated and entered in a lease, that can be used to determine payments by a tenant to the landlord unrelated to the tenant's actual (natural) breakpoint.[15]

urban areas   [GENERAL] Incorporated localities with a population of 2,500 or more; residences of already settled suburban areas surrounding major cities. Population densities in excess of 1,500 persons per square mile.[6]

urban centers   [GENERAL] Contributors to the revitalization of downtown areas, urban centers are usually part of a city's urban-renewal program.

They usually include a pedestrian mall or covered walkways (particularly in areas of climate extremes) and are built right in the traditional shopping district. Characteristically, urban centers feature a parklike atmosphere, absence of cars, freedom to move about among a variety of retail stores, and, in many cases, a food court.[12]

use clause   [LEASING/LEGAL] A clause inserted into a shopping center retail lease that restricts the category of merchandise or items that a retailer is allowed to sell.[7]

An outline of the exact type of merchandise to be sold or business to be conducted in the premises.[7]

Tenants are restricted to providing the categories of merchandise or services specified in their leases and must obey any lease restrictions on how they operate.[9]

useful life   [RETAIL/OPERATIONS] The period of time that a purchaser expects to get value for a particular purchase, regardless of how long it is actually in use.[15]

utilities expenses   [ACCOUNTING] This major category includes the cost of all utilities used in the common area of the center. It includes expenses for electricity, gas, and oil related to the common area, including exterior lighting. It does not include utilities purchased by the center and resold to individual tenants for consumption within their lease premises.[10]

utilities revenue   [ACCOUNTING] Any receipts from tenants for electrical or other utilities.[10]

V

vacancy loss   [ACCOUNTING] A rate, which an appraiser applies to gross revenue, that recognizes that a property will not always be 100 percent leased; for example, a 5 percent vacancy loss rate anticipates that the shopping center is likely to be 95 percent occupied.[15]

vacancy rate   [FINANCE/ACCOUNTING] The square footage that is unoccupied, even if leases are signed and rents are being collected, expressed as a percentage of the total occupancy area of each store category.[10]

value   [FINANCE] A determination about a company, set in the marketplace, that is based on the income it produces year after year; it is calculated by dividing net operating income (NOI) by the cap (capitalization) rate.[15] Retail: As defined by consumers, the balance of price, selection, and quality.[20]

value megamall   [GENERAL] A project that exceeds 700,000 square feet and has a tenant mix that includes mostly value-oriented retailers, including some outlet retailers.[20]

value retailing   [RETAIL/FINANCE] The retail sale of branded or quality merchandise, usually at less than traditional department store prices prior to markdowns.[19]

vandalism   [SECURITY] Willful or malicious destruction or defacement of public or private property.[5]

vanilla box   [LEASING/CONSTRUCTION] A space partially completed by the landlord based on negotiations between tenant and landlord. Although every landlord's definition is different, a vanilla box normally means HVAC (heating, ventilation, and air-conditioning), walls, floors, stockroom wall, basic electrical work, basic plumbing work, rear door, and storefront.[7]

variable expenses   [ACCOUNTING] Also called direct expenses; operating expenses that are affected by increases or decreases in sales volume.[7]

variance report   [ACCOUNTING] Usually part of the financial package provided to managers on a periodic basis. It shows the difference between budgeted expectations and actual results.[7]

venture capital [FINANCE] The process by which investors fund early stage, more risk-oriented business endeavors. A venture capital funding arrangement will typically entail relinquishing some level of ownership and control of the business. Offsetting the high risk the investor takes is the prospect of high return on the investment.[20]

vertical [GENERAL] A term used to relate a shopping center to a department store in urban areas.[2]

vertical retailer [RETAIL] Retailers that sell only their own branded merchandise; these goods aren't found anywhere except in their own stores or catalogues (also called lifestyle retailer).[20]

vertical-shaped center [DEVELOPMENT/GENERAL] A high-rise mall, which has escalators and elevators to carry people from floor to floor. Frequently the stores are placed around a central atrium. Such centers are usually in downtown areas or close to other high-density developments.[12]

video [MARKETING] The visual portion of a television broadcast.[2]

viewers per set (VPS) [MARKETING] The number of individuals in a demographic group viewing a particular spot, divided by the number of households reached by that same spot. VPS times homes equals audience expressed as persons.[5]

village center [GENERAL] An architecture style of open-air shopping center comprising several wings, sometimes connected to each other; more compact than a strip center.[20]

VPS [MARKETING] *See* viewers per set.

W X Y Z

wait order　[MARKETING] An instruction by the advertiser to hold purchased schedules until instructed to proceed.[2]

waiver　[LEGAL] The surrender of a legal right.[7]

waiver of subrogation　[INSURANCE/LEGAL] Each party to the lease gives up the right for its insurer to bring suit against the other party's insurer.[7]

warm brick　[LEASING] Term for the unfinished space a tenant is given in a shopping center; the tenant is responsible for paying for all costs of store construction.[7]

warranty　[INSURANCE] A statement that conditions will exist during the policy term and if found untrue, or not in existence, would invalidate the policy.[7]

Web site　[E-COMMERCE] A site (location) on the World Wide Web. Each Web site contains a home page, which is the first document users see when they enter the site. The site might also contain additional documents and files. Each site is owned and managed by an individual, company or organization.[27]

welcome book　[MARKETING/GENERAL] Pamphlet given to tenants after signing a lease; it explains the ownership philosophy and introduces them to the center.[7]

white space　[MARKETING] Print media term referring to the blank space in an advertisement.[2]

work period　[LEASING/CONSTRUCTION] The time that the landlord gives a tenant to construct the store, usually without paying rent; anywhere from 60 to 180 days or more, and spelled out in the tenant lease.[17]

working capital　[FINANCE] The difference between current assets and current liabilities.[15]

World Wide Web　[E-COMMERCE] A system of Internet servers that support specially formatted documents. The documents are formatted in a language called HTML (HyperText Markup Language) that supports links to other documents, as well as graphics, audio, and video files. Not all Internet servers are part of the World Wide Web.[27]

wrap-up, or **owner-controlled insurance program** [INSURANCE] Consolidation of insurance coverage for all contractors and subcontractors working on a construction project into one program managed and paid for by the owners. Advantages of such a program can include reduced insurance costs, expanded coverage, a centralized safety program, and more effective claims management; disadvantages can include contractor resistance and administrative costs for the owner.[17]

yield [FINANCE] The effective return on an investment, as paid in dividends or interest. Expressed as a percentage, yield is computed by dividing the market price for a stock or bond into the dividend or interest paid in the preceding period.[25]

zero lot line [DEVELOPMENT] The construction of a building on the boundary of a lot.

zero-based budgeting [FINANCE] A method of developing a budget without basing it on any previous year's budget.[15]

Translations
of
Shopping Center
Terms

	FRANÇAIS	DEUTSCH	PORTUGUÊS	ESPAÑOL
ABC Report	rapport ABC	ABC-Bericht	Relatório da ABC	Informe ABC
absorption	absorption	Absorption	absorção	Absorción
abstract	extrait	Abstrakt	sumário	Resumen
accelerated depreciation	dépréciation accélérée	Beschleunigte Abschreibung	depreciação acelerada	Depreciación acelerada
access time	temps d'accès	Einstiegszeit	tempo de acesso	Tiempo de acceso
account executive	chargé de compte	Kundenbetreuerin	director de contas	Ejecutivo de cuentas
accounts payable	comptes à payer	Verbindlichkeiten	contas a pagar	Cuentas por pagar
accounts receivable	comptes à recevoir	Forderungen	contas por cobrar; contas a receber	Cuentas por cobrar
accrual	produits à recevoir et charges à payer	Rechnungsab-grenzungsposten	acumulação e provisão contábil	Acumulación
accrual basis of accounting	comptabilité d'exercice	periodengerechte Aufwands und Ertragsrechnung	acumulações básicas em contabilidade; regime de competência	Contabilidad en valores devengables

	FRANÇAIS	DEUTSCH	PORTUGUÊS	ESPAÑOL
accrued liabilities	charges à payer	Rückstellungen von Passiven	passivo acumulado	Pasivo acumulado
accumulated depreciation	dépréciation accumulée	ansteigende Abschreibung	depreciação acumulada	Depreciación acumulada
activity report	rapport d'activité	Aktivitätsbericht	relatório de actividades de segurança	informe de actividades
ad grid	grille des tarifs de publicité	Tariflist in Bezug auf die Zeitperiode	sistema de tarifas em relação a cada período	Sistema de tarifas según cada período
adaptive re-use	réutilisation par adaptation	Umbau im Rahmen von Sanierungsmaßnahmen	aproveitamento de edifícios para reutilização	Acondicionamiento de locales / edificios para su reutilización
add-on rent charges	frais supplémentaires frais locatifs	Mietnebenkosten	adicionais despesas de arrendamento; despesas adicionais de locação	cargos de alquiler adicionales

	FRANÇAIS	DEUTSCH	PORTUGUÊS	ESPAÑOL
ADI	aire d'influence dominante	Hauptsendegebiet (ADI)	área de influência dominante	Área de influencia dominante
adjacency	adjacence	angrenzendes Programm	contiguidade; adjacência	Adyacencia
administration fee	frais administratifs	Verwaltungsgebühr	honorário de administração	Honorarios de administración
administrative marketing costs	frais administratifs Marketing-Kosten	Verwaltungstechnische marketing	custos de marketing administrativos	Costos administravos de marketing
advance	distribution préliminaire	Vorausabdruck	comunicação antecipada	Ejemplar de anticipo
advance rental	loyer payé d'avance	Mietvorauszahlung	Rendas locativas pagas com antecipação	Anticipo del alquiler
advertising	publicité	Werbung	publicidade	Publicidad
advertising campaign	campagne publicitaire	Werbekampagne	campanha publicitária	Campaña publicitaria

	FRANÇAIS	DEUTSCH	PORTUGUÊS	ESPAÑOL
advertising fund	fonds publicitaire	Werbefonds	fundos para despesas publicitárias	Fondo para gastos de publicidad
advertising plan	plan publicitaire	Werbeplan	plano publicitário	Plan publicitario
agate lines	ligne agate	Agate-Zeile	linhas de ágata	Líneas ágata
aggregate	granulat	Aggregat	agregado; material granular	agregado
aided recall	rappel facilité	Erinnerung mit Gedächtnisstütze	recordação assistida	Recordatorio guiado
air check	copie d'émission aux fins de vérification	Kontrollaufnahme	avaliação do conteúdo de uma emissão gravada	Cinta de archivo de una emisión para evaluación de su contenido
alarm system	système d'alarme	Alarm- und Überwachungssystem	sistema de alarmes	Sistema de alarmas
alligatoring [Also known as alligator cracks]	crocodilage [ou fendillement]	Krokodilnarben (auch unter dem Begriff "Krokodilrissbildung" bekannt)	rachas (também conhecido como rachas de jacaré)	Resquebrajamiento [también conocido como grietas irregulares]

	FRANÇAIS	DEUTSCH	PORTUGUÊS	ESPAÑOL
alteration costs	frais d'altération	Änderungskosten	despesas de alterações; custos de alterações	Costos de reformas
amortization	amortissement	Amortisation	amortização	Amortización
anchor store	magasin pilier	Ankergeschäft/ Hauptmieter	loja principal; loja âncora	Tienda ancla
ancillary charges	frais secondaires	Nebenkosten	encargos condominiais específicos, custos adicionais	cargos anexos
angle	accent ou point de vue	Gesichtswinkel	ângulo (de um artigo de imprensa); ponto de vista	Ángulo (de una historia)
annual basic rental	loyer annuel de base	jährliche Grundmiete	Renda básica anual de arrendamento; aluguel básico anual	Base anual del alquiler
annual percentage rent	loyer annuel en pourcentage	jährliche Umsatzmiete (%)	Percentagem anual de arrendamento; aluguel percentual anual	Porcentaje anual del alquiler
answer print	épreuve composite	Kopiervorlage	gravação de réplica	Impresión compuesta

	FRANÇAIS	DEUTSCH	PORTUGUÊS	ESPAÑOL
apportionment	répartition	proportionale Aufteilung	divisão proporcional	Imputación de gastos e ingresos
appraisal	évaluation	Einschätzung	avaliação	Tasación
appraisal rent	loyer basé sur l'évaluation	eingeschätzte Miete	cálculo do valor do aluguer	Alquiler calculado
approach (outdoor)	approche (extérieur)	Kontaktzone (Außenwerbung)	distância de visualização (no exterior)	Distancia de visualización (exterior)
arbitron	arbitron	Arbitron (Mediaforschung)	Direcção de Pesquisa Norte-Americana	Dirección Estadounidense de Investigación
area of dominant influence (ADI)	aire d'influence dominante	Hauptsendegebiet (ADI)	área de influência dominante	Área de influencia dominante
artificial breakpoint	seuil de rentabilité artificielle	künstliche Rentabilitätsschwelle	ponto de equilíbrio artificial	punto de equilíbrio artificial

	FRANÇAIS	DEUTSCH	PORTUGUÊS	ESPAÑOL
as-built plans	plans tels que construit	Baubestandspläne	planos finais de planificação de construção; plantas conforme a construção	Planos conforme a obra
asphalt	asphalte	Asphalt	asfalto	Asfalto
asphalt emulsion	émulsion d'asphalte	emulgiertes Bindemittel für Asphalt	emulsão asfáltica	Emulsión de asfalto
assault and battery	coups et blessures	Körperverletzung	vias de facto, agressão	Asalto con lesiones
asset	actif	Aktivposten	activo; ativo	Activo
asset turnover	coefficient de rotation de l'actif	Verhältnis von Umsatz zu Aktiven	rotação do activo; giro de ativos	Rotación de activos
assignee	cessionnaire	Zessionar	cessionário	Cesionario
assignment	cession	Zession	cessão	Cesión
attractive nuisance	source de danger pour les enfants	Gefahrenquelle, die Kinder anzieht	perturbação atraente para crianças	Objeto de atracción peligroso para niños

	FRANÇAIS	DEUTSCH	PORTUGUÊS	ESPAÑOL
audience	auditoire	Publikum/Zuhörerschaft	público	Público
audit trail	piste de vérification	Wirschaftsprüfungsnachweis	documentação de auditoria	Registro de auditoría
avails	liste d'émissions de télévision disponibles	verfügbare Werbesendezeit	disponibilidade de programas	Listas de programas disponibles
average	moyenne	Mittelwert/Durchschnitt	média	Promedio
average household income	revenu moyen des ménages	durchschnittliches Haushaltseinkommen	rendimento médio por família; renda média por família	Ingreso familiar promedio
average inventory	stocks moyens	durchschnittlicher Lagerbestand	inventário médio	Inventario promedio
average quarter-hour persons (AQH)	nombre moyen de personnes écoutant la radio pendant au moins 5 minutes durant une période de 15 minutes	durchschnittlicher Viertelstunden-Zuschauer	média do número de pessoas que escutam programas de rádio por um mínimo de cinco minutos	Cálculo del número medio de personas que escuchan [radio] cinco minutos como mínimo

	FRANÇAIS	DEUTSCH	PORTUGUÊS	ESPAÑOL
back of the house or back room	arrière-boutique	Bereich ausser der Verkaufsfläche, Hinterräume	Parte das traseiras da loja (armazenamento, casas de banho, etc.)	Parte posterior del local
back-to-back	publicités/émissions consécutives	unmittelbar aufeinanderfolgende Sendungen	programas sucessivos	programas seguidos
bad debt allowance [Also known as credit loss]	provisions pour créances douteuses	Forderungsabschreibung (auch unter dem Begriff "Kreditverlust" bekannt)	reserva para dívidas incobráveis (também conhecido como créditos incobráveis); fundo de loja-depósitos	Reserva para deudas incobrables [también conocido como pérdida de crédito]
balance sheet	bilan	Bilanz	mapa de balanço; balanço patrimonial	Balance general
balloon risk	risque de non-paiement du versement final	Risiko der Nichtbezahlung des Endbetrags	empréstimo com juros antecipados e amortização inicial reduzida, utilizado como meio para antecipar taxas melhores a longo prazo	Riesgo de no poder cubrir el pago del préstamo al vencimiento

	FRANÇAIS	DEUTSCH	PORTUGUÊS	ESPAÑOL
bank reconciliation	réconciliation bancaire	Bankkontoabstimmung	reconciliação bancária	Reconciliación bancaria
banner heading	titre en bannière	Balkenüberschrift	cabeçalho	Título del aviso
banning	interdiction	Zutrittsverbot	proibição de acesso por um período de tempo limitado	Prohibición temporal de acceso
base rent	loyer de base	Grundmiete	renda básica; aluguel básico	Alquiler base
base sheet	couche de base	Dachgrundeindeckung	cartão alcatroado; primeira camada para insulação de telhado	Hoja base
basis	base	Abschreibungsgrundlage	base	Base
baton	bâton	Schlagstock	bastão; cacete	bastón
benchmarking	évaluation par rapport à certains points de repère	objektive Vergleichsmöglichkeit mit einem Standard	avaliação comparativa	Medición de resultados
Best Company ratings	cotes de Best Company	Bewertung der A. M. Best Company	índices de classificação de companhias de Best	Calificación de compañías de Best

	FRANÇAIS	DEUTSCH	PORTUGUÊS	ESPAÑOL
big box	grande surface	Großgeschäft mit einzigem Zweck (Fläche von ca. 930 m² bis 9300 m²)	Loja singular ocupando uma vasta superfície (de 930 a 9.300 metros quadrados)	Local amplio (para un único fin, de 930 a 9.300 metros cuadrados)
bill-backs	refacturations/ facturations rétroactives	verrechnete Nebenkosten	facturação de contas pagas; facturamento retroativo	Reintegro del arrendatario al arrendador por los gastos abonados por este último
billboard	panneau d'affichage/ panneau-réclame publicitaire	Reklametafel	placard de informações	Cartelera
birdbath	affaissement ou bain d'oiseaux	Delle (im Asphalt-pflaster, wo sich Wasser ansammelt)	poça de água	Área baja donde se acumula el agua
bitumen	bitume	Bitumen	betume	Betún

	FRANÇAIS	DEUTSCH	PORTUGUÊS	ESPAÑOL
blacktop	revêtement bitumineux	Schwarzdecke	pavimentação de asfalto; superfície asfaltada	Superficie bituminosa
blanket or rolling wrap-up	assurance contrôlée par le propriétaire couvrant une série de projets de rénovation	firmeneigene Gemeinschaftsversicherung	seguro de cobertura global	Seguro global
bleeding [Also known as fat spots]	ressuage	Ausschwitzen (auch unter dem Begriff "Fettflecken" bekannt)	exsudação (também conhecido como manchas gordurosas)	Exudación también denominados puntos grasos
blistering	cloquage	Blasenbildung	formação de bolhas	Formación de ampollas
blue line	épreuve diazoïque	Blauabzug	cópia de prova de linhas a azul	Hoja de prueba con colores
bodily injury	lésions corporelles	Körperverletzung	lesões físicas; ferimento corpóreo	Lesiones físicas
boiler and machinery insurance	assurance des chaudières et des machines	Dampfkessel- und Maschinenparkversicherung	seguro de maquinaria e de caldeiras	Seguro de calderas y maquinaria

	FRANÇAIS	DEUTSCH	PORTUGUÊS	ESPAÑOL
boilerplate	clauses standard	vorformulierte Vertragsklauseln	cláusulas fixas normalizadas	Modelo de contrato
bookkeeping	tenue des livres	Buchhaltung	escrituração contábil	Teneduría de libros
bottom line	résultat net	Endergebnis	resultado final de lucro (prejuízo)	Resultado final
box ads	réclames regroupées sous un même titre	Kastenzeigen unter einer Überschrift	conjunto de anúncios sob o mesmo título	Conjunto de avisos uniformes bajo un mismo título
break	pause entre deux programmes	Werbesendung zwischen zwei Programmen	pausa entre dois programas	Posición de un comercial entre dos programas
break even point	seuil de rentabilité	Kostendeckungspunkt	liminar de rentabilidade	Punto de equilibrio
breakdown method	méthode de ventilation	Aufschlüsselungs-methode	método de desdobramento	Método de desglose

	FRANÇAIS	DEUTSCH	PORTUGUÊS	ESPAÑOL
breakpoint	point de rencontre du loyer en pourcentage avec le loyer minimum	Rentabilitätsschwelle	ponto limite; ponto de equilíbrio	Punto de equilibrio
bridge/mezzanine	financement provisoire	Zwischenfinanzierung	empréstimo financeiro temporário	Financiamiento transitorio
British thermal unit (BTU)	unité de quantité de chaleur anglaise (BTU)	britische Wärmemengeneinheit (BTU)	Unidade Térmica Britânica (BTU)	Unidad térmica británica
broker	courtier	Makler	Corretor	Corredor
brokerage	courtage	Vermittlungsgeschäft	corretagem	Corretaje
BTU	BTU (unité de quantité de chaleur anglaise)	BTU	BTU – unidade térmica británica	Unidad térmica británica/BTU
buckling	gondolage	Ausbeulung	deformação	Deformación
budget	budget	Budget	orçamento	Presupuesto
budget billing	facturation suivant le budget	Rechnungstellung nach Budget	facturação orçamental annual; facturamento segundo o orçamento	Facturación según presupuesto

	FRANÇAIS	DEUTSCH	PORTUGUÊS	ESPAÑOL
budgeted rent	loyer budgétisé	budgetierte Miete	renda de aluguer orçamentada; aluguel segundo o orçamento	Alquiler presupuestado
building code endorsement	avenant au code de la construction	Nachtrag zur Bauordnung	endosso das normas regulamentares de construção	Cláusula añadida de cumplimiento del código de edificación
built-up roof (BUR)	toit multicouche	mehrlagige Dachpappeneindeckung	telhado de camadas alternadas; telhado armado	Techo armado
bulk mail	envois postaux déposés en nombre	Postwurfsendung	correio ordinário em quantidade	Envío postal de gran volumen
bulk rate contract	contrat à tarif dégressif sur le volume	Vertrag über Preisnachlässe aufgrund der Jahreszeilenzahl	contrato de tarifa reduzida	Contrato de tasa reducida de publicidad
bullet loans	prêts à remboursement à l'échéance	Anleihe, die am Ende der Laufzeit in einer Gesamtsumme getilgt wird	empréstimo reembolsável de uma só vez após o seu vencimento	Préstamo reembolsable al vencimiento

	FRANÇAIS	DEUTSCH	PORTUGUÊS	ESPAÑOL
bulletin	panneau d'affichage à panneaux multiples	Anschlagwand	placard de informações	Cartelera
BUR	toit multicouche	Dachdeckung (BUR)	telhado de camadas alternadas; telhado armado	Techo armado
burglary	cambriolage	Einbruch	furto com arrombamento	Robo con escalamiento
business interruption insurance	assurance pour les pertes d'exploitation	Geschäftsunterbrechungsversicherung; Betriebsunterbrechungsversicherung	seguro de lucros cessantes	Seguro de pérdida del ingreso neto
business plan	plan d'affaires	Unternehmensplan	plano de negócios	plan comercial
buyout	rachat/acquisition	Geldmittel zum Aufkauf eines Unternehmens oder Produktlinie	acordo de recompra	Oferta de compras
byline	ligne portant le nom de l'auteur	Autorenzeile	linha em que aparece o nome do autor	Pie de autor
CAM	les charges; entretien des aires communes	Wartung der Gemeinschaftsflächen (CAM)	manutenção de áreas comuns	Mantenimiento de áreas comunes

	FRANÇAIS	DEUTSCH	PORTUGUÊS	ESPAÑOL
CAM administration fee	frais administratifs des charges; frais d'administration pour entretien des aires communes	Verwaltungsgebühren (CAM); Gemeinschaftskosten	honorários da administração pela manutenção das áreas comuns	Honorarios de administración del mantenimiento de áreas comunes
camera ready	prêt à photographier	Reproduktionsfähig	arte final para reprodução	Listo para reproducir
cancellation clause	clause de résiliation	Kündigungsklausel	cláusula de cancelamento	Cláusula de cancelación
cap	plafond	obere Grenze	limite máximo	Tope
cap (capitalization) rate	taux de capitalisation	Kapitalisierungsfaktor	taxa de capitalização	Tasa de capitalización
capital budget	budget des immobilisations	Kapitalauslagen-Budget	orçamento de capital	Presupuesto de gastos de capital
capital costs	frais d'immobilisations	Investitionskosten/ Kapital Kosten	custos de colocação de capital	Costos de inversión
capital expenditures	dépenses en capital	Investitionsausgaben	despesa de capital	Desembolso de capital

	FRANÇAIS	DEUTSCH	PORTUGUÊS	ESPAÑOL
capital expense	dépense d'immobilisations	Kapitalaufwand	desembolso de capital	Gasto de capital
capitalization	capitalisation	Kapitalisierung	capitalização	Capitalización
capsheet	couche supérieure de toit multicouche	Decklage (Dach)	camada de protecção superior no telhado	Capa superior de ciertos techos armados
captive brand stores	magasins à marques captives	Geschäfte, die Waren verkaufen, die nirgendwo sonst zu erwerben sind	lojas de marcas cativas	Tiendas de marcas cautivas
capture rate analysis	analyse du taux d'attraction des clients	Standortanalyse	análise da taxa de captura; análise da taxa de captação	Análisis de la tasa de captación
card holder	support de carte	Metallständer für Informationsblätter; Display-Ständer	suporte para exibição de avisos	Soporte para avisos o señales
carded	marchandise fixée à une carte de présentation	an eine Schaupackung befestigte Waren	pequeno cartaz de exibição descrevendo a mercadoria	mercadería con tarjeta de identificación
carrier	assureur	Versicherungs-gesellschaft	companhia de seguros	Compañía aseguradora

	FRANÇAIS	DEUTSCH	PORTUGUÊS	ESPAÑOL
cart	chariot	Verkaufswagen (Karren)	carrinho	Carro de mercaderías
case history	étude historique	Studie ähnlicher Projekte auf Erfolg und Nichterfolg	estudo de projectos semelhantes para avaliação de sucesso e insucesso comercial; case history	Estudio de proyectos similares para la evaluación de las posibilidades de éxito y fracaso comercial
cash basis	comptabilité de caisse	Buchführung auf Barmittel-Basis	contabilidade de caixa	Base de efectivo
cash disbursement journal	journal des débours	Kassenausgabebuch	livro de saídas de caixa	Diario de desembolso de efectivo
cash discount	une remise	Skonto	desconto por pronto pagamento; desconto para pagamento a vista ou por pagamento em dinheiro	Descuento por pago al contado
cash flow	trésorerie; flux monétaire	Kapitalfluss	fluxo de caixa	Flujo de fondos

	FRANÇAIS	DEUTSCH	PORTUGUÊS	ESPAÑOL
cash flow analysis	analyse du bilan; analyse du flux monétaire	Kapitalfluss-Analyse	análise do fluxo de caixa	Análisis de flujo de fondos
cash flow statement	bilan de trésorerie; état de l'encaisse	Kapitalflussrechnung	relatório de fluxo de caixa	Estado de flujo de fondos
cash method	méthode de comptabilité de caisse	Barmittelmethode	método de caixa	Método de efectivo
cash-wrap	caisse et emballage	Kasse und Einpacktisch	área de pagamento/caixa-embrulhos	Sección caja-empaque
CBD	centre d'affaires; quartier principal des affaires	Geschäftsviertel in der Innenstadt (CBD)	centro comercial central; distrito comercial central	Distrito Comercial Central
census tracts	secteurs de recensement	Zensusgebiete	área de recenseamento	Sectores censales
center mayor	maire du centre	Bürgermeister eines Einkaufszentrums	« Prefeito » do centro comercial	"Alcalde" del centro
center rate	taux réduit de publicité dont bénéficie le centre	reduzierter Werbetarif	taxa de desconto de publicidade; taxa reduzida de publicidade em benefício do centro	Tasa reducida de publicidad

	FRANÇAIS	DEUTSCH	PORTUGUÊS	ESPAÑOL
center spread	annonce sur les deux pages centrales ou sur deux panneaux extérieurs adjacents	Mittelseiten-Werbung	anúncio nas páginas duplas centrais	Artículo de doble página central
central business district (CBD)	centre d'affaires; quartier principal des affaires	Geschäftsviertel in der Innenstadt (CBD)	centro comercial central	Distrito comercial central
central city	centre urbain	Innenstadt	central urbana	Casco urbano
central/urban city center	centre urbain d'une ville	Einkaufszentrum einer Zentralstadt	centro urbano da cidade/ baixa; centro da cidade/ centro da cidade urbana	Centro en una gran ciudad / ciudad urbana
centralized administrative system	système administratif centralisé	Zentralisiertes Verwaltungssystem	sistema centralizado administrativo	Sistema administrativo centralizado
certificate of insurance	attestation d'assurance	Versicherungszertifikat	certificado de seguro; apólice de seguro	Certificado de seguro
certificate of occupancy	certificat d'occupation	Beziehbarkeits- bescheinigung	certificado de habitação; habite-se	Certificado de habilitación

	FRANÇAIS	DEUTSCH	PORTUGUÊS	ESPAÑOL
chain of command	l'hiérarchie	Befehlskette	cadeia de comando	Cadena de mando
chart of accounts	plan comptable	Kontenplan	plano de contas	Plan de cuentas
Christmas decor/ events	décoration/ manifestations pour les Fêtes	Weihnachtsschmuck - veranstaltungen	decoração de natal/ eventos	artículos de decoración / eventos especiales de Navidad
chuckhole	nid de poule	Schlagloch	buraco na estrada	Bache
circular/shopper	circulaire	Werbeprospekt	circular	Circular
circulation	circulation	Auflagenhöhe	circulação	Circulación
circulation plan	plan de circulation	Zirkulationsplan	plano de circulação	Plano de circulación
city zone	zone urbaine	Stadtzone	zona de distribuição na cidade e arredores	zona urbana
civil liability	responsabilité civile	zivilrechtliche Haftung	responsabilidade civil	Responsabilidad civil
claim	réclamation	Forderung	reclamação	Reclamo

	FRANÇAIS	DEUTSCH	PORTUGUÊS	ESPAÑOL
Class A/B/C rates	taux des classes A/B/C	Werbekosten der Klassen A/B/C	estrutura de preços de classe A/B/C	Estructura de tarifas por clases A/B/C
close	clôture	Schlussstadium	prazo limite encerrado	Cierre
closing entries	écritures de clôture	Abschlussbuchungen	regularização de fim de exercício	Asientos de cierre
cluster shaped shopping center	centre commercial; en forme de grappe centre commercial	Einkaufszentrums in rechteckiger Anordnung	formação de lojas numa área rectangular centro comercial; shopping center com formato voltado para a concentração de lojas, geralmente rectangular	Centro de compras conglomerado
clutter	encombrement/ excès de messages	Anhäufung von Werbemitteln	publicidade excessiva	Publicidad excesiva
CMBS (Commercial Mortgage-Banked Securities)	TACH (titres adossés à des créances hypothécaires commerciales)	Gewerbliche Hypothek avalisiert mit Wertpapieren	títulos mobiliários lastrados em hipoteca (comercial)	hipoteca comercial— títulos avalados
coal tar	goudron de houille	Steinkohlenteer	alcatrão	Alquitrán mineral

	FRANÇAIS	DEUTSCH	PORTUGUÊS	ESPAÑOL
COD (cash on delivery)	PSL (payable sur livraison)	Nachnahme	pagamento contra entrega	Entrega contra reembolso
coinsurance clause	clause de coassurance	Mitversicherungsklausel	cláusula de co-seguro	Cláusula de co-seguro
collateral	bien donné en garantie	Sicherheit, Besicherung	garantia adicional; caução	Garantía colateral
color key	photomécanique couleur	Farbschlüssel	explicação das cores	Clave de color
column depth/width	profondeur/largeur de colonne	Spaltentiefe/-höhe	largura/comprimento da coluna	Profundidad / ancho de columna
combination rate	taux combiné	Kombinationstarif	tarifa de combinação de anúncios	Tarifa combinada de anuncios
commencement date	date de début	Datum des Pachtbeginns	data de início	Fecha de inicio
commercial general liability policy	police de responsabilité générale commerciale	allgemeine gewerbliche Haftpflichtversicherungs-police	apólice geral comercial contra terceiros	Póliza de responsabilidad general comercial

	FRANÇAIS	DEUTSCH	PORTUGUÊS	ESPAÑOL
commercial length	durée d'une publicité (en secondes)	Werbespotlänge	duração do anúncio	Duración del aviso
common area	partie commune	Gemeinschaftsfläche	área comum	Área común
common area HVAC energy	frais énergétiques de chauffage, ventilation et climatisation pour les parties communes	Kosten für Heizung, Lüftung und Kühlung in den Gemeinschaftsanlagen	despesas de energia para aquecimento, ventilação e ar condicionado na área comum	Gastos de energía para calefacción, ventilación y aire acondicionado en el área común
common area maintenance (CAM)	les charges; entretien des aires communes	(Vom Pächter zu zahlende) Wartungskosten für die Gemeinschaftsanlagen	despesas de manutenção da área comum	Mantenimiento de áreas comunes
community acceptance	acceptation par la communauté	Akzeptanz als Gemeindezentrum	aceitação da comunidade	Aceptación de la comunidad
community center	centre communautaire	Gemeindeeinkaufszentrum	centro comunitário	Centro comunitario

	FRANÇAIS	DEUTSCH	PORTUGUÊS	ESPAÑOL
community rooms	salles communautaires	Räumlichkeiten für kommunale Veranstaltungen	salões comunitários	Salas comunitarias
compaction	compactage	Verdichtung	compactação	Compresión
comparative lease analysis	analyse comparée des baux	vergleichende Mietvertragsanalyse	análise comparativa de locação	Análisis comparativo del alquiler
comparison goods	marchandises comparables	Vergleichswaren	mercadorias comparáveis	Mercaderías de comparación
competing business	entreprise concurrentielle	Konkurrenz	negócios de concorrência	Empresa competidora
competitive effectiveness	efficacité compétitive	Konkurrenzbezogene Wirksamkeit	eficiência competitiva	Eficiencia competitiva
competitive evaluation	évaluation de la concurrence	Konkurrenzbezogene Bewertung	avaliação competitiva	Evaluación competitiva
competitive facilities	installations concurrentes	Konkurrenzunternehmen	instalações competitivas	Instalaciones competitivas

	FRANÇAIS	DEUTSCH	PORTUGUÊS	ESPAÑOL
compound interest	intérêts composés	Zinseszins	juros compostos	Interés compuesto
comprehensive	exhaustif/d'ensemble; maquette soignée d'une réclame	allgemeiner Layout	abrangente	Global
compressor	compresseur	Kompressor	compressor	Compresor
concession	concession	Konzession	concessão	Concesión
consequential loss coverage	couverture des pertes indirectes	Versicherungsschutz gegen Folgeschäden	protecção contra perdas consequenciais	Cobertura de daños indirectos
consideration	contrepartie	Entgelt	contraprestação contratual	Contraprestación
constant dollar projections	projections en dollars constants	Prognosen bei gleichbleibendem Dollar	projecções em dólares constantes	Proyecciones en dólar constante
construction allowance	allocation de construction	Bauzuschuss; Baukostenzuschüsse	condições financeiras especiais dadas a lojista para a construção de sua loja	Reserva para gastos de construcción

	FRANÇAIS	DEUTSCH	PORTUGUÊS	ESPAÑOL
construction management	gestion de construction	Bauleitung	administração das obras de construção; gerente de obras	Administración de las obras de construcción
construction manager (CM)	directeur de la construction	Bauleiter	gestor de obras em construção	Administrador de las obras de construcción
constructive eviction	éviction implicite	konstruktive Besitzentziehung	despojamento implícito; evicção implícita	Desalojo implícito
consumer benchmarks	repères de consommation	Vergleich des Konsumentenverhaltens	padrão de referência de consumidores	Cotas de referencia del consumidor
consumer market research	études de marché de consommation	Konsumentenmarktforschung	prospecção do mercado de consumidores; pesquisa de mercado junto a consumidores	Investigación de mercado sobre el consumidor
Consumer Price Index (CPI)	Indice des prix à la consommation (IPC)	Lebenshaltungskostenindex	índice de preços do consumidores	Índice de precios al consumidor

	FRANÇAIS	DEUTSCH	PORTUGUÊS	ESPAÑOL
Consumer Price Index Adjustment	ajustement selon l'Indice des prix à la consommation	Anpassung des Preisindexes für die Lebenshaltung	ajuste do Índice de Preços ao Consumidor	Ajuste del índice de precios al consumidor
consumer survey	sondage auprès des consommateurs	Verbraucherbefragung	inquérito ao consumidor; levantamento junto a consumidores	Encuesta a consumidores
contingency plans	plans de contingence	Pläne für Notfälle	planos de emergência	Planes de contingencia
continuity	en mode continue	kontinuierliche Werbung	continuidade	Continuidad
continuous occupancy clause	clause d'occupation continue	Betriebspflicht Klausel	cláusula de operação contínua	Cláusula de operación continua
continuous scheduling	présentation régulière continue	zu regelmäßigen Zeitpunkten wiederkehrende, gleichbleibende Werbung	programação contínua	Programación continua
contra-asset account	compte de contrepartie d'actif	Aktivengegenkonto	conta de rectificação do activo; conta de contrapartida de ativos	Cuenta contra-activos

	FRANÇAIS	DEUTSCH	PORTUGUÊS	ESPAÑOL
contract	contrat	Vertrag, Vereinbarung	contrato	Contrato
contract security	agents de sécurité à contrat	Vertraglich verpflichteter Wach- und Sicherheitsdienst	contrato para serviços de segurança	Contrato para servicios de seguridad
contractors	entreprises	Auftragnehmer	empreiteiros	Contratistas
convenience goods	articles de consommation courante	Verbrauchsgüter	artigos e serviços de consumo rápido; bens/artigos de conveniência	Artículos de compra rápida
convenience shopping center	centre commercial utilitaire; centre commercial d'achats rapides	Einkaufszentrum für Verbrauchsgüter	centro de compras de artigos de consumo rápido; shopping center de artigos de conveniência	Centro comercial de artículos de compra rápida
conversion	conversion	Umwandlung	conversão	Conversión
cookie	mouchard électronique	Cookie	cookie	"Cookie"
cooperative pages	pages coopératives	Gemeinschaftsseiten	páginas cooperativas	Páginas cooperativas
cooperative section	section coopérative	Werbeprospekt	secção cooperativa	Sección cooperativa

	FRANÇAIS	DEUTSCH	PORTUGUÊS	ESPAÑOL
copy and layout	texte et montage	Text und Layout	cópia e composição; cópia & lay-out	Copia y composición
copy and layout deadline	échéance texte et montage	Stichtag für den Fahnenabzug	prazo limite de cópia e composição	Plazo para copia y composición
copy research (Also known as copy testing)	recherche concernant le texte publicitaire (ou essai du texte publicitaire)	Werbetextanalyse (auch unter dem Begriff "Textprüfung" bekannt)	estudo do efeito de determinada campanha publicitária (também conhecido como teste de cópia)	Investigación del efecto de un aviso o campaña de publicidad (También conocido como prueba del efecto publicitario)
core samples	carottes d'échantillon	Hauptbeispiele	amostras de núcleo	Muestras del sondeo
cost	coût	Kosten	custo	Costo
cost approach	méthode du coût	Wertermittlung	proposta de custo	Método de costos
cost of capital	coût du capital	Kapital Kosten	custo do capital	Costo de capital

	FRANÇAIS	DEUTSCH	PORTUGUÊS	ESPAÑOL
cost per thousand (CPM)	coût par millier (CPM)	Tausenderpreis (TP)	custo por milhar	Costo por mil
cost-plus contract	contrat à coût majoré	Selbstkostenerstattungsvertrag mit begrenztem oder prozentualem Zuschlag	contrato de custos acrescido de honorários	Contrato al costo más honorarios
co-tenancy	clause de co-location	Mitpächterklausel	co-arrendamento; co-locação	Co-arrendamiento
course	rangée	Schicht	revestimento	Curso
covenant	stipulation	Abkommen	cláusula; acordo	Cláusula
cover page	page couverture	Umschlagseite	capa	Portada
coverage	couverture	Reichweite	cobertura	Cobertura
CPI (Consumer Price Index adjustment)	ajustement selon l'IPC (Indice des prix à la consommation)	Anpassung des Preisindexes für die Lebenshaltung	ajuste IPC (do índice de preços no consumidor)	Ajuste del (Índice de precios al consumidor)

	FRANÇAIS	DEUTSCH	PORTUGUÊS	ESPAÑOL
CPI (Consumer Price Index rents)	loyers indexé selon d'IPC (Indice de prix à la consommation)	Mieten gemäß dem Preisindex für die Lebenshaltung	rendas IPC (índice de preços no consumidor); alugueis segundo o IPC (índice de preços ao consumidor)	Alquileres según (Índice de precios al consumidor)
CPM	CPM (Coût par millier)	TP (Tausenderpreis)	custo por milhar	Costo por mil
CPM/PCM	CPM/ par minute commerciale	TP/Werbeminute	custo por milhar/ por minuto de anúncios	Costo por mil por minuto comercial
CPR	réanimation cardio-respiratoire	kardiopulmonale Reanimation	RCP - ressuscitação cardio pulmonar	Reanimación cardiopulmonar
credit	crédit	Guthaben	crédito	Crédito
credit loss	créance irrécouvrable	Kreditverlust	perdas por contas incobráveis	Pérdida de crédito
credit tenants	locataires jouissant d'un bon crédit	kreditkräftiger Mieter	locatários com crédito	Locatarios con solidez financiera

	FRANÇAIS	DEUTSCH	PORTUGUÊS	ESPAÑOL
cricket	pente de toiture qui évacue l'eau de pluie dans une certaine direction	Dachneigung	contrafeito de sanca; caimento do telhado (para aguas pluviais)	Declive del techo para orientar el agua de lluvia
Crime Prevention Through Environmental Design (CPTED)	Prévention du crime par conception de l'environnement	Kriminalitätsvorsorge durch Gestaltung des Umfeldes	Prevenção do Crime através de Conceitos Ambientais	Prevención de delitos a través de políticas de diseño ambiental
criminal liability	responsabilité criminelle	strafrechtliche Verantwortlichkeit	responsabilidade penal	Responsabilidad penal
critical mass	masse critique	kritische Menge	massa crítica	masa crítica
critical path method (CPM) schedule	calendrier à chemin critique; calendrier selon la méthode du chemin critique	Bauplanung nach der kritischen Wegmethode (CPM)	programação do método do caminho crítico	Método del camino crítico
cross-collateralization	garanties croisées	gesamtschuldnerische Besicherung	garantía cruzada	Garantía recíproca
cross-promotion	promotion croisée	kombinierte Absatzförderung	promoção cruzada	Promoción cruzada

	FRANÇAIS	DEUTSCH	PORTUGUÊS	ESPAÑOL
cross-shopping	achats croisés	Einkauf von Komplementärgütern	compras múltiplas	Compras múltiples
cume	cumulatif	kumulierte	acumulativo	Acumulativo
cumulative attraction	attraction cumulative	kumulative Attraktion	atracção cumulativa	Ventaja acumulativa
curb stone	bordure	Abstützsystem	lancil; pedra de meio fio	Sistema de tirantes
current asset	élément d'actif à court terme	Umlaufvermögen	activo circulante	Activo corriente
current dollar projections	projections en dollars courants	Planung in gegenwärtigen Dollars	projecções em dólares actuais	Proyecciones en dólar corriente
current liability	dette à court terme	kurzfristige Verbindlichkeit	passivo circulante	Pasivo corriente
current ratio	ratio du fonds de roulement	Liquiditätskoeffizient	coeficiente de liquidez	Relación corriente
customer profile	profil des consommateurs	Kundenprofil	perfil do consumidor	Perfil del consumidor

	FRANÇAIS	DEUTSCH	PORTUGUÊS	ESPAÑOL
cutline	légende d'illustration	Bildlegende	legenda	Pie de foto o ilustración
daypart	partie de la journée	Sendezeitsegment	parte do dia	Segmento del día
daytime business population data	données sur la population d'affaires le jour	Informationen über die Beschäftigten-population in einem Absatzgebiet	dados sobre a população trabalhadora	Datos sobre la población obrera
DB	diffusion retardée	verschobene Sendung (DB)	transmissão adiada	Emisión en diferido
debentures	obligations	Schuldverschreibungen	obrigações	Obligaciones
debit	débit	Belastung	débito	Débito
debt coverage ratio	coefficient de couverture de la dette	Kennziffer der Schulden-rückzahlungskapazität	coeficiente de cobertura de débito	Relación de cobertura de deuda
debt service	service de la dette	Schuldendienst	servicio da dívida; serviço da dívida	Servicio de la deuda

	FRANÇAIS	DEUTSCH	PORTUGUÊS	ESPAÑOL
decentralized administrative system	système administratif décentralisé	Dezentralisiertes Verwaltungssystem	sistema administrativo descentralizado	Sistema descentralizado de administración
deck	base de toit	Dachpappeneindeckungsfläche	laje	Base de aislamiento del techo
declaration	déclaration	Erklärung des Versicherten	declaração	Declaración
deductible	franchise	Selbstbehalt	franquia	Franquicia
default	défaut	Fristversäumnis	não cumprimento	Incumplimiento
default rate	taux d'intérêt pour défaillances	Zahlungsverzugszinsen	(taxa de) juros de mora	Tasa de mora
delamination	délaminage	Ablösung	delaminação	Delaminación
delayed broadcast (DB)	diffusion retardée	verschobene Sendung	transmissão adiada	Emisión en diferido
demising studding	montants autour de l'espace loué	Stahlträger um eine gemietete Fläche herum	tabique de aço; tabique/parede separando lojistas	Entramado

	FRANÇAIS	DEUTSCH	PORTUGUÊS	ESPAÑOL
demographic characteristics	caractéristiques démographiques	demographische Merkmale	características demográficas	Características demográficas
demographic market	marché démographique	demographischer Markt	mercado demográfico	Mercado demográfico
demographic multiplier	multiplicateur démographique	demographischer Multiplikator	multiplicador demográfico	Multiplicador demográfico
demographic study	étude démographique	demographische Studie	estudo demográfico	Estudio demográfico
demographics	aspects démographiques	demographische Struktur	estudos da população	Datos demográficos
department store type merchandise (DSTM)	marchandise de type grand magasin	in Warenhäusern bzw. Kaufhäusern angebotenes Warensortiment	mercadorias do tipo vendido em grandes armazéns	Mercadería tipo tienda de departamentos
depreciation	amortissement; dépréciation	Abschreibung	depreciação	Depreciación
depth of selection	éventail	Umfang eines Warensortiments	vasta gama de selecção	Amplia gama de selección

	FRANÇAIS	DEUTSCH	PORTUGUÊS	ESPAÑOL
design criteria	critères de conception	Design-Kriterien	critério de *design*	Criterio de diseño
designated market area (DMA)	aire de marché désignée	designiertes Marktgebiet (DMA)	área designada de mercado	Área designada de mercado
development area	aire de développement	Baugebiet	área de desenvolvimento	Área de desarrollo
difference-in-conditions (insurance)	(assurance) de carence	Versicherung unterschiedlicher Zustände	apólice de seguro para as diferenças de condições	(Seguro) por diferencia en las condiciones
differential advantage	avantage différentiel	Differenzierungsvorteil	vantagem diferencial	Ventaja diferencial
digital certificate	certificat numérique	digitales Zertifikat	certificado digital	Certificado digital
digital wallet	portefeuille numérique	digitale Brieftasche	carteira digital	Billetera digital
direct writing company	compagnie à souscription directe	Direktversicherungs-gesell-schaft	companhia de subscrição directa	Compañía de suscripción directa

	FRANÇAIS	DEUTSCH	PORTUGUÊS	ESPAÑOL
directors and officers liability insurance	responsabilité des administrateurs et dirigeants assurance	Haftpflichtversicherung für Direktoren und leitende Angestellte	responsabilidade civil dos diretores e dos funcionários seguro; seguro de responsabilidade civil dos diretores e executivos	Seguro de Responsabilidad civil de directores y gerentes
discount-anchored shopping center	centre commercial avec grande surface à prix d'usine; centre commercial avec magasin principal à escompte	Einkaufszentrum, dessen Hauptmieter ein Discounter ist	centro comercial com uma loja principal de descontos; shopping center com loja(s) âncora(s) de descontos	Centro de compras con una tienda principal de descuentos
discount rate	taux d'escompte	Diskontsatz	taxa de desconto	Tasa de descuento
discount retailing	vente au détail d'articles à rabais	Discounter (Discount—Handel)	venda a retalho com desconto; venda a varejo com desconto	Rebaja minorista
discounted cash flow	rentabilité interne	discounted Kapitalfluss	fluxo de caixa futuro, descontado a valor presente	Flujo de fondos actualizado

	FRANÇAIS	DEUTSCH	PORTUGUÊS	ESPAÑOL
display advertising	grande annonce	Werbung mit Hilfe von Großanzeigen	publicidade apresentada com destaque	Publicidad gráfica
disposable income	revenu disponible	verfügbares Einkommen	rendimento disponível; renda disponível	Ingresos disponibles
distribution	distribution	Verbreitungsgebiet	distribuição	Distribución
DMA	aire de marché désignée	DMA, designiertes Marktgebiet	área designada do mercado	Área designada de mercado
documentation	documentation	Dokumentation	documentação	Documentación
door busters	marchandise à prix très réduits, avec peu de sélection	Lockvogelangebote	mercadorias incompletas com preços extremamente reduzidos	Mercadería incompleta a precios reducidos
double decker	réclames extérieures l'une par-dessus l'autre	Doppeldeckerplakat	anúncios no exterior sobrepostos	Material publicitario exterior superpuesto
double-dumbbell shaped	en forme de double haltère	hantelförmig angelegtes Einkaufszentrum	em forma de haltere duplo	En forma de mancuerna doble

	FRANÇAIS	DEUTSCH	PORTUGUÊS	ESPAÑOL
double-entry bookkeeping	comptabilité en partie double	doppelte Buchführung	contabilidade por partidas duplas	Contabilidad por partida doble
double truck	les deux pages centrales opposées de réclames	doppelseitige Anzeige	páginas centrais duplas com anúncios	Doble página central con anuncios
draw tenant	locataire attrayant	Magnet-Mieter	inquilino (loja) com grande poder de atratividade	Tienda de gran atracción
dress code	code relatif à la tenue vestimentaire	Bekleidungsordnung	regulamento de uniformes/ tipo de roupa a ser usada pela segurança	Código de vestimenta
drive time	période de conduite aux heures d'affluence; heure de grande écoute (radio)	Anfahrzeit	tempo em automóvel	Horas pico de tránsito de vehículos
dry sheet	couche sèche	Unterlagspapier	revestimento	Revestimiento

	FRANÇAIS	DEUTSCH	PORTUGUÊS	ESPAÑOL
DSTM	marchandise de type grand magasin	in Warenhäusern angebotenes Warensortiment (DSTM)	mercadorias do tipo vendido em grandes armazéns; tipo de mercadoria vendido em loja de departamento	Mercadería tipo tienda de departamentos
due diligence	diligence raisonnable	sorgfältige Kontrolle	auditoria geral (fiscal, contábil, jurídica e patrimonial) aplicável a lasos de aquisições de empresas	Debida diligencia
dumbbell-shaped shopping center	en forme d'haltère centre commercial	hantelförmig angelegtes Einkaufszentrum	centro comercial/shopping center em forma de halteres	Centro de compras en forma de mancuerna
early fringe	période précédant le temps de grande écoute	Periode vor der Hauptsendezeit	horários antecedentes ao chamado "horário nobre"	Horario previo a las horas de mayor audiencia

	FRANÇAIS	DEUTSCH	PORTUGUÊS	ESPAÑOL
EBITDA	revenu avant intérêts, impôts, dépréciation et amortissement	Ertrag bevor Zins, Steuern, Abschreibungen Amortisation (EBITDA)	benefícios antes de juros, impostos, depreciação e amortização; receitas antes de juros, impostos, depreciação e amortização	Ganancias antes de la aplicación de intereses, impuestos, depreciación y amortización
e-commerce	commerce électronique	E-commerce	comércio electrónico; e-commerce	Comercio electrónico
economic base	base économique	wirtschaftliche Basis	base económica	Base económica
EDI	échange électronique de données	elektronischer Datenaustausch	transferência electrónica de dados; intercâmbio eletrónico de dados	Intercambio electrónico de datos
EDI Gateway	passerelle d'échange électronique de données	EDI Gateway	porta de transferência electrónica de dados; portal de intercâmbio eletrónico de dados	Portal de intercambio electrónico de datos
EDLP	bas prix tous les jours	kleine Dauerpreise	preços baixos todos os dias	Precios bajos constantes

	FRANÇAIS	DEUTSCH	PORTUGUÊS	ESPAÑOL
effective circulation (outdoor)	public effectif voyant un panneau d'affichage (extérieur)	wirksame Anschlagreichweite (Außenwerbung)	circulação efectiva (exterior)	Circulación real (exterior)
effective date	date d'entrée en vigueur	Datum des Inkrafttretens	Data de vigência	Fecha de entrada en vigencia
effective reach	portée effective	tatsächliche Reichweite	alcance eficaz	Alcance eficaz
effective rent	loyer effectif	tatsächlicher Mietzins	renda mínima e percentual combinada; aluguel mínimo e percentual combinado	Alquiler mínimo y porcentual combinado
efficiency	efficacité	Werbeträgerkosten je 1.000 Zielpersonen	eficiência	Eficiencia
elasticity factor of spending	facteur d'élasticité des dépenses	Kaufselastizitätsfaktor	factor de elasticidade de gastos	Factor de elasticidad de gastos
eligibility list	liste d'admissibilité	Liste qualifizierter Kandidaten (als Polizisten)	lista de candidatos elegíveis para emprego na polícia	Lista de candidatos idóneos

	FRANÇAIS	DEUTSCH	PORTUGUÊS	ESPAÑOL
emergency book	livret sur les urgences	Notfallmaßnahmen zum Nachschlagen	livro de emergências	Panfleto para emergencias
enclosed common area	partie commune close	Überdachte Gemeinschafts-fläche	área comum fechada	Área común cerrada
enclosed mall	centre commercial clos	Überdachtes Einkaufszentrum	centro comercial fechado; mall fechado	Centro comercial cerrado
end-of-month (EOM) dating	datage depuis la fin (EOM) dating	Datierung zum Monatsende	data para pagamento de contas no final do mês	Cierre de fechas a fin de mes
endorsement	avenant	Nachtrag	endosso	Endoso
engineering design forms	formulaires de conception d'ingénierie	Ingenieurtechnische Design-Pläne	formulários de concepção técnica	Formularios de diseño técnico
entertainment complex	complexe axé sur les divertissements	Unterhaltungskomplex	complexo de diversões	Complejo de entretenimientos
EOM	fin du mois	Monatsende (EOM)	final do mês	Fin de mes
EOP	fin de période	Periodenende (EOP)	final do período	Fin del periodo
equity	valeur nette	Eigenkapital	patrimônio líquido	Patrimonio neto

	FRANÇAIS	DEUTSCH	PORTUGUÊS	ESPAÑOL
equity offerings	offre de titres de participation	Aktienemissionen	oferta de acções	Ofertas de acciones
equity related loan	prêt lié à des titres de participation	Anleihe mit Optionsscheinen	empréstimo em forma de participação patrimonial	Préstamo en forma de participación en el capital
errors and omissions insurance coverage	couverture erreurs et omissions assurance	Haftpflichtversicherung für Fehler und Unterlassungen	cobertura de erros e omissões seguro	Cobertura de seguro de errores y omisiones
escalation clause	clause d'indexation	Kostenanpassungs-Klausel	cláusula de ajuste; clausula de indexação	Cláusula de indexación
estoppel letter	lettre d'estoppel / lettre de préclusion	Valutabescheinigung	carta de "estoppel"; carta de impedimento legal	Carta de impedimento legal
excepted property	propriété exclue	ausgeschlossene Vermögensgegenstände	propriedade exceptuada	Bienes exceptuados
excessive force	force excessive	unangemessene Gewaltanwendung	força excessiva	Fuerza excesiva

	FRANÇAIS	DEUTSCH	PORTUGUÊS	ESPAÑOL
exclusion	exclusion	Ausschluss	exclusão	Exclusión
exclusives	droits d'exclusivité	Alleinvertrieb, Exklusivvertrieb	exclusividade	Derechos exclusivos
exclusivity clause	clause d'exclusivité	Ausschließlichkeits- klausel	cláusula de exclusividade	Cláusula de exclusividad
exhibits	annexes	Anlagen	apêndices; anexos	Apéndices
expansion	expansion	Expansion	expansão	Expansión/ ampliación
expansion contribution	contribution à l'expansion	Beitragszahlung des Mieters an einen Expansions-Fonds	Contribuição para fundos de expansão	Contribución para gastos de ampliación
expense recovery	recouvrement de frais	Mietnebenkosten- rückerstattung	recuperação de despesas	Recuperación de los gastos
expenses	frais	Betriebskosten	despesas	Gastos
expiration date	date d'expiration	Fristablaufdatum	data de vencimento	Fecha de vencimiento
export	exportation	Export	exportação	Exportación

	FRANÇAIS	DEUTSCH	PORTUGUÊS	ESPAÑOL
exposure	risque; exposition	Verbanddeckung	exposição	Exposición
extended coverage insurance	couverture étendue assurance	Erweiterte Deckung Versicherung	cobertura adicional apólice de seguros	Seguro con extensión de cobertura
face out	devant vers l'extérieur	von der Vorderseite	roupa exposta pendurada de frente	Vestimenta exhibida colgada de frente
fact sheet	fiche d'informations	Informationsblatt	folha de dados	Hoja de datos
factory outlet	magasin d'usine	Fabrikladen (Factory Outlet)	Loja de fábrica	Tiendas de renta de fábrica
fair market value	juste valeur marchande	Verkehrswert	valor justo de mercado	Valor justo de mercado
fall	chute	Gefälle	declividade	Caída
fashion/specialty center	centre axé sur la mode/spécialisé	Mode-/Fachgeschäfte-Zentrum	centro de modas/ especialidade	Centro de modas / especialidad

	FRANÇAIS	DEUTSCH	PORTUGUÊS	ESPAÑOL
fat spots	ressuage	Fettflecken	manchas gordurosas no pavimento; manchas negras pegajosas no estacionamento	Puntos negros pegajosos en el pavimento
feasibility study	étude de faisabilité	Durchführbarkeitsstudie	estudo de viabilidade	Estudio de factibilidad
feature story	article vedette	Sonderbeitrag	artigo de fundo	Artículo de interés particular
fee manager	gestionnaire à contrat	Managementunternehmen	administração por comissão	Administrador por comisión
felony	acte délictueux grave/crime	Kapitalverbrechen	acto delituoso; crime doloso	Delito grave
felt	feutre	Filz	feltro	Fieltro
FFO	rentrées nettes d'exploitation	Mittel aus der laufenden Geschäftstätigkeit	fundos resultantes de operações	Fondos provenientes de las operaciones
fidelity bond	garantie de fidélité	Kaution gegen Veruntreuung	seguro-fidelidade	Fianza

	FRANÇAIS	DEUTSCH	PORTUGUÊS	ESPAÑOL
field survey	enquête sur le terrain	Primärerhebung	estudo em campo; levantamento	Reconocimiento de campo
FIFO	premier entré, premier sorti (PEPS)	Prioritätsprinzip, nach dem zuerst eingegangene Waren auch zuerst verbraucht werden (FIFO)	fluxo das mercadorias que se vendem pela ordem por que foram compradas	Salida en el orden de adquisición
fills	matière de remplissage	Füllmaterialien	materiais de enchimento	Materiales de relleno
financial reports	rapports financiers	Finanzberichte	relatórios financeiros	Informes financieros
financial statement	bilan financier	Jahresabschluss, Jahresbilanz	mapa da situação financeira; demonstrativo financeiro	Estado financiero
finished mechanical	montage fini d'une réclame	Reinlayout	layout/montagem pronta para impressão	Montaje acabado listo para ser impreso
fire insurance	assurance-incendie	Feuerversicherung	seguro contra incêndios	Seguro contra incendio

	FRANÇAIS	DEUTSCH	PORTUGUÊS	ESPAÑOL
first in, first out (FIFO)	premier entré, premier sorti (PEPS)	Prioritätsprinzip, nach dem zuerst eingegangene Waren auch zuerst verbraucht werden (FIFO)	fluxo das mercadorias que se vendem pela ordem por que foram compradas	Salida en el orden de adquisición
first stage	premier niveau	erste Phase	primeira fase	Primera etapa
fiscal year	année fiscale	Geschäftsjahr	ano fiscal	Año fiscal
fixed assets	immobilisations	feste Anlagen	activos fixos	Activos fijos
fixed contributions	contributions fixes	feste Beiträge	contribuições fixas	Contribuciones fijas
fixed expenses	frais fixes	feste Auslagekosten	despesas fixas	Gastos fijos
fixed minimum rent	loyer minimum fixe	feste Grundmiete	renda mínima fixa; aluguel mínimo fixo	Alquiler mínimo fijo
fixed position spot	spot à position fixe	fest plazierte Werbesendung	espaço (spot) publicitário em posição fixa	Espacio publicitario de posición fija
fixed rate	taux fixe	fester Zinssatz	taxa fixa	Tasa fija

	FRANÇAIS	DEUTSCH	PORTUGUÊS	ESPAÑOL
flashing	bande de solin	Blechverwahrung	placas de protecção; tapajuntas	Tapajuntas
flat rate	taux uniforme	Pauschalsatz	tarifa uniforme	Tarifa uniforme
flat rent	loyer invariable	Pauschalmiete	renda fixa; aluguel fixo	Alquiler fijo
flight (Also known as flighting)	vague publicitaire	Werbephase	série de promoções repetidas	Serie de promociones repetidas
floating rate	taux fluctuant	variabler Zinssatz	taxas flutuantes	Tasa flotante
flood coat	couche à l'épreuve des intempéries	bituminöse, zum Schutz gegen Regen während der Arbeiten am Haus auf der Dachpappe applizierte Schicht	camada de betume sobre o feltro para protecção contra as intempéries	Capa de betún sobre fieltro expuesto para protección contra la intemperie
fluorescent light	éclairage fluorescent	fluoreszierendes Licht	luz fluorescente	Luz fluorescente
FOB	franco à bord (FOB)	FOB	FOB (free-on-board)	Franco a bordo
focus group	groupe d'étude	Befragtengruppe	grupo em foco; "focus group"	Grupo enfocado

	FRANÇAIS	DEUTSCH	PORTUGUÊS	ESPAÑOL
follow-on/later stage	étape suivante ; investissement subséquent	Folgeinvestition	seguimento/ fase posterior	Seguimiento/ etapa posterior
food court	zone de restauration ; aire d'alimentation	food court	Pátio de comidas; praça de alimentação	Patio de comidas
food court expenses	frais de zone de restauration; frais de l'aire d'alimentation	die Spesen eines F.C.	despesas referentes à operação do pátio de comidas; despesas da praça de alimentação	Gastos de patios de comida
footcandle	lumen par pied carré	Fußkerze	pé-vela; unidade de iluminação medida	Bujía-pie
force majeure	force majeure	höhere Gewalt	força maior	Fuerza mayor
foreseeability	prévisibilité	Vorhersehbarkeit	previsibilidade	Previsibilidad
format	format	Format	formato	Formato
four-way rack	présentoir à quatre voies	Kleiderständer mit vier Armen	prateleira a quatro níveis; estante	Perchero de cuatro vías
free on board (FOB)	franco à bord (FOB)	frei an Bord (FOB)	franco a bordo; livre a bordo (FOB)	Franco a bordo

	FRANÇAIS	DEUTSCH	PORTUGUÊS	ESPAÑOL
freestanding stores	magasins autonomes	autonome Geschäfte	lojas autónomas	Tiendas autónomas
frequency	fréquence	Häufigkeit	frequência	Frecuencia
fringe time	heures précédant ou suivant immédiatement la période de grande écoute	Sendezeit vor und nach der Hauptzeit	horários antecedentes e posteriores ao chamado "horário nobre"	Horario previo a las horas de mayor audiencia
frontage	la façade; devanture	Fassade	fachada	Fachada
full position	position privilégiée	Vorzugsplatzierung	Posição preferida de um anúncio num jornal	Posición preferencial de un aviso en un periódico
funds from operations (FFO)	rentrées nettes liées à l'exploitation	Mittel aus der laufenden Geschäftstätigkeit	Fundos resultantes de operações	Fondos provenientes de las operaciones
future value (FV)	valeur capitalisée	Zukunftswert	valor futuro	Valor futuro

	FRANÇAIS	DEUTSCH	PORTUGUÊS	ESPAÑOL
GAAP	P.C.G.R. (principes comptables généralement reconnus)	GoB	GAAP – princípios contábeis geralmente aceitos	Principios de contabilidad generalmente aceptados
GAFO	GAFO (marchandise générale, vêtements, ameublement et autre marchandise)	Gemischtwaren, Bekleidung, Einrichtungsgegenstände und sonstige Waren (GAFO)	GAFO - mercadorias gerais, vestuário, móveis e outras mercadorias	Mercadería general, vestuario, muebles y otras mercaderías
general and administrative expenses	frais généraux et administratifs	allgemeine und verwaltungstechnische Ausgaben	despesas gerais e administrativas	Gastos generales y de administración
general conditions	conditions générales	Allgemeine Bedingungen	condições gerais	Condiciones generales
general contractor (GC)	entrepreneur général	Generalunternehmer	empreiteiro geral	Contratista general
general ledger	grand livre	Hauptbuch	razão geral	Libro mayor

	FRANÇAIS	DEUTSCH	PORTUGUÊS	ESPAÑOL
generally accepted accounting principles	principes comptables généralement reconnus	Grundsätze ordnungsgemäßer Buchführung	GAAP – princípios contábeis geralmente aceitos	Principios de contabilidad generalmente aceptados
GLA	surface locative brute	brutto vermietbare Geschäftsfläche (GLA)	ABL - área bruta alugável	Área bruta locativa
glossies	épreuves glacées	Hochglanzphotos	impressão em papel lustroso	Impresos en papel satinado
gondola	gondole	beiderseitig offenes Warenauslageregal	gôndola	Góndola
goodwill	achalandage	Geschäftswert	valor extrínseco; fundo de comércio	Fondo de comercio positivo
graduated lease	bail à loyer par paliers	gestaffelte Miete	arrendamento graduado; aluguel gradual	Alquiler gradual
grand opening date	date de la grande ouverture	Eröffnungsdatum	data de inauguração	Fecha de inauguración
granules	granules	Mineralgranulat	grânulos	Grânulos

	FRANÇAIS	DEUTSCH	PORTUGUÊS	ESPAÑOL
graphics	graphismes	graphische Kunst	Gráficos	Gráficos
grease pans	bacs à graisse	Fettfänger	recipientes para recolha de massa gordurosa	Colectores de grasa
grooving	ornières	Spurrillen	Sulcos	Acanalado
gross collectibles	sommes encaissables brutes	insgesamt einziehbare Ausgaben	cobranças brutas	Cobranzas brutas
gross floor area	superficie brute	Gesamtfläche	superfície bruta; área total construída	Superficie bruta
gross income	revenu brut	Bruttoeinkommen	rendimento bruto; renda bruta	Ingreso bruto
gross leasable area (GLA)	surface locative brute	brutto vermietbar Geschäftsfläche (GLA)	ABL - área bruta alugável	Área bruta locativa
gross lease	bail brut	Bruttomietvertrag	arrendamento bruto; aluguel bruto	Alquiler bruto
gross margin	marge brute	brutto Handelsspanne	margem bruta	Margen bruto

	FRANÇAIS	DEUTSCH	PORTUGUÊS	ESPAÑOL
gross potential revenue	revenus bruts potentiels	potentieller Bruttoertrag	rendimento potencial bruto	Ingresos potenciales brutos
gross profit	bénéfice brut	Bruttogewinn	lucro bruto	Ganancia bruta
gross rating points (GRPs)	points de cote brute	Bruttoreichweite (GRP)	volume de audiência ou alcance de uma mensagem, dentro do público alvo (target) desejado	Puntos de índice de audiencia bruto
gross sales	ventes brutes	Bruttoumsatz	vendas brutas	Ventas brutas
GRPs	points de cote brute	Bruttoreichweite (GRP)	escala de pontos de contacto bruta	Puntos de índice de audiencia bruto
guaranteed maximum price (GMP)	prix maximum garanti	garantierter Maximalpreis (GMP)	preço máximo garantido	Precio máximo garantizado
gutter space	petits fonds	Bundsteg	medianiz	Margen del medianil

	FRANÇAIS	DEUTSCH	PORTUGUÊS	ESPAÑOL
half run	carte publicitaire placée dans la moitié des wagons	Werbeanschlag in jedem zweiten Wagen	cartaz publicitário colocado alternadamente em veículos de transporte público	Tarjeta publicitaria colocada alternativamente en los automóviles del sistema de tránsito
hard costs	coût de base	"harte Kosten"	custos para terreno, edifício e melhoramentos	Costos gravosos
hard goods	marchandise durable	Gebrauchsgüter	mercadorias de consumo duradouro	Bienes duraderos
head	titre	Überschrift	título	Titular
head-on position	position face à la circulation	Plakatanschlagsposition frontal zum vorüberfliessenden Verkehr	cartaz visando o trânsito numa auto-estrada	Cartel de posición frontal en una autopista
heat pump	pompe de chaleur	Wärmepumpe	bomba de aquecimento	Bomba de calor

	FRANÇAIS	DEUTSCH	PORTUGUÊS	ESPAÑOL
heating, ventilation and air-conditioning (HVAC) units	appareils de chauffage, ventilation et climatisation (CVC)	Heizungs-, Lüftungs- und Kühlungs-Anlagen	unidades de aquecimento, ventilação e ar condicionado	Unidades de calefacción, ventilación y aire acondicionado
hiatus	lacune	Werbepause	intervalo	Intervalo
high end	haut de gamme	Geschäfte der oberen Qualitäts- und Preisklasse	de qualidade superior	De nivel superior
high income per capita	revenu élevé par tête	hohes Einkommen pro Kopf	rendimento elevado per capita; renda elevada per capita	Ingreso alto per cápita
hired car automobile liability insurance	responsabilité automobile pour voitures de location	Kfz-Haftpflichtversich-erung für Mietwagen	responsabilidade civil para carros de aluguer seguro; seguro de responsabilidade civil para carros de aluguel	Seguro de responsabilidad civil por automóviles de alquiler
historical sales performance (of tenants)	rendement au mètre carré des ventes; performance historique des ventes (des locataires)	Absatzleistung (der Mieter) in der Vergangenheit	resultados históricos de venda (dos locatários)	Resultados históricos de ventas (de los locatarios)

	FRANÇAIS	DEUTSCH	PORTUGUÊS	ESPAÑOL
hold-harmless agreement	accord d'exonération de responsabilité	Schadloshaltungsvereinbarung	contrato de isenção de responsabilidade	Acuerdo liberatorio de responsabilidad
holdup alarm	alarme de hold-up	Überfallalarm	alarme indicando a ocorrência de um assalto	Alarma contra robo
house organ	publication interne	Betriebszeitschrift	Publicação interna	Publicación interna
household	ménage	Haushalt	conjunto de pessoas que vivem numa casa	Casa familiar
housekeeping expenses	frais d'entretien	Unterhaltskosten	despesas de serviços de conservação	Gastos de mantenimiento
housing unit	unité d'habitation	Wohneinheit	unidade de habitação	Unidad de vivienda
hurdle rate	taux de rendement minimum	erwartete Mindestrendite	custo de oportunidade de capital que a taxa interna de rendibilidade deve exceder	Tasa crítica de rentabilidad

	FRANÇAIS	DEUTSCH	PORTUGUÊS	ESPAÑOL
HUT level	niveau HUT (ménages utilisant la télévision)	Anteil der effektiven Fernsehhaushalte (HUT)	Percentagem de casas que vêem televisão durante um determinado período de tempo	Porcentaje de hogares que miran televisión durante un plazo determinado
HVAC	chauffage, ventilation et climatisation; CVC	Heizung, Lüftung, Kühlung	aquecimento, ventilação e ar condicionado	Calefacción, ventilación y aire acondicionado
hybrid decentralized administrative system	système administratif décentralisé hybride	Mischform eines dezentralisierten	sistema administrativo descentralizado híbrido	Sistema administrativo descentralizado híbrido
image-building	renforcement d'image	Image-Pflege	projecção de imagem favorável; criação e proteção de imagem favorável	Construcción de la imagen
import	importation	Import	importação	Importación

	FRANÇAIS	DEUTSCH	PORTUGUÊS	ESPAÑOL
inboard	partie d'une zone commerciale vers la ville centrale	Einkaufsgebiet, das aus der Sicht eines Einkaufszentrums in Stadteinwärtsrichtung liegt	parte da área comercial situada na direcção da cidade central	Parte del área comercial situada en dirección a la ciudad central
incandescent lighting	éclairage incandescent	Weißlichtbeleuchtung	iluminação incandescente	Luz incandescente
inch	pouce	Spaltenzoll	polegada	Pulgada
incident reports	rapports d'incident	Berichte über Vorfälle	relatório do incidente	Informes sobre incidentes
income, net	revenu, net	Einkommen, Netto-	renda líquida	Ingreso, neto
income, per capita	revenu, par personne	Einkommen, Pro-Kopf-	rendimento, per capita; renda per capita	Ingreso, per cápita
income, real	revenu, réel	Einkommen, Real-	rendimento, real; renda real	Ingreso, real
income, total	revenu, total	Einkommen, Gesamt-	rendimento, total; renda tota	Ingreso, total
income, total personal	revenu, personnel total	Einkommen, Gesamtprivat	rendimento, total pessoal; renda pessoal total	Ingreso, total personal

	FRANÇAIS	DEUTSCH	PORTUGUÊS	ESPAÑOL
income approach	méthode du revenu	Einkommensbewertungsansatz	abordagem de rendimento; método de avaliação de alugueis (renda)	Método de ingresos
income statement	bilan financier; état des résultats	Gewinn- und Verlustrechnung	demonstrativo de resultados/receitas	Estado de ganancias y pérdidas
indemnification	indemnisation	Schadloshaltung	indemnização; indenização	Indemnización
indemnity agreement	accord d'indemnisation	Schadloshaltungsvereinbarung	acordo de indemnização; acordo de indenização	Acuerdo de indemnización
index	indice	Index	índice	Índice
industry averages	moyennes industrielles	Durchschnitte der Branche	média de vendas da indústria; médias da indústria ou do segmento	Promedios de la industria
inflow market	marché d'arrivée	Tertiärmarkt	mercado de entrada	Mercado de afluencia
in-house agency	agence interne	betriebsinterne Werbeagentur	agência interna (própria) de publicidade	Agencia de publicidad dentro de la empresa

	FRANÇAIS	DEUTSCH	PORTUGUÊS	ESPAÑOL
initial assessment	cotisation initiale	einmalige, vom Mieter zu entrichtende Vorauszahlung der Mietnebenkosten	avaliação inicial	Tasación inicial
initial markup	majoration initiale	erster Gewinnaufschlag	margem de lucro inicial	Margen de beneficio inicial
initial/seed	capitaux initiaux/ de lancement	Startkapital	investimento inicial para comprovação de um conceito	Capital generador / iniciador
insert	encart	Werbebeilage	encarte	Encarte
insertion order	ordre d'insertion	Anzeigenauftrag	ordem de encarte; ordem de inserção	Pedido de encarte
insolvency	insolvabilité	Insolvenz	insolvência	Insolvencia
inspection	inspection	Inspektion	inspecção	Inspección
institutional advertising	publicité institutionnelle	institutionelle Werbung	publicidade institucional	Publicidad institucional
insulation layer	couche isolante	Isolierschicht	camada isoladora	Capa aislante
insurance	assurance	Versicherung	seguro	Seguro

	FRANÇAIS	DEUTSCH	PORTUGUÊS	ESPAÑOL
insurance expense	frais d'assurance	Versicherungskosten	despesas de seguro	Gastos de seguros
insurance revenue	revenus d'assurance	eingehende Gelder für Versicherungskosten	receita relativa ao custo do seguro	Ingresos por seguros
insuring agreement	contrat d'assurance	Versicherungsverein-barung	contrato de seguros	Sección de una póliza de seguros que estipula lo que cubre la póliza
intangible assets	actifs incorporels	immaterielle Aktiva	Activos intangíveis	Activos intangibles
integrated commercial	réclame intégrée	integrierte Werbesendung	anúncio integrado	Aviso publicitario integrado

	FRANÇAIS	DEUTSCH	PORTUGUÊS	ESPAÑOL
intercept survey	enquête par interception de consommateurs	Studie zum Käuferverhalten	inquérito elaborado ao interceptar os compradores no centro comercial; levantamento/ pesquisa feita por abordagem a consumidores (geralmente dentro do mall)	Encuesta a los consumidores en el mismo centro de compras
interest	intérêts	Zinsen	juros	Interés
interest-only loan	prêt à intérêts seulement	Darlehen nur mit Zinsen	empréstimo apenas juros	Préstamo con amortización al vencimiento
interest rate	taux d'intérêt	Zinssatz	taxa de juro	Tasa de interés
internal controls	contrôles internes	interne Kontrollen	controlos internos; controles internos	Controles internos
internal rate of return (IRR)	taux de rendement interne	Kapitalrendite der Investition	taxa interna de rendimento; taxa de retorno interna	Tasa de rentabilidad interna
Internet	internet	Internet	Internet	Internet
inventory	stocks	Inventar	inventário; estoque	Inventario

	FRANÇAIS	DEUTSCH	PORTUGUÊS	ESPAÑOL
inventory average	moyenne des stocks	durchschnittlicher Lagerbestand	média de inventário; estoque médio	Promedio del inventario
inventory turnover	rotation des stocks	Umschlagsgeschindig-keit des Lagers, Lagerumschlag	rotação das existências; giro do estoque	Rotación de existencias
investigation	enquête	Ermittlungsverfahren	investigação	Investigación
investment bank	banque d'investissement	Investment-Bank, Effekten- und Emissionsbank	banco de investimento	Banco de inversiones
IPO	première offre publique de titres	Aktienneuemission (IPO)	oferta publica inicial	Oferta pública inicial
IRR	taux de rendement interne	interne Kapitalrendite	taxa interna de rendimento; taxa de retorno interna	Tasa de rentabilidad interna
irregularity reports	rapports d'irrégularité	Berichte über außer-ordentliche Vorfälle	relação de condições irregulares; relatórios das irregularidades	Informe sobre irregularidades
irregulars	marchandise irrégulière	Waren mit geringen Qualitätsmängeln	mercadorias com defeitos	Mercadería fallada

	FRANÇAIS	DEUTSCH	PORTUGUÊS	ESPAÑOL
jointly and severally	conjointement et solidairement	gesamtschuldnerisch	conjunta e solidariamente	Colectiva e individualmente
journal	journal	Journal	diário	Diario
journal entry	écriture de journal	Einzelposten	lançamento de diário	Asiento en el libro diario
junior department store	grand magasin; grand magasin junior	Juniorwarenhaus	loja de departamentos intermédia; loja de departamento de pequeno ou médio porte	Tienda de departamentos intermedia
junior unit	unité junior	Miniseitenformat	tamanho de página que permite ao anunciante usar a mesma chapa em páginas grandes e pequenas	Tamaño de página que permite al anunciante utilizar las mismas planchas para páginas pequeñas y grandes

	FRANÇAIS	DEUTSCH	PORTUGUÊS	ESPAÑOL
kettle	chaudière	Vergussmasseofen	pote de aquecimento; caldeira	Recipiente para calentar betún de techo
key money	cession de droit au bail ; pas-de-porte	Abstandssumme	dinheiro pago pelo arrendatário ao proprietário pela posse da chave; luvas	Dinero pagado por el inquilino al arrendador por el derecho a operar una tienda en el centro comercial
keystone price	prix qui est le double du prix coûtant	hoher Preis für spätere Preisreduzierung	preço base que reflete o dobro do custo do produto	Precio clave (alcanzado en el momento en que éste dobla el valor de compra abonado por el minorista)
kick-out clause	clause de résiliation	vermieterseitige Kündigungsklausel	cláusula de opção para terminar o aluguer antes do seu termo; cláusula de despejo	Cláusula de rescisión anticipada

	FRANÇAIS	DEUTSCH	PORTUGUÊS	ESPAÑOL
king size poster	affiche grand format	übergroßes Plakat	cartaz gigante	Cartel de tamaño extra grande
kiosks	kiosques	Kiosks	quiosques	Quioscos
L-shaped center	centre en forme de L	L-förmiges Einkaufszentrum	centro em forma de L	centro en forma de L
land charges	frais d'augmentation des impôts fonciers	Liegenschaftlasten	despesas prediais adicionais; encargos adicionais por impostos prediais e territoriais	Cargos adicionales por impuestos territoriales
land use regulations	réglementations de zonage	Landbenutzungsregelungen	regulamentos sobre a ocupação do solo	Reglamentaciones sobre el uso del suelo
landlord	propriétaire	Vermieter	proprietário	propietario
landlord's building	bâtiment du propriétaire	Strukturen des Vermieters	edifícios/prédios do locador	edificio del propietario
landlord's floor area	surface totale locative	die vom Vermieter vermietbare Fläche insgesamt	superfície para arrendar	Superficie para arrendar

	FRANÇAIS	DEUTSCH	PORTUGUÊS	ESPAÑOL
landscaping expenses	frais d'aménagement paysager	Gartenanlagekosten	despesas com a criação de zonas verdes; despesas com ajardinamento/paisagismo	Gastos de jardinería ornamental
last in, first out (LIFO)	dernier entré, premier sorti (DEPS)	zuletzt eingegangen, zuerst verbraucht (LIFO)	último que entra primeiro que sai	Última entrada, primera salida
layout	montage	Layout	maqueta; layout	composición
lead	paragraphe introductif	kurz zusammenfassende Einleitung	introdução de um artigo	párrafo introductorio de un artículo
leader	article de réclame	Lockartikel	chamariz	artículo de reclamo
lease	bail	Mietvertrag	contrato de aluguer; aluguel	Contrato de arrendamiento
lease abstract	résumé de bail	Kurzversion des Mietvertrags	sumário do contrato de aluguer; sumário do contrato de aluguel	Resumen del contrato de alquiler

	FRANÇAIS	DEUTSCH	PORTUGUÊS	ESPAÑOL
lease outline drawing (LOD)	dessin de l'espace loué	Nutzungsplan der zu vermietbaren Fläche	plano especificando o espaço para alugar	Croquis de la superficie en alquiler
lease summary report	rapport récapitulatif de location	Zusammenfassender Bericht über die vermietbare Fläche in einem Einkaufszentrum	relatório sumário do espaço para alugar; relatório resumido do contrato de aluguel	Resumen del contrato de arrendamiento
leasehold value	valeur locative; valeur d'une tenure à bail	Mietbesitzwert	valor da propriedade arrendada	Valor del alquiler
leasing fees and commissions	frais et commissions de location	Mietgebühren und –kurtagen	honorários e comissões para assegurar arrendatários; honorários e comissões referentes a locação	Honorarios y comisiones de alquiler
ledger	journal	Hauptbuch	razão	Libro mayor
legal and audit expenses	frais juridiques et frais de vérification	Anwalts- und Wirtschaftsprüfungsgebühren	despesas de contencioso e auditoria	Gastos de abogados y auditoría

	FRANÇAIS	DEUTSCH	PORTUGUÊS	ESPAÑOL
lessee	locataire	Mieter	arrendatário	Locatario
lessor	bailleur	Vermieter	arrendador	Arrendador
let	louer	Vermieten	alugar	Alquilar
lethal-weapons policy	politique relative aux armes dangereuses	Richtlinien für tödliche Waffen	normas referentes ao uso de armas letais	Política de armas letales
letter of intent	lettre d'intention	Absichtserklärung	carta de intenção	Carta de intención
letterpress	impression typographique	Buchdruck	tipografia	Tipografía
leverage	effet de levier de la dette; levier	Hebeleffekt durch Fremdfinanzierung	alavanca financeira; alavancagem	Apalancamiento
liability	responsabilité financière	Verbindlichkeit	responsabilidade financeira	Responsabilidad
liability insurance	assurance-responsabilité	Haftpflichtversicherung	seguro de responsabilidade civil	Seguro de responsabilidad civil
liability limit	limite de responsabilité	Haftungsgrenze	limite de responsabilidade	Límite de responsabilidad

	FRANÇAIS	DEUTSCH	PORTUGUÊS	ESPAÑOL
LIBOR	Libor	LIBOR	LIBOR - (taxa)	LIBOR - tasa de interés ofrecida en el mercado interbancario de Londres
lien	privilège, droit de gage	Pfandrecht	gravame	Gravamen
lifestyle data	données sur le mode de vie	Lebensstil-Daten, Life-Style-Daten	dados sobre o estilo de vida	Datos sobre el estilo de vida
LIFO	dernier entré, premier sorti (DEPS)	zuletzt eingegangenen, zuerst verbraucht (LIFO)	último que entra primeiro que sai	Últimas entradas, primeras salidas
lifts	couches	Einbauschicht	camada de asfalto	Capa de asfalto
limited-time station (daytimer)	station de radio diffusion à temps limité (de jour)	Tagessender zu beschränkten Zeiten	estação de rádio durante períodos limitados (diurnos)	Estación radial de tiempo limitado (durante el día)
line	ligne	Zeile	linha	Línea

	FRANÇAIS	DEUTSCH	PORTUGUÊS	ESPAÑOL
line art	dessin au trait	Strichzeichnung	material ilustrativo não fotográfico	Material ilustrativo no fotográfico
liquidated damages	indemnités ; dommages-intérêts fixés à l'avance	bezifferter Schadensersatz	danos apurados; danos liquidados por infração contratual	Daños liquidados
liquidation	liquidation	Liquidation	liquidação	Liquidación
liquidity	liquidité	Liquidität	liquidez	Liquidez
list price	prix de catalogue, prix courant	Katalogpreis	preço de tabela	Precio de lista
local ad rate	taux publicitaire local	Anzeigenpreis für ortsansässige Werbungtreibende	tarifa local publicidade	Tarifa local por publicidad
local alarm	alarme locale	lokale Alarmanlage	alarme local	Alarma local
local tenant	locataire local	lokaler Mieter	arrendatário local	Inquilino local

	FRANÇAIS	DEUTSCH	PORTUGUÊS	ESPAÑOL
lock-box structure	structure de dépôt sécurisé	gesicherte Deponierungsstruktur	valores de empréstimo, resgatados diretamente pelo lojista, depositados em conta especial do favorecido e deduzidos das primeiras receitas, para assegurar pagamento	Sistema en que los pagos de alquiler se mandan directamente al administrador fiduciario
logo (logotype) [Also known as sig cut]	logo (logotype) [également emblème]	Bildmarke	logo (logotipo)	Logo (logotipo)
LOI	lettre d'intérêt ou d'intention	Absichtserklärung	carta de intenções	Carta de intención
long term lease	bail à long terme	Mietvertrag auf lange Sicht	arrendamento a longo prazo	Alquiler a largo plazo
long-term liabilities	dettes à long terme	langfristige Verbindlichkeiten	passivo a longo prazo	Obligaciones a largo plazo
loss	perte	Verlust	perda	Pérdida
loss control specialist	spécialiste en contrôle des sinistres	Verlustkontrollexperte	especialista na avaliação de factores que possam causar danos e prejuízos	Especialista en el control de riesgos

	FRANÇAIS	DEUTSCH	PORTUGUÊS	ESPAÑOL
loss leader	produit d'appel vendu à perte	Lockangebot	artigo vendido com prejuízo	Artículo vendido con pérdida
low-end merchandise	bas de gamme marchandise	untere Preisklasse Waren	mercadoria de baixa gama	De nivel inferior mercadería
lump-sum contracts	contrats à montant forfaitaire	Vertrag mit Festpreisen	contrato por preço global	Contratos por una suma global
mace	macis	Tränengas	lacrimogéneo; mace para defesa pessoal	Gas para defensa personal
made-for-outlet goods	marchandise fabriquée pour centre de magasins d'usine	Fabrikverkaufsware	produtos fabricados especialmente para outlets	Productos fabricados para tiendas de fábrica
mailer	publipostage	Briefwerbematerial	envelope publicitário	Sobre publicitario
maintained markup	majoration maintenue	beibehaltene Handelsspanne	subida de preço mantida	Aumento sostenido

	FRANÇAIS	DEUTSCH	PORTUGUÊS	ESPAÑOL
maintenance	entretien	Wartung	Manutenção	Mantenimiento
maintenance and repair expenses	frais de maintenance et de réparation	Wartungs- und Reparaturkosten	despesas de manutenção e reparos	Gastos de mantenimiento y reparaciones
major tenant	locataire principal	Hauptmieter	loja principal	principal locatario
makegood	reprise, réclame gratuit de remplacement	Ersatzinserat	publicação suplementar grátis	Publicación adicional sin cargo
mall	centre commercial clos	Einkaufszentrum	centro comercial	Centro comercial cerrado
mall manager	directeur du centre commercial	Center-Manager	gerente do centro comercial	Administrador de un centro comercial
mall mayor	maire du centre commercial	Bürgermeister eines Einkaufszentrums	Prefeito de um centro comercial	"alcalde" de un centro comercial

	FRANÇAIS	DEUTSCH	PORTUGUÊS	ESPAÑOL
management fee	frais de gestion	Verwaltungsgebühren	comissão de gestão; taxa/ honorários de administração	Honorarios por administración
management vision	vision de la direction	Management-Vision	visão da administração	Visión del personal gerencial
mandatory advertising	publicité obligatoire	vertraglich vorgeschriebe Werbung	publicidade obrigatória	Publicidad obligatoria
marginal cost of capital	coût marginal du capital	marginale Kapitalkosten	custo marginal do capital	Costo marginal del capital
markdown	solde	Preisabschlag	descontos especiais; remarcação de preços para menos	Reducción del precio
market analysis	analyse de marché	Marktanalyse	análise do mercado	Análisis de mercado
market area	aire de marché	Absatzgebiet	área de mercado	Área de mercado
market benchmarks	repères de marché	Vergleiche mit anderen Märkten	padrões de referência do mercado	Cotas de referencia del mercado

	FRANÇAIS	DEUTSCH	PORTUGUÊS	ESPAÑOL
market cap	capitalisation boursière	Marktkapital	capitalização de mercado	Capitalización de mercado
market data	données de marché	Marktdaten	dados de mercado	Datos de mercado
market-data approach	méthode d'évaluation basé sur les données du marché	Marktwertermittlungsverfahren für Grundstücke	avaliação baseada nos dados de mercado	Método de tasación basado en los datos del mercado
market penetration	pénétration du marché	Marktdurchdringung	penetração de mercado	Penetración del mercado
market plan	plan de marché	Marktplan	plano de mercado	Plan de mercado
market population	population du marché	Marktpopulation	população de mercado	Población del mercado
market potential	potentiel du marché	Marktpotential	potencial de mercado	Potencial del mercado
market profile	profil de marché	Marktprofil	perfil de mercado	Perfil del mercado

	FRANÇAIS	DEUTSCH	PORTUGUÊS	ESPAÑOL
market rent	loyer du marché; loyer établi en fonction du marché	Marktübliche Miete	renda orçamentada; aluguel de mercado	Alquiler calculado en base al mercado
market research	étude de marché	Marktforschung	pesquisa de mercado	Investigación de mercado
market research process	processus d'étude de marché	Marktforschungs- verfahren	processo de pesquisa de mercado	Proceso de investigación de mercado
market sales approach	méthode d'évaluation basé sur les ventes sur le marché	Marktwertermittlungs- verfahren für Verkäufe	avaliação baseada nas vendas do mercado	Método de tasación basado en las ventas del mercado
market segmentation	segmentation du marché	Marktsegmentierung	segmentação do mercado	Segmentación del mercado
market share	part de marché	Marktanteil	participação no mercado	Participación en el mercado
market study	étude de marché	Marktstudie	estudo de mercado	Estudio de mercado

	FRANÇAIS	DEUTSCH	PORTUGUÊS	ESPAÑOL
market universe	univers de marché	statistische Masse eines Markts	universo de mercado	Universo del mercado
market value	valeur marchande	Marktwert	valor de mercado	Valor de mercado
marketing	marketing ; techniques de commercialisation	Marketing	marketing	Marketing
marketing direction	orientation du marketing	gezieltes Marketing	alvo de marketing	Orientación del mkt.
marketing director	directeur du marketing, directeur commercial	Marketing-Direktor	director de marketing	Director de marketing
marketing fund	fonds de marketing	Marketing-Fonds	fundo para despesas de marketing	Fondo para gastos de marketing
marketing fund advisory board	comité consultatif du fonds de marketing	Beratender Ausschuss bezüglich des - Marketing Fonds	grupo consultivo do fundo para despesas de marketing; conselho consultivo para o fundo de marketing	Junta de asesoramiento del fondo para gastos de marketing

	FRANÇAIS	DEUTSCH	PORTUGUÊS	ESPAÑOL
markup	majoration	Handelsspanne	margem de benefício; preço com margem de lucro	Margen de beneficio
marriage mail	publipostage combiné	Gemeinschafts briefwerbung	envelope de publicidade combinada	Sobre publicitario combinado
masthead	bloc-générique, placard administratif	Masttopp	cabeçalho de uma publicação	Mancheta
mat	matériel dont une publicité est imprimé	Matrize	matriz	Matriz
maximum milline rate	tarif maximum par ligne (taux de ligne x 1,000,000 divisé par la circulation)	Anzeigenpreis pro Agate-Zeile für eine Auflage von einer Million	tarifa máxima por linha de coluna por milhão de exemplares	Tarifa máxima de la línea de una columna por millón de ejemplares
mean	moyenne	Mittelwert	média; meio-termo	Media; medio (promedio)
mechanical	maquette de mise en page	Reinlayout	modelo	Molde

	FRANÇAIS	DEUTSCH	PORTUGUÊS	ESPAÑOL
media	médias	Medien	meios de comunicação; mídia	Medios (de comunicación)
media alert	alerte médias	Media Alert	ângulos do artigo; sumário publicitário com os fatos básicos de um artigo	Alerta de los medios
media kit	pochette d'informations aux médias	Pressemappe	comunicados aos media; kit/pacote de informações à mídia	Paquete de información para los medios
media plan	plan de médias	Medienplan	plano dos media; plano de mídia	Esquema de los medios considerados
media representative	représentant auprès des médias	Vertreter der Medien	representante dos meios de comunicação	Representante de los medios
median	médian; médiane	Medianwert	mediana; mediano	Mediano/a
membrane	membrane	Dachhaut	membrana	Membrana
merchandise manager	directeur du service de marchandises	Produkt-Manager	gerente comercial; gerente de produto	Gerente comercial

	FRANÇAIS	DEUTSCH	PORTUGUÊS	ESPAÑOL
merchandise mix	éventail de marchandises	Produkt-Mix	mistura de mercadorias; mix de mercadorias	Variedad de mercaderías
merchandise plan	plan de marchandises	Produktprognose	plano de comercialização	Plan de comercialización
merchandising	marchandisage	Merchandising	comercialização; merchandising	Comercialización
merchants' association	association des commerçants	Einzelhandelsverband	associação de comerciantes; associação de lojistas	Asociación de comerciantes
merchants' association articles of incorporation	acte constitutif de l'association de commerçants/marchands	Gründungsurkunde des Einzelhandelsverbands	estatutos de uma sociedade associação de comerciantes; instrumento de incorporação à associação de lojistas	Escritura de constitución de la asociación de comerciantes
merchants' association by-laws	statuts de l'association des commerçants; statuts/règlements de l'association de commerçants/marchands	Satzungen des Einzelhandelsverbands	estatutos de associação de comerciantes; estatutos da associação de lojistas	Estatutos de la asociación de comerciantes

	FRANÇAIS	DEUTSCH	PORTUGUÊS	ESPAÑOL
merchants' association dues	frais de cotisation à l'association de commerçants/marchands	Einzelhandelsverbandsgebühren	obrigações financeiras da associação de comerciantes; contribuições da associação de lojistas	Cuotas de la asociación de comerciantes
metropolitan area	zone métropolitaine	Stadtgebiet	área metropolitana	Área metropolitana
metropolitan statistical area (MSA)	zone statistique métropolitaine	statistisches Stadtgebiet (MSA)	área estatística metropolitana	Área estadística metropolitana
midnight sale	vente de minuit	einmaliger, bis etwa Mitternacht dauernder Abendverkauf	liquidação até à meia-noite, apenas numa noite	Liquidación de una sola noche hasta la medianoche
milline rate	tarif par ligne (taux de ligne x 1.000.000 divisé par la circulation)	Anzeigenpreis pro Agate-Zeile für eine Auflage von einer Million	tarifa por linha de coluna por milhão de exemplares	Tarifa por la línea de una columna por millón de ejemplares
minimum rent	loyer minimum	Mindestmiete	aluguer mínimo; aluguel mínimo	Alquiler mínimo

	FRANÇAIS	DEUTSCH	PORTUGUÊS	ESPAÑOL
misdemeanor	infraction	Vergehen	delito relativamente leve	Delito de menor cuantía
mix	composition	Marketing-Mix	mistura	combinación
mixed-use centers	centres à utilisation mixte	Mehrzweck-Center	centros de utilização mista	Centros de usos combinados
mode	mode	Modus	modo	Modo
modernization	modernisation	Modernisierung	modernização	Modernización
modified bitumen	bitume modifié	Modifiziertes Bitumen	betume modificado	Betún modificado
mom-and-pop store	magasin unique sans succursales souvent géré par une famille	Tante-Emma-Laden	loja cujos proprietários apenas possuem uma loja única; loja única de propriedade familiar	Tienda cuyos propietarios sólo poseen esa sola tienda
moonlight sale	vente de nuit	einmaliger, bis 23 Uhr dauernder Abendverkauf	liquidação de uma noite, geralmente indo até às 23 horas	Liquidación de una sola noche hasta las 11:00 P.M.
mortgage	prêt immobilier; hypothèque	Hypothek	hipoteca	hipoteca

	FRANÇAIS	DEUTSCH	PORTUGUÊS	ESPAÑOL
mortgage constant	hypothèque à paiements constants	Hypothekentilgung, ausgedrückt als Prozentsatz des Darlehens	constante hipotecária	Constante hipotecaria
mortgage, wraparound	deuxième hypothèque comprenant le premier hypothèque	Zweithypothek garantiert mit dem Gegenstand der ersten	segunda hipoteca	Hipoteca refinanciada
motion detector	détecteur de mouvements	Bewegungsmelder	detector de movimento	Detector de movimiento
MSA	zone statistique métropolitaine	statistisches Stadtgebiet (MSA)	área estatística metropolitana	Área estadística metropolitana
multiple percentage rate	taux de pourcentage multiple	mehrfacher Prozentsatz	taxas de percentagem múltiplas	Tasa porcentual múltiple
multiple prime contracts	contrats principaux multiples	mehrfache Hauptverträge	contratos principais múltiplos	Contratos principales múltiples
multiplex cinema	multiplex	Multiplex-Kinokomplex	complexo com várias salas de cinema; multiplex de cinemas	Multicine

	FRANÇAIS	DEUTSCH	PORTUGUÊS	ESPAÑOL
mystery shoppers	acheteurs mystérieux	Ladenbeobachtungsverfahren zur Bewertung des Personals, der Warenpräsentation usw.	compradores misteriosos	Compradores misteriosos
named insured	assuré nommé	benannter Versicherer	segurado nomeado	Asegurado nombrado
named-peril insurance	assurance à sinistres nommés	benannte Gefahrenpolice	seguro de sistema de individualização dos riscos cobertos	Seguro contra el riesgo nombrado
national rate	taux national	nationaler Ansatz	taxa nacional	Tasa nacional
national tenant	locataire national	Einzelhändler auf nationaler Ebene	retalhista a nível nacional; varejista a nível nacional	Minorista a nivel nacional
natural breakpoint	seuil de rentabilité naturel	Natürlicher Kostendeckungspunkt	ponto limite natural; ponto de equilíbrio natural	Punto de equilibrio natural
natural disaster	catastrophe naturelle	Naturkatastrophe	catástrofe natural	Desastre natural
negligence	négligence	Fahrlässigkeit	negligência	Negligencia

	FRANÇAIS	DEUTSCH	PORTUGUÊS	ESPAÑOL
negligent hiring	embauche négligente	Fahrlässige Personaleinstellung	contratação negligente	Contratación negligente
negligent retention	rétention négligente	Fahrlässige Belassung im Arbeitsverhältnis	retenção negligente	Retención negligente
negligent security training	formation négligente à la sécurité	Fahrlässige Ausbildung des Wach- und Sicherheitsdienst-personals	formação profissional e treino negligente; treinamento negligente ou insuficiente para empregado de segurança	Capacitación negligente sobre seguridad
negotiated bid	appel d'offres négocié	Freihändiges Angebot	proposta negociada; proposta concorrência para projeto	Licitación negociada
negotiated contract	contrat négocié	ausgehandelter Vertrag	contrato negociado	Contrato negociado
negotiated inducements	incitatifs négociés	ausgehandelte Anreize	Incentivos negociados	Incentivos negociados
neighborhood centers	centres de voisinage	Nachbarschafts-Einkaufszentren	centros de vizinhança	Centros del vecindario

	FRANÇAIS	DEUTSCH	PORTUGUÊS	ESPAÑOL
net	net	Netto	Líquido	Neto
net income	revenu net	Nettoeinkommen	Rendimento líquido	Ingreso neto
net lease	bail net	Nettomiete	arrendamento líquido	Alquiler neto
net operating income	revenu net d'exploitation	betriebliche Nettoerträge	rendimento operacional líquido	Ingresos netos de explotación
net present value (NPV)	valeur actualisée nette	aktualisierter Wert	valor actual líquido	Valor neto actual
net price	prix net	Nettopreis	preço líquido	Precio neto
net profit	bénéfice net	Reingewinn	lucro líquido	Ganancia neta
net profit projection	prévision de bénéfices nets	Nettoumsatzprojektion	projecção de lucro líquido	Proyección de la ganancia neta
net sales	ventes nettes	Nettoumsatz	vendas líquidas	Ventas netas
net worth	valeur nette	Reinvermögen	activo líquido; patrimônio líquido	Valor neto
news conference	conférence de presse	Pressekonferenz	conferência de imprensa	Conferencia de prensa

	FRANÇAIS	DEUTSCH	PORTUGUÊS	ESPAÑOL
news release	communiqué de presse	Pressemitteilung	comunicado de imprensa	Comunicado de prensa
nonanchors	locataires; locataires UCD ; locataires des magasins non principaux	Einzelhandelsgeschäfte, die nicht als Absatzmagnete des Einkaufszentrums wirken	lojas ou estabelecimentos que não operam como geradores primários de tráfego; lojas satélites	Tiendas secundarias (no anclas)
noncash charges	frais hors caisse	nicht ausgebenwirksame Kosten	encargos não monetários	Cargos no en efectivo
noncash expenses	frais non en espèces	bargeldlose Aufwendungen	despesas não monetárias	Gastos no en efectivo
noncurrent liabilities	passif à long terme	langfristige Verbindlichkeiten	passivo exigível a longo prazo	Pasivo no corriente
nondisturbance covenant	clause de jouissance paisible	Klausel, die dem Mieter unterbrechungs freien Geschäftsbetrieb zusichert	cláusula garantindo a não perturbação da operação contínua; cláusula assegurando a não interrupção da operação	Cláusula de garantía de operación continua
nonlethal weapons	armes non meurtrières	nichttödliche Waffen	armas não letais	Armas no mortales

	FRANÇAIS	DEUTSCH	PORTUGUÊS	ESPAÑOL
nonoperating tenants	locataires (qui n'exploitent pas d'activités commerciales)	Miete zahlende Mieter, die ihre Geschäfte aufgegeben haben	locatários não operacionais	Locatarios no operativos
nonpreemptible spots	les spots les plus chers qui ne peuvent pas être préemptées	unabsetzbare Werbesendungen	spots publicitários que não podem substituídos	espacios de publicidad no reemplazables
nonrecourse loans	prêt sans recours	Hypotheken, bei denen ein Rückgriff auf das persönliche Vermögen des Schuldners ausgeschlossen ist	empréstimos sem acesso a recursos	Préstamos sin recursos
nonretail tenants	locataires non détaillants	Mieter, die kein Einzelhandelsgeschäft betreiben	arrendatários não retalhistas; locatários não varejistas	Inquilinos comerciales no minoristas
notice to quit	avis d'expulsion; avis de congé	Kündigung des Mietvertrags	mandato de despejo; notificação de despejo	Intimación de desalojo

	FRANÇAIS	DEUTSCH	PORTUGUÊS	ESPAÑOL
NPV	valeur actuelle nette	aktualisierter Wert	valor actual líquido	Valor neto actual
occupancy area	surface d'occupation	gesamte Belegungsfläche	área de ocupação	Área de ocupación
occupancy cost	coût d'occupation	Kosten der Belegung	custo de ocupação	Costo de ocupación
occupancy cost ratio	coefficient du coût d'occupation	Quotient der Belegungs kosten/Gesamtumsatz	razão de custo de ocupação /volume anual de vendas	Relación volumen anual de ventas/costo de ocupación
occupancy rate	taux d'occupation	Belegungssatz	proporção de ocupação; taxa de ocupação	Proporción de ocupación
occurrence	survenance	Vorfall	ocorrência	Acontecimiento
OES	mise à l'horaire effective optimale	optimale Werbewirksamkeit (OES)	programação efetiva optimizada	Programación eficaz óptima
office equipment expenses	frais du matériel de bureau	Ausgaben für Büroausstattung	despesas de equipamento de escritório	Gastos de equipamiento de oficinas

	FRANÇAIS	DEUTSCH	PORTUGUÊS	ESPAÑOL
off-price advertising	publicité de la marchandise à prix réduits	Werbung für zeitlich begrenzte Sonderangebote	promoções de mercadorias a preço reduzido	Publicidad de mercaderías a precio reducido
off-price centers	centres de marchandise à prix réduits	Einkaufszentren, die Markenwaren erster Wahl zu reduzierten Preisen anbieten	centros de venda de mercadorias a preço reduzido	Centros de venta de mercadería a precios rebajados
off-price retailing	vente au détail à prix réduits	Verkauf von Markenwaren zu reduzierten Preisen	venda a retalho a preços reduzidos; venda no varejo a preços reduzidos	Venta minorista de productos de marca a precios reducidos
offset	compensation	Verrechnung	compensação	Compensación
offset printing	impression offset	Offset-Druck	impressão off-set	Impresión offset
on the break	pause entre deux programmes	Werbesendung zwischen zwei Programmen	anúncio entre dois programas	(comercial) entre dos programas
one-line budget	budget abrégé	abgekürzter Haushaltsplan	orçamento breve; orçamento abreviado	Presupuesto de un solo renglón

	FRANÇAIS	DEUTSCH	PORTUGUÊS	ESPAÑOL
on-site payroll and benefits	fiche de paie; salaires et avantages du personnel sur le site	Löhne und Gehälter sowie Nebenleistungen zahlbar an das Personal des Einkaufszentrums	folha de pagamentos e benefícios do pessoal directamente envolvido na administração do centro comercial	Nómina y beneficios del personal que administra directamente el centro comercial
open and operate provision	clause d'exploitation; clause de début et de maintien de l'exploitation	Klausel, die den Mieter verpflichtet, seine gemietete Fläche für Geschäftszwecke zu nutzen	cláusula requerendo que o locatário inicie ou mantenha as suas actividades comerciais no local que arrendou	Cláusula que exige al locatario iniciar o mantener la explotación del local que ocupa
open rate	taux ouvert	offener Tarif	tarifa aberta	Tasa abierta
open-to-buy	montant libre à l'achat	verfügbarer Betrag zum Einkauf	disponível para compra	Disponible para compra
open windows	vitrines ouvertes	offene Fenster	montras abertas; vitrinas abertas	Vitrinas abiertas
opening contribution	contribution à l'ouverture	einmaliger Beitrag zum Öffnungsfonds	Contribuição para o fundo de gastos de inauguração	Contribución para gastos de inauguración

	FRANÇAIS	DEUTSCH	PORTUGUÊS	ESPAÑOL
operating budget	budget d'exploitation	Funktionsbudget	orçamento operacional	Presupuesto de explotación
operating cost ratio	coefficient des frais d'exploitation	Verhältnis von Betriebskosten zu Nettoumsatzerlösen	rácio de custos operacionais; índice de custos operacionais	Relación costos de explotación
operating expenses	frais d'exploitation	Betriebskosten	custos operacionais	Gastos de explotación
operating margin	marge d'exploitation	Betriebsgewinnspanne	margem operacional	Margen de operación
operating statement	état d'exploitation	Gewinn- und Verlustrechnung	extracto de conta operacional; relatório das operações	Estado de resultados de operación
operating year	exercice d'exploitation	Geschäftsjahr	Ano operacional; exercício anual operacional	Ejercicio anual
optimum effective scheduling (OES)	mise à l'horaire effective optimale	Sendezeitplanung für optimale Werbewirksamkeit (OES)	programação efectiva optimizada	Programación eficaz optima
orbit	orbite	Orbit	órbita	órbita

	FRANÇAIS	DEUTSCH	PORTUGUÊS	ESPAÑOL
OTB	ouvert pour achats	verfübarer Betrag zum Einkauf	disponível para compra	Disponible para la compra
OTO (one time only)	OTO (une seule fois)	einmalige Werbesendung	apenas uma vez	Única vez
outboard	aire commerciale en sens opposé au district urbain central	Einkaufsgebiet, das aus der Sicht eines Einkaufszentrums in Stadtauswärtsrichtung liegt	zona comercial ao lado do centro comercial afastado do distrito central da cidade	Área comercial al lado de un centro comercial alejada del distrito urbano central
outlet centers	centre de magasins d'usine; centres de magasins entrepôts	Fabrikoutlet-Zentren	centros de lojas de fábrica tiendas de	Centros de fábrica
outlet retailer	magasin d'usine	Einzelhandelsgeschäft, das Markenwaren zu einem verbilligten Preis anbietet	unidade retalhista com preços de fábrica; loja de fábrica	Negocio minorista con precios de fábrica

	FRANÇAIS	DEUTSCH	PORTUGUÊS	ESPAÑOL
outlot tenant	locataire en périphérie	freistehendes Einzelhandelsgeschäft, meist auf einem separaten Grundstück vor dem Einkaufszentrum	estabelecimento localizado numa parcela de terreno em frente de um centro comercial	Tienda situada en la parte del frente de un centro comercial
outparcels	parcelles du périmètre	unbenutzte Teile am Rand des Einkaufszentrums, exkl. Parkplätze	parcelas por utilizar num centro comercial constituindo as áreas do perímetro	Parcelas perimetrales del emplazamiento de un centro comercial
outposting	placement temporaire d'un locataire à des fins promotionnelles	temporärer Verkaufsstand	locatário colocado temporariamente para fazer uma promoção; colocação temporária de inquilino de loja satélite para promover um produto novo	Publicidad temporaria fuera del local

	FRANÇAIS	DEUTSCH	PORTUGUÊS	ESPAÑOL
overage rent	loyer excédentaire ; loyer sur ventes brutes excédentaires	auf den Bruttoumsatz, über die Gewinnschwelle hinaus des Mieters zu zahlende Prozentmiete	percentagem de renda paga sobre as vendas brutas que ultrapassam o ponto limite especificado	Porcentaje del alquiler abonado sobre las ventas brutas en exceso del punto de equilibrio estipulado
overages	loyer excédentaire	Zusatzmiete	pagamento excedente de aluguer; aluguel acima do mínimo	Alquiler excedente
overhead	frais généraux	fixe Kosten	despesas fixas	Gastos fijos
overstocks	stocks excédentaires	überfüllte Warenlager	estoques excedentes	existencias excesivas
owner's protection coverage	couverture de protection du propriétaire	Schutzhaftversicherung des Eigentümers	apólice de seguro de protecção do proprietário	Cobertura de protección del propietario
package	groupe	Pauschale	pacote	paquete

	FRANÇAIS	DEUTSCH	PORTUGUÊS	ESPAÑOL
pad	parcelle de terrain en périphérie ; parcelle de terrain où se situe un grand magasin	exakte Grundfläche des Landes, auf dem ein Einkaufszentrum steht	parcela de terreno onde se situa o edifício de um armazém; terreno de uma grande loja	Parcela de tierra donde se erige el edificio de una tienda de departamentos
pad tenant	locataire en périphérie	freistehendes Einzelhandelsgeschäft, meist auf einem separaten Grundstück vor dem Einkaufszentrum center	estabelecimento localizado numa parcela de terreno em frente de um centro comercial; inquilino em lote de frente para o shopping	Tienda situada en una parcela separada en la parte del frente de un centro comercial
paint unit	panneau d'affichage	bemalter Anschlag	placard de informações	Cartelera
parking area	aire de stationnement	Parkplatzbereich	estacionamento	Área de estacionamiento
parking lot cleaning/sweeping/repair expenses	frais de nettoyage/balayage/réparation du terrain de stationnement	Reinigungs-, Kehr- und Reparaturkosten für den Parkplatz	despesas de reparação/limpeza/varredura do parque de estacionamento	Gastos de limpieza/barrido/reparación del área de estacionamiento

	FRANÇAIS	DEUTSCH	PORTUGUÊS	ESPAÑOL
parking ratio	ratio de stationnement	Parkquotient	proporção de estacionamento	Relación de estacionamiento
pass-along reader	lecteur secondaire	Folgeleser	leitor de publicações gratuitas	Lector por transferencia
pass-through expenses	dépenses récupérables; frais récupérables; frais imputables	vom Mieter zu bezahlende Nebenkosten	despesas transferíveis	Gastos transferidos por el arrendador a las tiendas arrendatarias
patching	rapiéçage	Dach- und Ausbesserungsverfahren	procedimento de reparação; reparos no telhado ou piso	parcheo
pending nonrenewal	achat d'un spot en attendant le non-renouvellement	schwebend bis zur Nichterneuerung	spot publicitário pendente de renovação pelo anunciante, que já adquiriu o spot	Sin renovación pendiente
penetration ratio	taux de pénétration	Penetrationsquotient	relação de penetração; índice de penetração	Índice de penetración
per capita	par tête	pro Kopf	per capita	Per cápita

	FRANÇAIS	DEUTSCH	PORTUGUÊS	ESPAÑOL
per capita income	revenu par tête	Pro-Kopf-Einkommen	rendimento per capita; renda per capita	Ingreso per cápita
per capita retail sales	ventes au détail par tête	Einzelhandelsverkäufe pro Kopf	vendas a retalho per capita; vendas a varejo per capita	Ventas al por menor per cápita
per inquiry (PI)	par demande	Werbung auf Anfragebasis	por solicitação	Por orden
percentage rent	loyer variable	Prozentmiete	aluguer percentual; aluguel percentual	Alquiler porcentual
perils	périls	Gefahren	Perigos	Riesgos
perimeter protection	protection du périmètre	Schutz der Grenzen des Einkaufszentrums	protecção do perímetro	Protección perimetral
permitted use	usage permis ; utilisation autorisée	gestatteter Benutzungszweck	Uso permitido	Uso permitido
personal guarantee	garantie personnelle	persönliche Garantie	garantia pessoal	Garantía personal
personal injury	blessures corporelles	Personenschaden	acidente pessoal	Lesión personal
photo opportunity	occasion de photo	Photogelegenheit	oportunidade fotográfica	Oportunidad para fotografías

	FRANÇAIS	DEUTSCH	PORTUGUÊS	ESPAÑOL
pica	pica	Pica	Cícero; pica (tipografia/tipo de letra)	Pica
piece goods	marchandise à la pièce	Stückgut	materiais utilizados para a confecção de roupa	Mercadería por pieza
piggyback	en cascade	Huckepacksendung	transmissão publicitária de dois produtos	Promoción con producto añadido
pitch	vendre une idée	Verkaufspräsentation	apresentação ao chefe de redacção de um ângulo para um artigo; apresentação de uma ideia a um editor	Presentar al editor una idea para una historia
plainclothes officers	agents en civil	Sicherheitsbeamte in Zivil	policia à paisana	Policías de civil
plies	couches	Lagen der Dachpapp eneindeckung	camadas de feltro e betume edificadas durante a construção de um telhado com vários revestimentos	Capas de fieltro y betún formadas durante la creación de un techo armado

	FRANÇAIS	DEUTSCH	PORTUGUÊS	ESPAÑOL
plot plan	plan de terrain	Grundrissplanung	plano parcelar; plano do terreno	Plano de terreno
ply	couche	eine der Lagen der Dachpappeneindeckung	camada de material para telhados	Capa de material de techo
PNR (pending nonrenewall)	achat d'un spot en attendant le non-renouvellement	schwebend bis zur Nichterneuerung	spot publicitário pendente de renovação pelo anunciante, que já adquiriu o spot	Sin renovación pendiente
point-of-origin survey	sondage point d'origine	Erhebung über Kundenadressen	inquérito de ponto de origem; pesquisa de ponto de origem	Encuesta de punto de origen
point size	force de corps d'un caractère	Schriftkegelgröße	tamanho de letra	Cuerpo (de tipo de imprenta)
policy	police	Police	apólice de seguro	Póliza
policyholder	titulaire de police	Policenbesitzer	segurado	Tenedor de la póliza
ponding (Also known as ponds)	affaissement	Delle (im Asphalt-pflaster, wo sich Wasser ansammelt)	área de acumulação de águas	Área baja donde se acumula el agua

	FRANÇAIS	DEUTSCH	PORTUGUÊS	ESPAÑOL
poster	affiche	Plakat	cartaz	cartel
posting	report	Nachbuchung	lançamento nos livros	Pase de asientos
pothole	nid de poule	Schlagloch	cova no leito do pavimento	bache
power center	centre régional; megacentre; centre à plusieurs locataires importants	Einkaufszentrum mit mehreren Geschäften, die als Absatzmagnete fungieren	centro dominado por várias lojas principais; shopping com concentração de grandes marcas (lojistas)	Centro dominado por varios centros comerciales de gran magnitud
preaudit	prévérification	Vorprüfung	auditoria preliminar	Auditoria preliminar
preempt	préemptable	absetzbarer Verkauf	preempção	Comprar con derecho preferente
preemptible spots	spots vendu à prix réduit préemptables moyennant l'offre d'un tarif plus élevé	absetzbare Werbesendung	spots publicitários que podem ser substituídos	Espacios de publicidad preferenciales
preferred positioning	positionnement préférentiel	Vorzugsplatzierung	posicionamento preferido	Posicionamiento preferencial

	FRANÇAIS	DEUTSCH	PORTUGUÊS	ESPAÑOL
premium	prime	Prämie	prémio de seguro	Prima
prepaid expenses	frais payés d'avance	vorausbezahlte Kosten	despesas pagas antecipadamente	Gastos abonados por adelantado
present value (PV)	valeur actuelle	aktueller Wert	valor actual; valor presente	Valor actual
primary market	marché principal	Hauptabsatzgebiet	mercado primário	Mercado principal
primary research	recherche principale	Primärforschung	pesquisa primária	Investigación principal
primary trading area	marché principale ; zone de commerce principale	Haupteinzugsgebiet	área comercial primária	Área de comercio principal
prime rate	taux principale	Hauptzinssatz	taxa primária	Tasa principal
prime time	heure de grande écoute	Hauptsendezeit	hora de maior audiência; horário nobre	Horas de mayor audiencia

	FRANÇAIS	DEUTSCH	PORTUGUÊS	ESPAÑOL
private placement	placement privé	Privatplatzierung	colocação privada; venda de acções diretamente pela empresa emitente, as quais são oferecidas a um grupo limitado de investidores institucionais	Colocación de títulos o acciones en un círculo determinado de clientes exenta del cumplimiento de los requisitos exigidos por la Comisión de la Bolsa de Valores
pro forma	pro forma	Proforma	pró-forma	Pro forma
pro rata share	part proportionnelle	anteilige Kosten	comparticipação pro rata; participação pro-rata	Participación a prorrata
probability distribution	répartition des probabilités	Wahrscheinlichkeitsverteilung	distribuição de probabilidades	Distribución de probabilidades
process color	photogravure en couleur; couleur de la quadrichromie	Prozessfarbe	impressão de cores processadas	Color de proceso

	FRANÇAIS	DEUTSCH	PORTUGUÊS	ESPAÑOL
professional fee	honoraire professionnel	Honorar	honorários profissionais	Honorarios profesionales
profit	bénéfice	Gewinn	lucro	Ganancia
profit and loss statement	bilan financier; état des résultats	Gewinn- und Verlustrechnung	conta de ganhos e perdas; demonstrativo de lucros e perdas	Estado de pérdidas y ganancias
project delivery approaches	approches de livraison du projet	Projektausführungs-verfahren	métodos de abordagem para realização do projecto	Criterios de ejecución del proyecto
project management	gestion de projet	Projekt-Management	gestão do projecto	Administración del proyecto
promotion	promotion	Verkaufsförderung	promoção	Promoción
promotion fund contribution	contribution au fonds de promotion	Beitragszahlung des Mieters zum Marketing-Fonds	contribuição para o fundo de promoções	Contribución al fondo para promociones
promotional license agreement	contrat de permis promotionnel	Lizenzvereinbarung zur Verkaufsförderung	acordo de licença de promoção	Convenio de licencia de promoción

	FRANÇAIS	DEUTSCH	PORTUGUÊS	ESPAÑOL
promotions	frais de promotions ou de manifestations spéciales	Ausgaben für Verkaufsförderung und Sonderveranstaltungen	despesas com eventos especiais ou promoções	Gastos por promociones o eventos especiales
proof	épreuve	Korrekturbogen	prova tipográfica	Prueba (de imprenta)
property damage	dommages matériels	Sachschaden	danos materiais	Daños patrimoniales
property insurance	assurance de biens	Sachversicherung	seguro contra danos materiais	Seguros contra daños a la propiedad
property, plant, and equipment	propriété, usine et équipement	Vermögenswerte wie Grundstücke, Gebäude und Einrichtungen	activos corpóreos; ativo imobilizado/ propriedades	Propiedad, planta y equipo
proprietary security	sécurité interne	interne Sicherheitsmaß-nahmen des Einkaufszentrums	segurança interna	Seguridad interna
protected premises	lieux protégés	überwachte Bereiche	instalações protegidas	Instalaciones protegidas

	FRANÇAIS	DEUTSCH	PORTUGUÊS	ESPAÑOL
PruneYard court case	jugement PruneYard	Entscheidung im PruneYard-Fall	caso judicial PruneYard	Caso judicial PruneYard
PSAs	annonces de services publics	Ansagen des öffentlichen Dienstes (PSA)	notificações de serviço público	Anuncios de servicio público
psychographics	psychographie	Psychographie	psicográficos	Psicografía
psychological testing	tests psychologiques	psychologische Untersuchung	exame psicológico	Pruebas psicológicas
public relations	relations publiques	Public Relations	relações públicas	Relaciones públicas
public service announcements (PSAs)	annonces de service publiques	Ansagen des öffent-lichen Dienstes (PSA)	notificações de serviço público	Anuncios de servicio público
publicity	publicité	Werbung	publicidade	Publicidad
publicity release	communiqué de publicité	Werbemitteilung	informação/comunicado publicitário	Información publicitaria
pub-set	texte et montage	Satzanzeige	cópia e traçado	Copia y trazado

	FRANÇAIS	DEUTSCH	PORTUGUÊS	ESPAÑOL
put to bed	clôture	Redaktionsende	encerramento de uma publicação	Cierre de una publicación
PV	valeur actuelle	aktueller Wert	valor actual; valor presente	Valor actual
quick assets	actif disponible et réalisable	leicht realisierbare Aktiva	activos disponíveis	Activo disponible
quick ratio	coefficient de liquidité relative	Liquidität ersten Grades, leicht realisierbare Aktiva in Prozent der kurzfristigen Verbindlichkeiten	rácio de liquidez reduzida; quociente de liquidez imediata	Relación entre activo disponible y pasivo corriente
quiet enjoyment clause	clause de jouissance paisible	Klausel über die ungestörte Nutzung	cláusula de usufruto sem impedimento	Cláusula de goce sin impedimento
quote rates	taux établis	Kostensatz für die Wartung der Gemeinschaftsanlagen, Grundstückssteuer usw	taxas calculadas	Tasas calculadas
racetrack design	concept (piste de course)	Rennbahndesign	desenho do tipo pista de corrida	Diseño en forma de pista de corridas

	FRANÇAIS	DEUTSCH	PORTUGUÊS	ESPAÑOL
radio A time	temps radio A	Radiosendezeit A	Horário de rádio A	Horario radial A
radio AA time	temps radio AA	Radiosendezeit AA	Horário de rádio AA	Horario radial AA
radio AAA time	temps radio AAA	Radiosendezeit AAA	Horário de rádio AAA	Horario radial AAA
radius restriction	restriction de rayon	Radiusbeschränkung	Restrição de alcance	Restricción de alcance
radius (restriction) clause	clause de (restriction à un) rayon	Radiusklausel (Beschränkung)	cláusula (de restrição) de alcance	Cláusula (de restricción) de alcance
rate card	liste de tarifs	Tarifliste	Lista de tarifas de publicidade	Lista de tarifas de publicidad
rate holder	réclame de maintien du tarif	Tarifhalter	condições para manter um anúncio em determinada ocasião ou com desconto	Condiciones para que el anunciante se asegure una determinada hora o descuento

	FRANÇAIS	DEUTSCH	PORTUGUÊS	ESPAÑOL
rate of retention	taux de rétention	Mietpreis bei Verlänge-rung des Mietvertrag	valor de retenção	Tasa de retención
rate of return on assets	taux de rendement sur les actifs	Gewinn in % des inves-tierten Gesamtkapitals	taxa de rendibilidade dos activos	Tasa de rendimiento de los activos
rates and data book	livre des tarifs et données	Preisansätze über Veröffentlichung und Daten	livro de tarifas e dados	Libro de tarifas y datos
rating	cote	Einschaltquote	índice de audiência	Índice de audiencia
rating point	point de cote	Prozentpunkt der Zuschauerschaft	ponto de índice	Punto del índice de audiencia
raveling	érosion	Erosion	desmoronamento da textura do pavimento; desmoronamento da textura da pavimentação	Desmoron-amiento en el borde de carreteras
reach	portée	Reichweite	alcance	Alcance
reach and frequency	portée et fréquence	Reichweite und Frequenz	alcance e frequência	Alcance y frecuencia

	FRANÇAIS	DEUTSCH	PORTUGUÊS	ESPAÑOL
real income	revenu réel	Realeinkommen	rendimento real; renda real	Ingresos reales
recapture	récupération	Rückfluß	recuperação	Recuperación
recapture rate	taux de recouvrement	Rückflußssatz	taxa de recuperação	Tasa de recuperación
receipt of goods (ROG) terms	modalités réception de la marchandise	Bedingungen des Wareneingangs	termos referentes à recepção de mercadorias	Términos acerca de la recepción de mercaderías
receivable collection	encaissement des comptes clients	Einzug von Forderungen	cobrança de contas a receber	Cobranza de cuentas
recoating	application d'une nouvelle couche	Neubeschichtung	novo revestimento	Nuevo revestimiento
reconfiguration	reconfiguration	Neukonfiguration	reconfiguração	Reconfiguración
recourse basis	prêt avec recours	Regresshypothek	à base de garantia pessoal	A base de préstamos con aval
re-covering	recouvrement	Neubedachung durch Aufbringen eines neuen Dachs auf dem alten	aplicação de um telhado novo sobre o telhado existente	Colocación de un techo nuevo sobre un techo existente

	FRANÇAIS	DEUTSCH	PORTUGUÊS	ESPAÑOL
redevelopment	redéveloppement	Neugestaltung	reorganização	Reorganización
reflection crack	fissuration réfléchissante	Schwell- und Schwindriss	rachas de reflexão	Grieta de reflexión
regional center	centre régional	regionales Einkaufs-zentrum	centro regional; shopping center regional	Centro regional
regional tenant	locataire régional	regionaler Einzelhändler	locatário regional	Arrendatario regional
reinvestment rate	taux de réinvestissement	Wiederanlagesatz	taxa de reinvestimento	Tasa de reinversión
REIT	fonds de placement immobilier	Immobilienfonds (REIT)	sociedade comercial especializada em investimento imobiliário; fundo de investimento imobiliário	Fondo de inversión en bienes raíces
relative draw analysis	analyse de l'attraction relative	relative Analyse Anziehungskraft	análise relativa de atratividade	Análisis de atracción relativo
release	communiqué	Pressemitteilung	comunicados	Comunicados

	FRANÇAIS	DEUTSCH	PORTUGUÊS	ESPAÑOL
relocation clause	clause de relocalisation; clause de réinstallation	Standortveränderungsklausel	cláusula de translação; cláusula de transferência	Cláusula de traslado
renewal option	option de renouvellement	Erneuerungsoption	opção de renovação	Opción de renovación
renovation	rénovation	Renovierung	renovação	Renovación
rent leveling	égalisation des loyers	Mieteinkommenausgleich	nivelamento da renda de arrendamento	Nivelación del alquiler
rent roll	liste des espaces locatifs	Verzeichnis der Mieträumlichkeiten	lista sucinta de todos os espaços disponíveis e ocupados, com informações sobre tamanho de loja, atividade e alugueis	Lista de datos sobre los espacios de alquiler
rent/sales index	indice loyer/ventes	Miete-/Umsatz-Index	índice de vendas/arrendamento	Índice de alquiler/ventas
rent steps	paliers prévus d' augmentation de loyer	Mietstaffelungen	aumentos escalonados da renda	Aumentos programados del alquiler

	FRANÇAIS	DEUTSCH	PORTUGUÊS	ESPAÑOL
rent-to-sales ratio	ratio loyer/ventes	Quotient der Miete zu Umsatz	proporção entre arrendamento e vendas; índice/relação entre aluguel e vendas	Relación alquiler a ventas
rental area	superficie locative	vermietbare Fläche	área de aluguer; superfície alugável	Área de alquiler
rental year	année location	Mietjahr	Ano de aluguel	Año de alquiler
replacement	remplacement	Wiederbeschaffung	substituição	Reposición
replacement cost	coût de remplacement	Wiederbeschaffungs-kosten	custo de substituição	Costo de reposición
replacement value	valeur de remplacement	Wiederbeschaffungswert	valor de substituição	Valor de reposición
reports	rapports	Berichte (über Vorfälle)	relatórios	Informes
repositioning	repositionnement	Umpositionierung	reposicionamento	Reposiciona-miento
representative (rep)	représentant	Vertreter	representante	Representante
request for proposal (RFP)	appel d'offres	Angebotsantrag	solicitação para proposta	Solicitud de propuesta

	FRANÇAIS	DEUTSCH	PORTUGUÊS	ESPAÑOL
reserve for replacement	réserve de remplacement	Wiederbeschaffungsreserve	reservas para reposições	Reserva para reposiciones
residual analysis	analyse résiduelle	Restanalyse	análise residual	Análisis residual
retail	prix de détail	Einzelhandelspreis	preço de retalho; preço da mercadoria no varejo	Al por menor
retail expenditures	frais d'achat au détail	Ausgaben der Einzelhandelsgeschäfte	despesas de retalhistas; despesas de varejo	Gastos minoristas
retail merchandising unit (RMU')	unité de commerce de détail	Verkaufwagen	quiosque fixo	Unidad de comercialización minorista
retailer survey	sondage auprès des détaillants	Erhebung des Einzelhandels	pesquisa sobre as expectativas dos retalhistas	Encuesta a los minoristas
retailing	vente au détail	Verkauf über den Einzelhandel	venda a retalho; venda a varejo	Venta al por menor
retained earnings	bénéfices non distribués	unverteilter Gewinne	lucros acumulados	Ganancias retenidas
retained income	bénéfices non répartis	einbehaltener Gewinn	lucros não distribuídos	Ganancias retenidas

	FRANÇAIS	DEUTSCH	PORTUGUÊS	ESPAÑOL
return on assets	rendement sur les actifs	Ertrag aus Aktiven	taxa de rendibilidade do activo; rendimento dos ativos	Rendimiento de los activos
return-on-equity (ROE) ratio	coefficient du rendement sur les fonds propres	Kennziffer der Kapitalrendite (ROE)	taxa de rendibilidade dos capitais próprios; rentabilidade sobre patrimônio	Relación del rendimiento del capital
return on investment (ROI) analysis	analyse du rendement sur le placement	Rentabilitätsrechnung	análise da taxa de rendibilidade do investimento; analise sobre retorno do investimento	Análisis de rendimiento de la inversión
return on sales	rendement sur les ventes	Umsatzrendite	taxa de rendibilidade das vendas; índice de lucros sobre vendas	Rendimiento de las ventas
revenue growth	croissance du revenu	Ertragszuwachs	taxa de crescimento de rendibilidade; crescimento de receita/rentabilidade	Crecimiento de los ingresos
revenues	revenu	Einkünfte	receitas	Ingresos

	FRANÇAIS	DEUTSCH	PORTUGUÊS	ESPAÑOL
reverse allowance	allocation inverse	Betrag für Baukosten zusätzlich zur Miete	pagamento específico ao proprietário efectuado pelo arrendatário para o custo de construção do espaço	Pago adicional al arrendador por parte del arrendatario por el costo de construcción del espacio
rider	avenant	Zusatzklausel	acto adicional; adendo	Cláusula adicional
right of subrogation	droit de subrogation	Subrogationsrecht	direito de sub-rogação	Derecho de subrogación
ring road	routes annulaires	Ringstraßen	estradas que rodeiam o centro comercial; anel rodoviário periférico (dentro) de um shopping center	Carreteras periféricas al centro de compras
ripple	ondulation	Schwankungen im Verkehrsfluss an Ampeln	ondulação	Onda
risk	risque	Risiko	risco	Riesgo

	FRANÇAIS	DEUTSCH	PORTUGUÊS	ESPAÑOL
risk management	gestion des risques	Risiko-Management	gestão de risco	Administración de riesgos
risk premium	prime de risque	Risikoprämie	prémio de risco	Prima de riesgo
Risk Retention Act companies	sociétés en vertu du Risk Retention Act (loi sur la rétention du risque)	Firmen, die sich unter dem Risikozurückbehaltunggsgesetz versichern	companhias operando segundo o Decreto de Retenção de Riscos	Compañías que se acogieron a la Ley de Retención de Riesgos
robbery	vol	Raubüberfall	roubo	Robo
ROE	coefficient du rendement sur les fonds propres	Kennziffer der Kapitalrendite (ROE)	taxa de rendibilidade dos capitais próprios; rentabilidade sobre patrimônio	Rendimiento del patrimonio
ROG	réception de la marchandise	Wareneingang	termos referentes a recepção de mercadorias	Términos de le recepción de mercaderias

	FRANÇAIS	DEUTSCH	PORTUGUÊS	ESPAÑOL
ROI	rendement sur l'investissement	Kapitalrendite	análise da taxa de rendibilidade do investimento; retorno sobre o investimento	Rendimiento de la inversión
roof cement	ciment pour réparation de toitures	Dachpappenklebemasse	cimento para reparações no telhado	Cemento para reparación de techos
roof deck	base de toiture	Dachpappeneindeckungsfläche	tecto; plataforma de telhado	Plataforma de techo
roof repair	réparation de toiture	Dachreparatur	reparação do telhado; conserto de telhado	Reparación de techo
ROP	positionnement de la réclame au choix du journal	ohne Vorzugsplatzierung (ROP)	Impressão de um anúncio em qualquer parte dum jornal conforme determinado pela publicação	Colocación de un aviso en cualquier parte que determine la publicación
ROR	taux de rendement sur les actifs	Gewinn in % des investierten Gesamtkapitals	taxa de rendibilidade do activo (ROR); taxa de retorno sobre ativos	Tasa de rendimiento de los activos

	FRANÇAIS	DEUTSCH	PORTUGUÊS	ESPAÑOL
ROS	positionnement des spots au choix de la station	ohne Sendezeitverein-barung (ROS)	spots publicitários para transmissão em qualquer altura determinada pela programação da estação	Transmisión de espacios publicitarios en cualquier parte a ser determinada por la programación de una estación
run of paper (ROP)	positionnement de la réclame au choix du journal	ohne Vorzugsplatzierung (ROP)	Impressão de um anúncio em qualquer parte dum jornal conforme determinado pela publicação	Colocación de un aviso en cualquier parte que determine la publicación
run of placement (ROP) color	positionnement aléatoire de couleur	ohne Vorzugsplatzierung (ROP)	aplicação ao acaso de uma ou duas cores num anúncio	Colocación aleatoria de uno o dos colores en un aviso publicitario

	FRANÇAIS	DEUTSCH	PORTUGUÊS	ESPAÑOL
run of station (ROS)	positionnement des spots au choix de la station	ohne Vorzugsplatzierung des Senders	spots publicitários para transmissão em qualquer altura determinada pela programação da estação	Transmisión de espacios publicitarios en cualquier parte a ser determinada por la programación de una estación
sales	vente; chiffre d'affaires	Umsatz	vendas	Ventas
sales analysis report	analyses du chiffre d'affaires	Absatzanalysenbericht	relatório de análise de vendas	Informe sobre análisis de ventas
sales area	superficie de ventes	Verkaufsfläche	área de vendas	Área de ventas
sales benchmarks	repères de ventes	Vergleich mit anderen Einkaufszentren	padrão de referência de vendas	Cotas de referencia de ventas
sales breakpoint	seuil de rentabilité des ventes	Gewinnschwelle	ponto limite de vendas; ponto de equilíbrio das vendas	Punto de equilibrio de ventas

	FRANÇAIS	DEUTSCH	PORTUGUÊS	ESPAÑOL
sales contribution	contribution des ventes	Beitrag zum Umsatz	contribuição de vendas	Contribución de ventas
sales efficiency ratio	ratio d'efficacité commerciale	Verkaufseffizienzquotient	coeficiente de eficiência de vendas	Índice de eficiencia de ventas
sales per square foot	chiffre d'affaires par mètre carré	Umsatz pro Quadratfuß	vendas por pé quadrado	Ventas por pie cuadrado
sales potential	potentiel du chiffre d'affaires	Absatzpotential	potencial de vendas	Potencial de ventas
sales projection	prévision du chiffre d'affaires	Absatzprognose	projeção de vendas	Proyección de ventas
sales/rent report	rapport de ventes/loyer	Umsatz-/Mietenbericht	relatório de vendas/aluguer	Informe de ventas/alquiler
sample size	taille de l'échantillon	Stichprobenumfang	volume de amostra; tamanho da amostra	Tamaño de la muestra
sans serif	sans empattements	serifenlose Schrift	sem cerifa	Caracteres sin trazos terminales
saturation	saturation	Sättigungswerbung	saturação	Saturación

	FRANÇAIS	DEUTSCH	PORTUGUÊS	ESPAÑOL
scatter plan	plan de diffusion	Streuplan	plano de difusão	Plan de difusión
screen halftones	similis tramés	Rasterhalbtöne	ilustrações fotográficas referentes a um anúncio cujas imagens resultam da aplicação de uma percentagem de tinta	Semitonos en ilustraciones fotográficas de un aviso
scupper	dalot	Überlaufpfanne	orifício para permitir o escoamento das águas	Abertura por drenaje
sealers	scellants	Versiegelungsmittel	selantes; vedantes	Selladores
search procedure	méthode de recherche	Durchsuchungsverfahren	procedimento de busca	Procedimiento de investigación
seasonality index	indice des ventes saisonnières	Saisonindex	índice de vendas de acordo com a estação	Índice de ventas por estación
second stage	second stade	zweite Phase	segunda fase	Segunda etapa
secondary market	marché secondaire	sekundärer Markt	mercado secundário	Mercado secundario
secondary public offering	offre publique secondaire de titres de participation	Zweitemission	oferta pública secundária	Oferta pública de acciones a secundaria

	FRANÇAIS	DEUTSCH	PORTUGUÊS	ESPAÑOL
secondary purchase	achat secondaire	Sekundärerwerb	compra secundária	Compra secundaria
secondary research	recherche secondaire	Sekundärforschung	pesquisa secundária	Investigación secundaria
secondary zone	zone secondaire	Sekundärzone	zona secundária	Zona secundaria
seconds	marchandise défectueuse	Waren zweiter Wahl	artigos de qualidade inferior de segunda clase	
secret shoppers	acheteurs secrets	Ladenbeobachtungsverfahren zur Bewertung des Personals, der Warenpräsentation usw.	compradores secretos	Compradores secretos
sector	secteur	Sektor	sector	Sector
sector analysis	analyse sectorielle	Sektoranalyse	estudo do sector; análises setoriais	Análisis sectorial
securitization	titrisation	Sekuritisierung	securitização	Titulización
security	sécurité	Sicherheit	segurança	seguridad
security chain of command	chaîne de commande de sécurité	Befehlskette innerhalb des Schließ- und Wachdienstes	cadeia de comando de segurança	Cadena de mando de seguridad

	FRANÇAIS	DEUTSCH	PORTUGUÊS	ESPAÑOL
security expenses	frais de sécurité	sicherheitstechnische Ausgaben	despesas de segurança	Gastos por seguridad
security revenue	revenus de sécurité	Einnahmen zur Deckung der sicherheitstechnischen Ausgaben	entradas para cobrir as despesas de segurança; receitas para cobrir despesas com segurança	Ingresos por seguridad
selectivity	sélectivité	Selektivität	selectividade; escolha da mídia pelo anunciante	Selectividad
self-managed REIT	Société de placement ; immobilier autogérée	selbstverwalteter REIT	fundo de investimento imobiliário auto administrado	Fondo de inversión en bienes raíces auto-administrado
series discounts	rabais en série	Serienrabatt	série de descontos; série de descontos oferecidos pelo fabricante ao varejista (comerciante)	Descuentos en serie
serifs	empattements	Serif	serifas	Serifs

	FRANÇAIS	DEUTSCH	PORTUGUÊS	ESPAÑOL
SET	SET (transaction électronique sûre)	sichere elektronische Transaktion	transacção electrónica de segurança	Transacción electrónica protegida
share	part	Anteil	participação	Participación
share of market	part de marché	Marktanteil	quota de mercado; participação de mercado	Participación de mercado
share-of-the-market analysis	analyse de part du marché	Marktanteils-Analyse	estudo da quota do mercado; análise da participação de mercado	Análisis de participación en el mercado
shopper intercept survey	sondage par interception des acheteurs	Studie zum Käuferverhalten	inquérito elaborado ao interceptar os compradores	Encuesta mediante intercepción de compradores
shopping attitudes	attitudes de shopping	Einstellungen zum Einkaufen	atitudes relativas a compras	Actitudes de compra
shopping behavior	comportement de shopping	Kaufverhalten	comportamento relativo a compras	Comporta-miento de compra

	FRANÇAIS	DEUTSCH	PORTUGUÊS	ESPAÑOL
shopping center	centre commercial	Einkaufszentrum	centro comercial; shopping center	Centro comercial
shopping goods	marchandise	Waren	mercadorias à venda numa variedade	Mercaderías de lojas; mercadorias
shopping patterns	habitudes d'achat	Einkaufsmuster	padrões de compra	Patrones de compra
short rate	tarif réajusté (pour ne pas avoir rempli les conditions de la remise)	Rabattrückbelastung	tarifa superior por falta de cumprimento do contrato	Tarifa mayor por incumplimiento contractual
short-term debt	dettes à court terme	kurzfristige Verbindlichkeit	dívida com uma maturidade a curto prazo; dívida a curto prazo	Deuda a corto plazo
short-term lease	bail à court terme	kurzfristiger Mietvertrag	arrendamento a curto prazo; locação a curto prazo	Alquiler a corto plazo
shrinkage	contraction	Schrumpfung	contracção; a diferença no estoque de mercadorias encontrada pela auditoria física versus o valor contabilizado; redução	Encogimiento

	FRANÇAIS	DEUTSCH	PORTUGUÊS	ESPAÑOL
shrinkage cracks	fissures de contraction	Schwindrisse, Schwundrisse	rachas devido a contracção	Grietas por encogimiento
sidewalk sale	vente de trottoir	Bürgersteig-Verkauf	mercadorias vendidas ao desbarato no passeio; liquidação de rua	Liquidación de vereda
sig cut	logo	Bildmarke	logotipo	Logotipo
single ply	une seule couche	einlagig	camada única	Capa individual
single-family house	maison unifamiliale	Einfamilienhaus	unidade de habitação monofamiliar; residência unifamiliar	Vivienda unifamiliar
site	site	Standort	parcela de terreno	Emplazamiento
site-specific demand analysis	analyse de la demande spécifique à un site	standortspezifische Nachfrageanalyse	análise da procura para renovação de um local específico; análise da demanda específica de uma determinada área, por ocasião de uma renovação ou mudança	Análisis de las exigencias para el desarrollo de un sitio específico
slab	dalle	Dachplatte	laje	Losa

	FRANÇAIS	DEUTSCH	PORTUGUÊS	ESPAÑOL
sleepers	poutres	Lagerbalken	dormentes de suporte	Largueros
slightly imperfect	légère imperfection	mit geringen Qualitätsmängeln	ligeramente imperfeito	Con leves imperfecciones
slip and fall litigation	poursuites pour chute	von einem Kunden, der im Einkaufszentrum ausgerutscht und gefallen ist, angestrengter Prozess	acção judicial por escorregadela súbita e queda	Litigio por resbalón y caída
slippage cracks	fissures de glissement	Risse aufgrund der Ablösung der Straßendecke	rachas por deslocamento da camada superior do pavimento; rachaduras no piso (por tração)	Rajaduras por desplazamiento
slurry	laitance, scellant d'asphalte	Asphaltversiegelung	tipo de selante de asfalto	Lechada
small town rural	petite ville en zone rurale	Kleinstadt außerhalb des Großstadtgebiets	cidade pequena rural	Pequeña ciudad rural
S/MIME	S/MIME	S/MIME	S/MIME	S/MIME

	FRANÇAIS	DEUTSCH	PORTUGUÊS	ESPAÑOL
SMSA	aire statistique métropolitaine standard	statistisches städtisches Standardgebiet (SMSA)	área padrão de estatística metropolitana	Área estadística metropolitana estándar
snipe	bande de texte	Plakatüberkleber	faixa contendo informações especiais	Tira adicional de información
snow removal expenses	frais de déneigement	Schneebeseitigungs-kosten	despesas para remoção da neve	Gastos por remoción de nieve
sodium light	lampe au sodium	Natriumlicht	luz de sódio	Luz de sodio
soft costs	coûts accessoires	"weiche Kosten"	custos referentes a um projeto de renovação; todos os custos de um projeto, excluídos os custos de construção, contrário de "hard-costs"	Costos accesorios
soft goods	marchandise non durable	kurzlebige Gebrauchsgüter	artigos têxteis pouco duráveis; artigos têxteis (de caráter não durável)	Mercaderías perecederas
source of sales	source des ventes	Quelle für Verkaufsdaten	fonte de dados	Fuente de ventas

	FRANÇAIS	DEUTSCH	PORTUGUÊS	ESPAÑOL
space deadline	échéance d'espace	Anzeigenannahmeschluss	prazo limite estipulado para reserva de espaço publicitário	Plazo límite para reservar espacios publicitarios
special event	événements spéciaux	Sonderveranstaltungen	eventos especiais	Eventos especiales
special (marketing) assessment	cotisation spéciale (pour marketing)	Sonderbeitrag zum Marketing	avaliação especial (de marketing)	Evaluación especial (de marketing)
specialty leasing program	programme de location spécialisée	Programm zur Vermietung an vorübergehende Mieter	programa para locatários temporários	Plan para locatarios temporarios
specific performance clause	clause d'exécution spécifique	spezifische Erfüllungs-Klausel	cláusula de execução do estipulado	Cláusula de cumplimiento específico
split run	alternance de réclames	Anzeigensplit	publicação alternada de anúncios publicitários diferentes	Publicación fraccionada de avisos publicitarios
spot	spot	Werbesendezeit in einem Lokalsender	mensagem publicitária; spot publicitário	Espacio publicitario

	FRANÇAIS	DEUTSCH	PORTUGUÊS	ESPAÑOL
spot color	application localisée de couleurs	Zusatzfarbe in einer Anzeige	aplicação de cor em um ou dois lugares num anúncio	Aplicación de color a uno o dos lugares de un aviso publicitario
sprinkler contribution rate	taux de contribution au système de gicleurs	Beitragssatz zum Unterhalt der Sprinkleranlage	contribuição para manutenção do sistema aspersor; taxa de contribuição para o sistema de sprinklers	Tasa de contribución al fondo para aspersores
SSL	protocole SSL (couche des sockets sécurisés)	SSL-Protokoll	protocolo de segurança de privacidade	Protocolo de la seguridad de privacidad
staggered schedule	calendrier alterné	Wechselstreuung	programação alternada	Programación alternada
standard inspection	inspection standard	normale Inspektion	inspeção de norma; inspeção padrão	Inspección estándar
standard metropolitan statistical area (SMSA)	aire statistique métropolitaine standard	statistisches städtisches Standardgebiet (SMSA)	área padrão de estatística metropolitana	Área estadística metropolitana estándar

	FRANÇAIS	DEUTSCH	PORTUGUÊS	ESPAÑOL
standard operating procedure	méthodes de fonctionnement normalisées	Standard-Arbeitsverfahren	procedimento operacional padrão	Procedimiento operativo estándar
standard operating procedures manual	manuel des méthodes de fonctionnement normalisées	Handbuch der Standard-Arbeitsverfahren	manual de procedimento operacional padrão	Manual de procedimiento operativo estándar
statement of cash flows	état de l'encaisse	Kapitalflussrechnung	demonstração dos fluxos de caixa	Estado de flujo de fondos
statement of changes in financial position	état de l'évolution de la situation financière; tableau de trésorerie	Ausweis der Veränderungen im Finanzstatus	declaração de alterações relativas à posição financeira	Estado de cambios en la posición financiera
statement of retained earnings	état des bénéfices non répartis	Aufstellung über den unverteilten Gewinn	declaração de lucros não distribuídos	Estado de ganancias retenidas
step-down rents	loyers décroissants	Mieten mit reduziertem Prozentsatz	rendas de percentagens reduzidas; alugueis decrescentes	Alquileres de porcentajes reducidos

	FRANÇAIS	DEUTSCH	PORTUGUÊS	ESPAÑOL
step-up rents	loyers croissants	Mieten mit erhöhtem Prozentsatz	rendas de percentagens aumentadas; aluguéis crescentes	Alquileres de porcentajes incrementales
stock turnover	roulement des stocks	Lagerumschlag	rotação de existências; giro de estoque	Rotación de existencias
straightlining	amortissement linéaire	lineare Abschreibung	linearidade, constância	lineal/rectilíneo
straight-line depreciation	amortissement linéaire; amortissement constant	lineare Abschreibungsmethode	método das quotas constantes; depreciação constante	Amortización lineal
straight-line rents	loyers constants	konstante Mieten	arrendamentos de amortização constante; aluguéis de amortização constantes	Alquileres de amortización lineal
strip center	centre commercial à ciel ouvert ; centre de quartier	kleiners Vorort-Einkaufszentrum	centro de lojas de retalho configurado em linha recta; centro de lojas de varejo configurado em linha reta	Centro de tiendas minoristas ubicados en franja

	FRANÇAIS	DEUTSCH	PORTUGUÊS	ESPAÑOL
stun gun	revolver paralysante	Betäubungsgerät	arma de descarga eléctrica; pistola de descarga elétrica temporariamente paralizante	Pistola de descarga eléctrica
subcontractors	sous-traitants	Unterlieferant	subempreiteiros	Subcontratistas
subgrade	hérisson	zubereitete Fläche zum Asphaltieren	superfície preparada para aplicação de asfalto	Capa de asiento
sublease	sous-location	Untervermietung	subarrendamento; sub-locação	Sublocación
submission date	date de soumission	Einreichungsdatum	data de submissão	Fecha de entrega
subordinated bonds or debentures	obligations ou débentures subordonnées	nachrangige Obligationen	obrigações subordinadas e obrigações garantidas; títulos ou debentures subordinados	Bonos u obligaciones subordinados
subordination	subordination	Untergebene	subordinação	Subordinación
subordination clause	clause de subordination	Rangnachfolge-Klausel	cláusula de subordinação	Cláusula de subordinación
subrogation	subrogation	Rechtsübergang auf den Versicherer	sub-rogação	Subrogación

	FRANÇAIS	DEUTSCH	PORTUGUÊS	ESPAÑOL
substrate	substrat	Dachhautträger	substrato	Sustrato
suburban center	centre de banlieue	vorstädtisches Einkaufszentrum	centro suburbano	Centro suburbano
suburban share	part du marché de banlieue	Marktanteil der Außenstadt	participação suburbana	Participación suburbana
superregional center	centre superrégional	überregionales Einkaufszentrum	centro super regional	Centro superregional
supervision fee	frais de supervision	Beaufsichtigungsgebühren	honorário de supervição; taxa de supervição	Honorario por supervisión
surety bonds	cautionnements	Kautionsversicherung	fianças	Fianzas
TAP	plan audience totale	Gesamtzuschauerschaftsplan	plano de público (audiência) total	Plan de audiencia total
T-shaped center	centre en forme de T	T-förmiges Einkaufszentrum	centro comercial em forma de T	Centro comercial en forma de T
T-stand	présentoir en T	T-förmiger Kleiderständer	banca em forma de T	Estand con forma de T

	FRANÇAIS	DEUTSCH	PORTUGUÊS	ESPAÑOL
tall-wall mall stall	présentoir construit à même un grand mur	Verkaufsstand entlang einer freien Wand	parede desocupada usada para comercialização	Pared utilizada para publicidad
tangible assets	biens corporels	Vermögenswerte	activos corpóreos; ativos tangíveis	Activos tangibles
target audience	audience visée	Zielpublikum	audiência; público alvo	Público objetivo
tear-off	enlèvement	Entfernung der Dachhaut	retirada de camada para substituição	Desprendi-miento de membrana para reemplazo
tear sheet	copie de la réclame publiée	Einzelbeleg für Werbungtreibende oder Autoren	cópia de um anúncio publicado	Copia impresa y fechada de un aviso publicitario
teaser ads	réclames d'essai	Neugier weckende Werbung	anúncios preliminares para despertar o interesse do público	Avisos publicitarios preliminares para atraer el interés del público

	FRANÇAIS	DEUTSCH	PORTUGUÊS	ESPAÑOL
telephone survey	sondage téléphonique	telefonische Umfrage	sondagem telefónica; pesquisa telefónica	Encuesta telefónica
temporary tenant	locataire temporaire	vorübergehender Mieter	inquilino temporário	Locatario temporáneo
temporary tenant program	programme pour locataires temporaires	Programm für Vermietung an vorübergehende Mieter	programa para locatários temporários	Plan para locatarios temporarios
tenant	locataire	Mieter	arrendatário	Arrendatario/locatario
tenant allowance (TA)	allocation au locataire	Genehmigung an den Mieter	concessão aos locatários; subsídio a lojista (condições especiais)	Concesión a locatarios
tenant evaluation	évaluation des locataires	Bewertung der Mieter	avaliação do arrendatário; avaliação do lojista	Evaluación de locatarios
tenant improvements	améliorations locatives	dem Mieter zugute kommende bauliche Verbesserungen	melhorias efectuadas pelo arrendatário; benfeitorias realizadas para realçar o espaço do inquilino (lojista)	Mejoras realizadas por el inquilino

	FRANÇAIS	DEUTSCH	PORTUGUÊS	ESPAÑOL
tenant mix	éventail de locataires	Mietermix-Plan	mistura de lojas num complexo de vendas a retalho; mix de inquilinos/lojistas	Distribución de tipos de tienda en un complejo minorista
tenant representatives	représentants des locataires	Vertreter der Mieter	representantes do locatário; representantes dos lojistas	Representantes del locatario
tenant roster	liste des locataires	Mieterverzeichnis	lista de informações sobre os arrendatários; cadastro dos lojistas	Lista de información sobre los locatarios
tenant trade name	appellation commerciale du locataire	Geschäftsname des Mieters	nome comercial do locatário; razão social do inquilino/lojista	Nombre comercial del locatario
tenant's floor area	superficie occupée par le locataire	die vom Mieter belegte Fläche insgesamt	área total do espaço do locatário; área total ocupada pelo lojista/inquilino	Superficie ocupada por el locatario
10 K	10K	10 K-Formular	impresso 10 K; formulário 10 K	Formulario 10 K

	FRANÇAIS	DEUTSCH	PORTUGUÊS	ESPAÑOL
10 Q	10Q	10 Q-Formular	impresso 10 Q; formulário 10 Q	Formulario 10 Q
term	durée	Laufzeit	período de duração; prazo da locação	Plazo
termination	résiliation ou congédiement	Kündigung	terminação; término	Finalización
tertiary zone	zone tertiaire	Tertiärzone	zona terciária	Zona terciaria
theme/festival center	centre à thème/festival	Themen/Festivalzentrum	centro temático/festival	Centro temático/festival
third-party insurance	assurance de tiers	Versicherung gegen dritte Parteien	seguro contra terceiros	Seguro contra terceros
three-party agreement	accord tripartite	Dreiparteien-Vereinbarung	acordo entre três partes	Convenio entre tres partes
till forbid (TF)	jusqu'à instructions ultérieures	bis auf Weiteres (TF)	até notificação em contrário	Hasta su prohibición
time value of money	valeur temporelle de l'argent	Geldzeitwert	valor temporal de dinheiro	Valor temporal del dinero

	FRANÇAIS	DEUTSCH	PORTUGUÊS	ESPAÑOL
tonnage	tonnage	Grenzlast	tonelagem	Tonelaje
total audience plan (TAP)	plan audience totale	Gesamtzuschauerschaftsplan	plano de público (audiência) total	Plan de público total
total income	revenu total	Gesamteinkommen	rendimento total; renda total	Ingreso total
total market coverage	couverture totale du marché	Gesamtmarktabdeckung	cobertura total do mercado	Cobertura total del mercado
total personal income	revenu personnel total	Gesamtprivateinkommen	rendimento pessoal total; renda total pessoal	Ingreso personal total
total rent	loyer total	Gesamtmiete	renda total pelo aluguer; aluguel total	Alquiler total
total survey area	aire totale du sondage	Gesamterhebungsgebiet	área total de sondagem; área total de pesquisa	Área total de encuesta
trade area	aire commerciale	Handelsgebiet	área comercial	Área comercial
trade area zones	segments de l'aire commerciale	Handelsgebietzonen	zonas comerciais segmentadas	Zonas de áreas comerciales
trade discount	remise commerciale	Wiederverkäuferrabatt	desconto comercial	Descuento comercial

	FRANÇAIS	DEUTSCH	PORTUGUÊS	ESPAÑOL
trade fixture	bien meuble du locataire	Geschäftseinrichtung	equipamento comercial; acessório próprio e específico de um lojista	Instalación comercial
trade name	nom commerciale, raison sociale	Handelsname	denominação comercial; razão social	Nombre razão social
traffic	trafic; circulation	Kundenverkehr, Besucherfluss	tráfego	Tráfico
traffic count	comptage (de passage des acheteurs ou acheteurs potentiels)	Verkehrszählung	contagem de consumidores	Censo del tránsito de compradores
traffic estimates	estimations du trafic	Käuferschätzung	estimativa de tráfego	Estimaciones de tráfico
traffic-building device	activité de marketing; activité pour attirer la clientèle	Werbemittel zum Aufbau des Besucherflusses in einem Einkaufszentrum	actividade promocional para estimular tráfego de compradores	Actividad promocional para estimular el tráfico de clientes

	FRANÇAIS	DEUTSCH	PORTUGUÊS	ESPAÑOL
training record	documentation de la formation	Ausbildungszeugnis	registo de formação profissional do pessoal de segurança; histórico de treinamento de pessoal de segurança	Registro del adiestramiento del personal de seguridad
transactions	transactions	Transaktionen	transacções	Transacciones
transfer	transfert	Übermittlung	transferência	Transferencia
trial balance	balance de vérification	Rohbilanz, Saldenbilanz	balancete	Balance de verificación
triangle-shaped center	centre de forme triangulaire	dreiseitig angelegtes Einkaufszentrum	centro comercial em forma de triângulo	Centro comercial en forma de triángulo
triple net lease	bail triple net	Mietvertrag, dem gemäß der Mieter 100% der Steuern, Versicherungs- und Wartungskosten zahlt	contrato de arrendamento líquido triplo	Contrato de arrendamiento neto triple

	FRANÇAIS	DEUTSCH	PORTUGUÊS	ESPAÑOL
turn key	clé en mains	schlüsselfertig	chave na mão	Llave en mano
turn-over	chiffre d'affaire	Umsatz	rotação das existências	Rotación de existencias; giro
two-party design/construct agreement	accord bipartite de conception/construction	Vereinbarung der Bauherr gemäß der Bauherr mit lizenzierten Architekten und Baufirmen arbeitet	acordo de concepção/construção envolvendo duas partes	Convenio de diseño/construcción de dos partes
U-shaped center	centre en forme de U	U-förmiges Einkaufszentrum	centro comercial em forma de U	Centro comercial en forma de U
umbrella excess liability	assurance responsabilité excédentaire générale	Überschusshaftpflicht	responsabilidade civil complementar abrangente	Seguro global de cobertura complementaria de excedente
underwriting	contrat de prise ferme	Übernahme einer Emission	tomada firme de uma emissão; subscrição de uma emissão de títulos mobiliários	Colocación de títulos/valores

	FRANÇAIS	DEUTSCH	PORTUGUÊS	ESPAÑOL
unnatural breakpoint	seuil de rentabilité superficiel	unnatürlicher oder künstlicher Kosten-deckungspunkt	ponto limite não natural; ponto de equilíbrio não natural	Punto de equilibrio no natural
urban areas	zones urbaines	Ballungsgebiete	áreas urbanas	Áreas urbanas
urban centers	centres urbains	innerstädtische Einkaufszentren,	centros urbanos	Centros urbanos
use clause	clause d'utilisation; clause d'usage; clause destination	Benutzungszweck-Klausel	cláusula de utilização	Cláusula de uso
useful life	durée de vie	Nutzungsdauer	vida útil	Vida útil
utilities expenses	frais de services publics	an öffentliche Versorgungsbetriebe zu zahlende Ausgaben	custos de serviços públicos	Gastos por servicios públicos
utilities revenue	revenus de services publics	Einnahmen für öffentliche Versorgungsbetriebe	receita de serviços públicos	Ingresos por servicios públicos
vacancy loss	perte d'inoccupation	Verlust der Nichtvermietung	perda por espaços deso cupados	Pérdida por espacio no alquilado

	FRANÇAIS	DEUTSCH	PORTUGUÊS	ESPAÑOL
vacancy rate	taux d'inoccupation	Freiraumanteil	índice de espaço de lojas desocupadas; taxa de vacância	Índice de tiendas desocupadas
value	valeur	Firmenwert	valor	Valor
value megamall	(grand centre offrant de la marchandise à valeur supérieur)	Megamall-Vorzugspreise	megamall objetivando valor (bom preço, preços de atacadista)	Gran centro comercial con mercadería de valor superior
value retailing	vente au détail d'articles de marque à prix réduits	Verkauf von Markenartikeln unter dem in Kaufhäusern gängigen Preisen	venda a preços inferiores aos dos grandes armazéns	Valor de venta inferior a los precios del centro de compras
vandalism	vandalisme	Vandalismus	vandalismo	Vandalismo

	FRANÇAIS	DEUTSCH	PORTUGUÊS	ESPAÑOL
vanilla box	espace aménagé avec les éléments de base	halbfertige Räumlichkeiten zur Fertigstellung durch den Mieter	espaço parcialmente terminado pelo proprietário baseado em negociações entre este e o arrendatário	Espacio parcialmente terminado por el arrendador de acuerdo a negociaciones entre éste y el arrendatario
variable expenses	frais variables	variable Kosten	despesas variáveis	Gastos variables
variance report	rapport d'écart	Varianzbericht	relatório de variância	Informe de la varianza
venture capital	capitaux de risque	Risikokapital	capital de risco	Capital de riesgo
vertical	vertical	vertikal	vertical	Vertical
vertical retailer	détaillant intégré	vertikaler Einzelhändler	varejista com fabricação própria	Minorista integral
vertical-shaped center	centre de forme verticale	vertikalförmiges Einkaufszentrum	centro comercial em forma vertical	Centro comercial de forma vertical
video	vidéo	Video	vídeo	Vídeo

	FRANÇAIS	DEUTSCH	PORTUGUÊS	ESPAÑOL
viewers per set (VPS)	téléspectateurs par spot	Zuschauer pro Fernsehgerät	número de telespectadores por aparelho de televisão	Espectadores por televisor
village center	centre de type (village)	Dorfzentrum	centro de compras em formato de vilarejo	centro de pueblo
VPS	téléspectateurs par spot	Zuschauer pro Fernsehgerät	número de telespectadores por aparelho de televisão	Espectadores por aparato televisor
wait order	ordre d'attente	Terminauftrag	ordem de espera	Orden de espera
waiver	renonciation	Verzicht	renúncia de direito	Renuncia a un derecho
waiver of subrogation	renonciation à la subrogation	Verzicht auf das Subrogationsrecht	renúncia de direito de sub-rogação	Renuncia al derecho de subrogación
warm brick	espace non fini que reçoit le locataire	unfertiger Raum zur Fertigstellung durch den Mieter	espaço por terminar num centro comercial	Espacio sin terminar en un centro comercial
warranty	garantie	Garantie	Garantia	Garantía
Web site	site web	Website	website	Sitio web/sitio en la red

	FRANÇAIS	DEUTSCH	PORTUGUÊS	ESPAÑOL
welcome book	livre de bienvenue	Willkommensschrift	livro informativo de acolhimento; livro de boas vindas e instrutivo (dado ao lojista após a assinatura do contrato de locação)	Libro de bienvenida
white space	espace blanc	Unbedruckte Stelle	espaço em branco	Espacio en blanco
work period	période de travail	gewährte Bauzeit	prazo dado pelo locador ao inquilino (lojista) para instalação de sua loja	Periodo permitido para la realización de obras de construcción
working capital	fonds de roulement	Betriebskapital	capital de exploração; capital de giro	Capital de trabajo
World Wide Web	World Wide Web	World Wide Web	World Wide Web	Red de extensión mundial

	FRANÇAIS	DEUTSCH	PORTUGUÊS	ESPAÑOL
wrap-up, or owner-controlled insurance program	programme d'assurance contrôlée par le propriétaire	Art der firmeneigenen Gemeinschaftsversicherung	plano integrado de riscos; consolidação do plano de seguros, controlado pelo proprietário	Plan de seguro global
yield	rendement	Ausbeute	rendimento	proporcionar/ otorgar/ producir/ rendimiento
zero lot line	ligne de démarcation du lot	Bau eines Gebäudes an der Grenzlinie eines Grundstücks	linha de demarcação de terreno	Edificación sobre el límite del lote
zero-based budgeting	budgétisation à base zéro	Budgetierung auf Nullbasis	orçamento a partir de zero	Elaboración del presupuesto a partir de cero